The Idea of Art as Propaganda in France 1750-1799

University of Toronto
Romance Series, No. 8

University of Toronto Press

The Idea of
Art as Propaganda
in France

1750-1799

A Study in the History of Ideas

JAMES A. LEITH

Associate Professor of French History,
Queen's University at Kingston

UNIVERSITY OF TORONTO ROMANCE SERIES

Preface

THE FOLLOWING STUDY is not a history of a period in art but rather an essay in the history of ideas. Its purpose is to examine the ideas about the social value of art developed during the last half of the eighteenth century in France by the *philosophes*, the *Encyclopédistes*, certain royal officials, and finally by revolutionaries. It is hoped that this study will clarify some of the implications of the *Weltanschauung* of both the Enlightenment and the Revolution.

Recently this sort of intellectual and cultural history has inspired increasing attention. For this period there have already been studies of the activities of artists during the French Revolution. However, these studies have been concerned with the organization of artistic societies, the struggle for the right of all artists to exhibit in the biennial Salons, the establishment of national museums, the activity of artists in revolutionary organizations, and other related developments.[1] No writer has focused his attention wholly on the development of the idea of art as propaganda. Consequently valuable unexplored material existed even for the radical phase of the Revolution which has been most studied. This study extends before and after that period. In order to understand the factors which contributed to the revival of art as propaganda it is essential to go back at least to the middle of the century, and in order to understand why it proved difficult to implement the idea, it is necessary to carry the study through the period of the Directory.

[1]Stanley J. Idzerda, "Art and the French State during the French Revolution 1789–1795," unpublished Ph.D. thesis (Western Reserve, 1952); David L. Dowd, "The French Revolution and the Painters," *French Historical Studies*, vol. I, 1959, no. 2, pp. 127–48. Other works by Idzerda and Dowd are listed in the bibliographical notes.

Before reading a study in the history of ideas the reader deserves
to be forewarned about the prejudices of the author. I am in
sympathy with much of the rational and secular outlook of the
philosophes, but do not share their view that a good work of art
must convey some social message. Nor do I like the totalitarian
implications inherent in the programme of directing all the various
arts toward some social goal. Like Camus I believe that all ideology
corrupts and that absolute ideology corrupts absolutely.

It is not, however, the function of the historian to refute those
whose ideas he is studying. Therefore I have attempted simply
to understand why the eighteenth-century philosophers and revolutionaries developed the kind of ideas they did about the value of
art in society. This does not mean that I have attained objectivity,
perhaps a vain hope, but that I have sought to enter into the minds
of those under study, despite a distaste for certain features of their
thought.

In what follows I have used the word "propaganda" to denote
any method of diffusing ideas without giving the term overtones
of disapprobation. By "art" I mean mainly painting and sculpture,
but occasionally I have mentioned other arts such as architecture
or poetry in order to clarify the aesthetic ideas of the *philosophes*
and revolutionaries. I have not dealt with the *fêtes civiques* which
have already been subjected to detailed study.[2] Besides, the perish-
able works of art employed in these state festivals could have a
lasting impact only when translated into permanent sculptured
figures or historical paintings.

My study is the result of research in Parisian libraries and
archives in recent years. I should like, therefore, to express warm
appreciation to the staffs of the Bibliothèque nationale, the Bibliothèque historique de la ville de Paris, the Bibliothèque de l'école
des beaux-arts, the Archives nationales, and the archives of the
Institut de France for their assistance and co-operation.

Also I should like to thank those bodies which granted me the
financial assistance which made my research in France possible: the
Royal Society of Canada, and the Arts Research Committee of

[2]David Dowd, *Pageant-Master of the Republic: Jacques-Louis David and the
Revolution* (Lincoln, 1948); A. Blum, "The National Festival in the French
Revolution 1794–7," unpublished Ph.D. thesis (Cornell, 1939).

Queen's University. This work has been published with the help of grants from the Humanities Research Council, using funds provided by the Canada Council, and from the Publications Fund of the University of Toronto Press.

More particularly, I wish to thank Professor R. M. Saunders of the Department of History at the University of Toronto for his guidance over a number of years, Professors C. D. Rouillard and R. D. C. Finch of the Department of French at Toronto for much helpful advice, and Monsieur J. Adhémar of the Print Division of the Bibliothèque nationale for assistance on a number of occasions. And, finally, my special gratitude is due to my wife whose patience and understanding have made the writing of this book a pleasure.

September 1, 1964   J. A. L.

Contents

The Idea of Art as Propaganda in France 1750-1799

Toward the Revival
of the Idea of
Art as Propaganda

1.

Ceux qui ont gouverné les peuples dans tous les tems, ont toujours fait usage des peintures et statues, pour leur mieux inspirer les sentiments qu'ils vouloient leur donner, soit en religion, soit en politique. CHEVALIER DE JAUCOURT[1]

TWO PRINCIPAL CONCEPTIONS of the value of art have competed with each other since classical times. Those who hold one point of view have insisted that the main value of art lies in its usefulness as an educational force in the service of religion or some secular ideology. Those holding the other view have asserted that the main value of art consists in its ability to give aesthetic satisfaction independent of any extraneous purpose. The artists of the Italian Renaissance, the art patrons of early eighteenth-century France, the Impressionists of the nineteenth century, and various groups in more recent times have expected art simply to delight the heart and please the eye. But medieval churchmen, the leaders of the Counter Reformation, the art officials at the court of Louis XIV, and the ministers of cultural affairs in certain modern states have all demanded that art convey a message to the masses. In France

---

[1]Chevalier de Jaucourt, "Peinture," *Encyclopédie*, 3e édition (36 vols., Genève, 1778–79), vol. XXV, pp. 120–21.

during the last half of the eighteenth century the latter concept, of art as propaganda, gradually gained support until it reached full development during the Revolution.

This revival of the idea of using art as a social weapon was partly the product of a reaction which set in around the middle of the eighteenth century against the fashionable art of the preceding half century. During the reign of Louis XIV, art had been employed to enhance the grandeur and celebrate the glory of the most powerful ruler in Europe. The King and his art ministers had encouraged a monumental style in which everything was cast in a heroic mould. But even before *le grand monarque* finally passed from the stage, art had begun to move out of the great chamber to the private apartment, to abandon the vast mural for the easel painting, to leave the great historical narrative for the amorous episode or genre scene; there was a shift from grandeur to intimacy, from pomp to elegance, from majesty to charm.

The Sun King and his ministers had largely succeeded in making Versailles the cultural centre of the nation, but in doing so they had turned life at court into an unending ritual. No sooner had Louis XIV died than this court began to disintegrate, never to be restored again in its old form. The Regent, Philippe d'Orléans, who had never liked his late uncle's way of doing things, dissolved the court completely for a time, and moved the centre of government from Versailles to Paris. At the Palais-Royal the Regent could enjoy the company of his favourites, free from the tiresome formalities of the old court. When Louis XV eventually came to the throne, he moved the centre of government back to Versailles, but he too showed a distaste for exacting ceremony, escaping as much as he could into the intimacies of private life. As royal direction of culture relaxed, the aristocracy and the upper *bourgeoisie* were able to make their taste felt more than before. The centre of cultural life tended consequently to shift from the public to the private domain. The upper classes began to demand a more natural life after an excessively ceremonial one.

To suit the new mood of the privileged classes a new style was evolved by the artists of the early eighteenth century. In the art of Watteau, Pater, Lancret, Natoire, Boucher, Nattier, and their contemporaries everything tended to become graceful, fluid, and sensuous. In response to the taste of their patrons, artists tended to avoid serious themes. Even historical painting[2] lost its former grave, austere, idealistic character and became pretty, feminine, and capricious. When painters did undertake historical subjects, they selected love scenes rather than noble themes from the classics or religious history. Thus the courtly baroque of the seventeenth century yielded to the rococo of the eighteenth. The emergence of this style reflected the change from the confident and resplendent absolutism of Louis XIV to the enervated and libertine monarchy of his great grandson.

Nothing dramatizes this change from baroque to rococo better than the transition from Le Brun (1619–1690) to Watteau (1684–1721). At Versailles Le Brun had commemorated the achievements of his royal patron in a gigantic series of allegories swarming with heroic figures. With Watteau everything became delicate and intimate. In his *fêtes galantes* he created a visionary world where lovers attired in rainbow finery strolled or lolled idly about exchanging gallantries and enjoying the delights of their surroundings. His gay figures moved in a halcyon setting of verdant parklands and lacy groves; his gardens were overgrown with roses, and his villages alive with festivities. Watteau's canvases quivered with movement, yet even in motion his figures seemed reposed, dwelling in a world where time stood still. His playful charm, his pastel colours, his nervous lines all announced the dissolution of the grand manner of the seventeenth century.

Boucher revealed other qualities of the new rococo manner. His art had a special appeal for the amorous and decadent court aristocracy of the age of Louis XV. His mythological paintings were full of classical gods and goddesses cavorting about in various settings, almost invariably accompanied by clouds of little cupids. For his pastoral scenes, he created a romantic countryside where, amid luxuriant vegetation, buxom shepherdesses, decked out in satin and ribbons, received the advances of their lovers. Obviously his country folk, with their soft hands and pretty feet, were all aristocrats masquerading as peasants. No other artist could portray

[2]As a genre historical painting—*la peinture d'histoire*—included any work in which were portrayed one or more characters drawn from history or classical literature.

voluptuousness with such skill and delicacy. With masterful strokes
he depicted undulating curves, provocative postures, inviting flesh,
and wanton gestures. The women whom Boucher loved to depict
in so many poses always appeared more undressed than naked. In
1740 his friend Piron summed up the spirit of Boucher's art in one
of his poems, in which he represented the artist as saying to Mme
de Pompadour:

> Je ne recherche, pour tout dire,
> Qu'élégance, grâces, beauté,
> Douceur, gentillesse et gaîté,
> En un mot, ce que respire
> Ou badinage, ou volupté. . . .[3]

Fragonard, the Goncourt brothers remind us, was the poet of the
ars amatoria of his age.[4] His art was sired by Boucher but it had
more liveliness and more passion. Love was his constant theme
whether the lovers pursued each other in mythological settings or
in eighteenth-century gardens. He became the popular painter for
fashionable women of the day, decorating their luxurious boudoirs
with scenes celebrating their life of frivolity. As we can see from
the four panels which he did for the Château de Louveciennes
depicting the course of true love in the hearts of young maidens,
his was a world in which innocence was always a pretence. His
gallant lovers pursued their ladies in a contest which was governed
by elegant rules, but which in the last analysis was a mock contest,
ending in inevitable surrender. In one panel, now often entitled
"Storming the Citadel," a young courtier climbs over a garden wall
while a young lady on the other side feigns astonishment. Seldom
has a fortress been so easily taken. Mme du Barry had commissioned the series, but she turned it down, perhaps because the
actors in this scene bore too close a resemblance to herself and
Louis XV.

Venus, goddess of beauty and pleasure, was the divinity adored
by the courtiers of the age of Louis XV. So popular was her cult
that a scholar named Larcher won a prize in 1775 from the
Académie royale des inscriptions et belles-lettres for recounting

[3]Quoted in G. V. Plekhanov, *Art and Social Life* (London, 1953), p. 154.
[4]Edmond and Jules de Goncourt, *French XVIII Century Painters*, transl. Robin
Ironside (London, 1948), p. 259.

her history.[5] Through this pagan goddess an epicurean aristocracy expressed its preoccupation with the pleasures provided by women. Everywhere the nude female form was to be seen: in murals in state apartments, easel paintings, book illustrations, upholstery fabrics, mantelpiece ornaments, and jewellery. Nudity became so commonplace that Greuze found that he could achieve an erotic effect in his paintings of young ladies simply by putting their clothes back on. There have been few ages when art has been so frankly dedicated to sensual beauty.[6]

Monumental painting shrank from lack of patronage during the early eighteenth century. The Crown did not commission many large works for royal palaces once the workshop at Versailles closed down, nor in an increasingly secular society did the Church offer many opportunities for great historical paintings. Artists were therefore compelled to do smaller paintings which would appeal to the wealthy private patrons who frequented the art exhibitions. After Watteau, a succession of painters executed *fêtes galantes* in which characters from the opera and the theatre were transported into a rustic setting. At the same time French artists catered to the vogue for Flemish genre paintings and landscapes. But above all artists turned out more and more portraits to satisfy the demand of both aristocrats and wealthy burghers. In this way *la petite manière* triumphed over *la grande manière* of the previous century.

Around the middle of the eighteenth century a reaction set in against the fashionable art of the day, and this reaction paved the way for the new cult of antiquity which eventually produced the neoclassical style of David. Various factors contributed to this assault on rococo. Some critics felt that contemporary art did not offer the same scope for artistic expression as had historical painting in the grand tradition. Others disapproved of its subjects and in so doing seemed to reflect the growing influence of bourgeois values in French society. Certainly most contemporary paintings and sculpture did not satisfy the emphasis on utility which was one sign of

[5]P.-H. Larcher, *Mémoire sur Vénus qui a remporté le prix à l'Académie royale des inscriptions et belles-lettres* (Paris, 1775).
[6]Arnold Hauser, *The Social History of Art* (2 vols., London, 1951), vol. II, pp. 520–21.

the expanding influence of the middle class. Works of art which idealized the erotic play of a bored aristocracy scarcely harmonized with the virtues of hard work and moral discipline cherished by the bourgeoisie as a group.

The attack on contemporary art was launched by La Font de Saint-Yenne whose *Réflexions sur quelques causes de l'état présent de la peinture en France* appeared in 1747.[7] Saint-Yenne was upset by the decline which he had observed in historical painting during the preceding decades. In his view the historical genre was the highest form of painting because it alone could transmit noble ideas to posterity; it did much more than just provide pleasure for the eye.[8] This admirable genre had fallen into neglect because the petty taste of the age preferred fashionable portraits and erotic scenes. In order to make a living artists were forced to flatter women by showing them either as classical goddesses, or in pretty little portraits. Saint-Yenne's reaction against the fashionable rococo style led him also to appeal to painters to re-establish the dignity of their art by devoting their talents to noble themes capable of instructing the mind by penetrating the soul.[9] Saint-Yenne continued his attack on fashionable art in various other works published during the following decade.[10]

This attack on rococo soon found considerable support. A growing number of art critics joined in condemning the delicately decadent style favoured by the aristocracy. For example, in his *Lettre sur l'exposition des ouvrages de peinture* in 1747, the Abbé Leblanc denounced the preoccupation with boudoir scenes, with the sexual pastimes of classical gods, or with amorous little cupids. He urged a return to the elevated themes which had inspired artists in earlier times to create compositions in a grand manner. Artists, he said, should study the human heart from a philosophical point of view in order not to expose the onlooker to any but noble

7La Font de Saint-Yenne, *Réflexions sur quelques causes de l'état présent de la peinture en France* (La Haye, 1747). On Saint-Yenne see T. Arnauldet, "La Font de Saint-Yenne," *Gazette des Beaux-Arts*, 1ère série, vol. IV, p. 45.

8Saint-Yenne, *Réflexions*, p. 8.

9*Ibid.*, p. 78.

10La Font de Saint-Yenne, *L'Ombre du Grand Colbert, le Louvre, et la Ville de Paris* (La Haye, 1749); *Le Génie du Louvre aux Champs-Elysées* (Paris, 1756); *Sentiments sur quelques ouvrages de peinture, sculpture et gravure écrits à un particulier en province* (1754).

actions.[11] Other art commentators echoed similar criticisms of the contemporary style.[12] Clearly there was a rising wave of dissatisfaction with the pretty but vacuous art typified by Boucher.

A number of critics also condemned the proliferation of small easel paintings, portraits, genre scenes, and landscapes. These critics felt that in catering to the demand for such trivial subjects painters were endangering the nobility of their art. Saint-Yenne had already complained that the growing demand for portraits was diverting the best artists from serious themes.[13] In his *Réflexions critiques sur les différentes écoles de peinture* d'Argens lamented the fact that the popularity of small genre paintings was undermining the taste for historical subjects. Amateurs were filling their collections with trivial genre scenes which in his opinion had no higher purpose than servile imitation of nature.[14]

Sorties against petty themes forced upon artists by the fashions of the time became quite common after the middle of the century. In 1758 Lacombe published *Le Spectacle des beaux-arts* in which he argued that the fine arts ought to fill an educative role by consecrating glorious events and immortalizing the virtues of illustrious men.[15] Another critic expressed similar views in an anonymous *Lettre sur l'exposition des ouvrages de peinture et de sculpture au Sallon du Louvre*, published in 1769. This critic lamented the sterility of the historical paintings on display, along with the profusion of small paintings and portraits. In his opinion this situation was not the fault of the artist but rather of the dominant taste of the period which demanded the *agréable* and the *délicieux*. Consequently, instead of treating great historical themes, the artist was forced to paint women bathing and children at play. There was a

[11]Abbé Jean-Bernard Leblanc, *Lettre sur l'exposition des ouvrages de peinture, sculpture, etc., de l'année 1747* (1747), pp. 154 ff.

[12]François-Cyprien-Antoine Lieudé de Sepmanville, *Réflexions d'un amateur des beaux-arts* (Paris, 1747); Saint-Yves, *Observations sur les arts et sur quelques morceaux de peinture et de sculpture exposés au Louvre en 1748* (Paris, 1748); Pierre Estève, *Lettre d'un ami sur l'exposition de 1753* (Paris, 1753); Baillet de Saint-Julien, *La Peinture* (1753); Marc-Antoine (le Père) Laugier, *Réflexions critiques sur les différentes écoles de peinture* (Paris, 1752); Louis Petit de Bachaumont, *Essai sur la peinture et l'architecture* (Paris, 1752).

[13]Saint-Yenne, *Sentiments sur quelques ouvrages*, p. 132.

[14]Jean-Baptiste d'Argens, *Réflexions critiques sur les différentes écoles de peinture* (Paris, 1752), p. 258.

[15]Lacombe, avocat, *Le Spectacle des beaux-arts ou considérations touchant leur nature, leurs objets, leurs effets et leurs règles principales* (Paris, 1758).

lack of encouragement for historical painting in the grand manner. Young artists inspired by great examples of historical painting were corrupted by fashionable taste almost as soon as they returned from Italy. Before long they were painting pretty, elegant little canvases with neither severity nor expression or even painting historical subjects *à la française*.[16]

Seen in a broader perspective, the objection which the *philosophes* were to raise against the art of their times formed part of a fairly widespread revulsion against contemporary taste by men who felt that art should serve some nobler purpose. In his *Correspondance littéraire* Grimm criticized the lack of virile emotions in the canvases produced by Boucher.[17] Diderot went further in his condemnation of Boucher by claiming that in this artist's work degradation of style had accompanied corruption of morals step by step.[18] The *Encyclopédie* ridiculed the current idea that the only purpose of art was a momentary gratification of the senses. Characteristically Rousseau was even more vehement than his fellow philosophers in condemning the art of his age.[19] And in *La Morale universelle*, published posthumously in 1776, d'Holbach called on artists to abandon lascivious mythological scenes in order to depict "quelques traits de grandeur d'âme, de bonté, de justice, de l'amour de la patrie. . . ."[20] Clearly it was a short step from revulsion against fashionable art to the notion of art as propaganda.

The revival of the concept of art as propaganda also grew out of the need to refute an accusation that art contributed to the degeneration of society. In eighteenth-century France the idea became familiar that art flourished only in a society where at least some of

[16]Anonymous, *Lettre sur l'exposition des ouvrages de peinture et de sculpture au Sallon* [sic] *du Louvre* (1769), in Collection Deloynes, tome IX, Item 120, p. 8.

[17]Friedrich Melchior Grimm, *Correspondance littéraire, philosophique et critique par Grimm, Diderot, Raynal et Meister* (16 vols., Paris, 1877–82), vol. II (Sept. 1753), p. 280.

[18]Denis Diderot, *Œuvres complètes*, ed. Assézat and Tourneux (20 vols., Paris, 1875–77), vol. X, p. 257.

[19]Jean-Jacques Rousseau, *Discours sur les sciences et les arts* (Genève, 1750), ed. G. R. Havens (New York, 1946), pp. 148–49.

[20]Paul-Henri Thiry, baron d'Holbach, *La Morale universelle ou les devoirs de l'homme fondés sur sa nature* (3 vols., Paris 1820; 1st edition Amsterdam, 1776).

the people could enjoy a life of affluence rather than have to struggle for their livelihood. But the same luxury which was thought to nourish art was often considered the main cause of moral decay which undermined the vigour of a society. Art thus became associated with the moral decline which luxury was supposed to produce. In his *Discours sur les sciences et les arts* published in 1750,[21] Rousseau gave a most eloquent exposition of this view. His main attack was on luxury, but his indictment implicated the arts as well.

In this famous discourse, which launched Rousseau on his controversial career, he took up the problem of whether or not the revival of the arts and sciences had contributed to the moral improvement of mankind. In attempting to answer this question he developed what we might describe as a philosophy of history. According to his theory, virtue had thrived in simple societies where habits were rude but natural. In such rustic communities men lived happy lives unspoiled by the sophisticated vices of cultured societies. At bottom these men were no better than in modern times, but at least they did not hide their motives behind deceptive social conventions (pp. 113 ff.). Unfortunately such natural simplicity vanished as luxury increased, bringing with it all the various arts and sciences. "Le luxe va rarement sans les sciences et les arts," claimed Rousseau (p. 113), "et jamais ils ne vont sans lui."

Rousseau rejected the idea that luxury contributed to the welfare of society. In his opinion, moral rectitude was absolutely essential to the very survival of society, and luxury was diametrically opposed to such rectitude. To be sure, luxury did indicate a certain amount of wealth, and might even contribute to the expansion of such wealth, but, he contended, such apparent advantages were completely outweighed by the disastrous consequences which luxury brought in its train (pp. 136 ff.). For, according to Rousseau, as the conveniences of life increased, as the arts were brought to perfection, as the influence of luxury spread through society, true courage flagged and the virtues gradually disappeared. Renaissance Italy had been easy prey for Charles VIII because her martial strength had been undermined by the cultural preoccupations of

---

[21]References will be given here to the edition of G. R. Havens (New York, 1946).

the princes and nobles of Italy (p. 142). In classical times the Romans themselves had recognized that military vigour had declined amongst them in proportion as they became connoisseurs of the fine arts (p. 143). Consequently, had the noble Fabricius had the misfortune to return to Rome, he would have called on his descendants to demolish their amphitheatres, break up their statues, and drive out their artists.

Luxury gave birth to the arts, but it corrupted its offspring. Relaxation of morality was the necessary consequence of luxury, bringing with it in turn the corruption of taste. In a decadent society the artist would find it almost impossible not to debase himself by working on puerile productions. If he tried to resist degradation, he would probably die in indigence and oblivion. Rousseau warned Carle and Pierre Vanloo that the time was already coming when their brushes, capable of producing sublime and holy images, would have to fall from their hands, or else be prostituted to adorning the panels of coaches with lascivious paintings. And the inimitable Pigalle, a worthy rival of Phidias and Praxiteles, whose chisel the ancients would have employed to carve themselves noble gods, would also have to remain idle, or else condescend to fashion the bellies of apes (pp. 139 ff.). Thus, in Rousseau's opinion, the arts, themselves depraved by voluptuous taste, added to the evil consequences which luxury brought in its train. Nothing, he claimed, could breathe new life into a society once it had been enervated by luxury and the arts (p. 111).

Rousseau thought that this historical law was already working itself out clearly in contemporary France. To him it was evident that luxury had undermined virtue, that wealth was powerless to buy morals or citizens, although it could buy almost everything else (pp. 150 ff.). Cultural progress had added nothing to the real happiness of his countrymen; instead it had corrupted their morals and that corruption in turn had vitiated taste. Rousseau thought that this moral decay was apparent, not only in the frivolous literature and the extravagant philosophies of the period, but also in the plastic arts:

Nos jardins sont ornés de statuës et nos Galeries de tableaux. Que penseriez-vous que représentent ces chefs-d'œuvres [*sic*] de l'art exposés à l'admiration publique? Les défenseurs de la Patrie? ou ces hommes plus grands encore qui l'ont enrichie par leurs vertus? Non. Ce sont des images de tous les égaremens du cœur et de la raison, tirées soigneuse-ment de l'ancienne Mythologie, et présentées de bonne heure à la curiosité de nos enfans; sans doute afin qu'ils ayent sous leurs yeux des modèles de mauvaises actions, avant même que de savoir lire. (p. 148 f.)

In 1753, Rousseau asked ironically that a correspondent prove to him that a beautiful statue was more valuable than a noble deed or "qu'un morceau de toile peinte par Vanloo vaut mieux que de la vertu."[22] Admittedly some of his remarks did imply that under favourable conditions, works of art could convey moral ideas. It was also true that in his *Considérations sur le gouvernement de Pologne* he recommended that all the various arts be mobilized in order to create a national spirit by impressing common ideas on the minds of the Poles.[23] But the main point of the famous essay continued to worry men right through the period of the Revolution, and thinkers repeatedly felt compelled to refute the idea that the arts, as the offspring of luxury, necessarily devitalized the moral energy of a society.[24] It was one of those arguments which continue to plague men even when it seems to have been rebutted repeatedly.

Obviously one of the best ways to answer the argument that art along with luxury contributed to social degeneration was to reply that art could be used to educate the masses provided that it was properly directed. Thus we shall see how the *Encyclopédie* attempted to answer Rousseau by arguing that art could make a valuable contribution to the education of the citizen.[25] At the peak of the Revolution we shall find some austere republicans echoing the arguments of Rousseau, thus forcing art lovers to show that art could serve a useful purpose.[26] And even under the Directory we

[22]*Correspondance générale de J. J. Rousseau*, ed. T. Dufour, vol. II, no. 153, p. 37.
[23]Rousseau, *Considérations sur le gouvernement de Pologne* (1772), *Œuvres de J. J. Rousseau*, ed. Didot (20 vols., Paris, 1827), vol. II, pp. 315–56.
[24]For example, L-P. de Bugny, "De l'influence des belles-lettres, des sciences, et des arts sur la situation politique des nations," *Magasin encyclopédique*, vol. X (1796), pp. 14–29.
[25]"Beaux-arts," *Encyclopédie*, vol. III, p. 489 a,b.
[26]For example, Durand de Maillane told the Convention that the higher arts were dangerous because luxury "ne peut pas compâter avec un gouvernement républicain. . . ." *Opinion sur les écoles primaires prononcée à la Convention nationale le 12 décembre 1792* (Paris, n.d.), p. 3.

shall discover the whole question debated at great length in the *Journal de Paris*, causing those who cherished the visual arts to restate once more the idea of using art for public education.

The revulsion against fashionable art, along with the need to show that art was not a social menace, contributed, then, to the growth of the idea of art as propaganda. But the principal reason for this development was a positive one—the desire of social reformers to make use of the emotional appeal of the fine arts. These *philosophes* were not philosophers in the usual sense of the word; they were not architects of complex structures of thought, but rather men of letters intent on popularizing ideas which they felt would improve the lot of their fellow men. Voltaire, Diderot, d'Alembert, Helvétius and their colleagues were primarily interested in ideas which could be applied, in practical verities, in truths which could set men free.

Certainly there was a crying need for practical reform. Eighteenth-century France was a mass of social abuses, useless privileges, vestigial institutions, and regional anomalies, all capped by the incomplete superstructure of a modern state. A man could be jailed by a note from the king. There was no official religious liberty. Haphazard censorship impeded free expression of ideas. Peasants bore an intolerable burden of taxation while wealthier groups enjoyed exemptions. Aristocrats who no longer filled any useful function exacted heavy dues from the peasants and enjoyed exclusive privileges. Laws were cruel and excessively complex. Institutions which had long since been superseded survived as a burden on the state. The country was still divided economically by innumerable tolls and customs barriers. And in piecing together a large state over the centuries the kings had permitted many provincial differences and inconsistencies to remain.

This social confusion stood in marked contrast to the picture of the physical universe presented by contemporary science—a universe which seemed like a great watch running smoothly according to unchanging laws. The *philosophes* wanted to impose a similar order on society. They believed that there must be natural laws governing human relationships just as there were laws which controlled the motions of the heavenly bodies. It was their ambition to discover these laws, publicize them, and induce men to obey them. They aspired to be the Galileos and Newtons of the social world.

Reason was now to take the place of revelation as the guiding light for mankind. The *philosophes* were confident that reason could reveal the right principles by which society could be reorganized. Reason did not always lead these men to the same conclusions, but they did agree on many objectives—the need to render government less arbitrary, to create a more equitable tax system, to uproot harmful social barriers, to codify the laws, to destroy hindrances to trade, to bring about religious toleration, and to gain freedom of expression for enlightened thinkers. Above all they agreed that brotherly love had to be secularized. Such objectives were thought to be some of the results of examining nature in the light of reason.

But there was a basic difference between the laws of nature as they applied to men and as they applied to heavenly bodies. The planets did not have to be shown the right course or persuaded to adhere to it. Why had men strayed from it in the first place? This was a disturbing question which eighteenth-century radicals never answered very satisfactorily. They accused priests of misleading mankind, but at best this answer only pushed the problem of evil back one step. They found it expedient to gloss over this difficulty or put it to one side. The immediate problem was considered more important—how to persuade men to return to the course indicated by nature.

Despite their faith in reason, the *philosophes* did not believe that cold logic alone could convert mankind. They realized that men had to be attracted, moved, and aroused by those who hoped to lead them. "D'ailleurs on ne conduit le peuple ni par des raisonnements, ni par des définitions," wrote Saint-Lambert in the *Encyclopédie*; "il faut imposer à ses sens . . ." (vol. XX, p. 552a). The eighteenth-century reformers consequently utilized all sorts of methods of presenting their message in an attractive fashion—essays, poems, stories, histories, and plays. Some of the reformers also began to consider the possibility of using the visual arts as a means of impressing their new gospel on the minds of men.

The psychological theory then in vogue encouraged the belief of these reformers that art could assist them. This theory repudiated belief in innate ideas in favour of the epistemology of Locke. According to the latter view, all ideas are transformations of primitive sensations, since at birth the mind is like a blank sheet of paper awaiting the imprint of sense perceptions. Such a doctrine was encouraging to reformers. It suggested that the mind was not sullied at birth by original sin, but was shaped by environmental forces. If from birth the mind were exposed to the right sort of impressions, then a desirable type of human being could be produced. It followed also that by manipulating the environment human nature could likewise be perverted, but eighteenth-century thinkers preferred to emphasize the happier possibilities. By surrounding a man from birth with images of social virtue they hoped to produce a good citizen.

Despite their rejection of innate ideas, the *philosophes* nevertheless usually ascribed a few basic instincts to mankind. Often they endowed man with an instinctive sympathy for his fellow men. They also believed that men naturally sought the good synonymous with pleasure and avoided evil associated with pain. This suggested that men could be led to desirable goals by associating them with pleasure and away from undesirable ones by reversing the technique. Such an application of association ought to be familiar to us in the twentieth century: it is the advertising trick which always pictures a glamorous female beside the new car so that the customer will associate the two in his mind. Eighteenth-century reformers thought that the fine arts could provide one medium where this process could be used to teach men to love virtue and shun vice.

The belief of reformers that art could assist their cause was also encouraged by their awareness that art had often been considered as a social weapon in the past. Since they had been nurtured in classical literature, the *philosophes* and later revolutionaries knew that the great Greek philosophers had been concerned about the moral influence of art. Plato, for example, had argued in *The Republic* that artists should be required to portray the image of the good in their works on pain of expulsion from the state if they did anything else. In the good society sculptors and other artists were to be allowed to practise their professions only so long as they impressed noble sentiments on the minds of youth (III. 401-2).

Again in *The Laws* (II. 656) Plato had suggested that artists should not be left free to follow their own fancy with no thought of their moral influence on youth. The arts should be controlled by artistic canon which would prevent them from having harmful consequences. In his *Politics* (VIII. 5, 21) Aristotle had argued that figures and colours were not only imitations but expressions of emotion which denoted moral habits. Although he had not been sure how extensive an influence works of art had, he did advise guiding youth toward certain works and away from others. Clearly utilitarian considerations had influenced Greek attitudes toward art.

The social critics and revolutionaries also remembered what certain Roman authors had said about the social impact of artistic images. For instance the *Encyclopédie* pointed out that Cicero had believed that constant exhibition of an image of virtue could create a lasting impression on his son.[27] Elsewhere it quoted the elder Pliny with approval because he had admired works of art primarily as a means of commemorating virtuous acts, thereby exciting emulation among the citizenry.[28] Later, during the Revolution, numerous commentators pointed out that in classical times the arts had been recognized as a way of instructing the public by means of pleasant sensations.[29]

The Church provided eighteenth-century reformers with further support for their belief that art could be a valuable educational weapon. Although the *philosophes* and their successors were not familiar with medieval theories on the value of images, they could see around them the cathedrals in which these theories had been applied. As Emile Mâle has demonstrated vividly in *L'Art religieux du treizième siècle en France*, the medieval cathedral had been a plastic presentation of the dogmas and traditions of the Church. Everything which was considered useful for a man to know had been depicted there for all to see: the life and passion of Christ, the lives of the various saints, the virtues contrasted with their corresponding vices, the history of the world since creation, as well as all the diverse activities of mankind dedicated to the Creator. From

27"Beaux-arts," *Encyclopédie*, vol. III, p. 486 b.
28*Ibid.*, vol. XXV, pp. 1336–42; the reference seems to have been to Pliny the Elder, *Natural History*, XXXV.I.
29For example, T-B. Emeric-David, *Recherches sur l'art statuaire chez les anciens et chez les modernes* (Paris, l'an IX), pp. 27, 107, and 111.

the statues, the low reliefs, the stained glass windows, and the embroidered tapestries, the common folk had learned almost all they knew about their faith. Through images the highest conceptions of medieval theology had been carried down to the most ignorant. Art had provided a Bible for the poor.[30]

Medieval apologists for religious art had marshalled arguments very like those which Frenchmen were to use for a different programme. Many churchmen had contended that images left a more lasting impression on the human mind than either the spoken or the written word. One of the clearest examples of this belief in the influence of visual presentations had been *An Essay on the Various Arts* by Theophilus,[31] a Benedictine monk who probably lived about the middle of the tenth century, although some scholars have dated him later. Theophilus had defended the practice of ornamenting the walls and windows of churches with glowing flowers and leaves on the grounds that it showed the beholder everything in creation praising God. But his main argument for the lavish use of art in churches had rested on the conviction that images conveyed lessons directly to the observer. The faithful could be moved by representations of the Passion, induced to live better by visions of heaven, and warned by sight of the torments of hell.

In the thirteenth century the assumptions behind the use of art as religious propaganda had been elucidated by William Durandus in his *Rationale Divinorum Officiorum*. Durandus had explained the value of art in terms similar to those we shall encounter among eighteenth-century reformers, although the faith which art was to serve was quite different. He had begun by asserting that the use of art in churches did not constitute worship of graven images as forbidden in the Old Testament. It was one thing to adore an image, but something completely different to learn from such a work what should be adored. Images used in churches were not idols, but instruments by which lessons were imprinted on the hearts of the laity who often could not read but could only look. Even if the laity

[30]Emile Mâle, *L'Art religieux du treizième siècle en France* (Paris, 1923), pp. i f.

[31]Theophilus, *An Essay upon Various Arts in Three Books by Theophilus, called also Rugerus, Priest and Monk, Forming an Encyclopedia of Christian Art of the Eleventh Century*, transl. Robert Hendrie (London, 1847), in E. G. Holt, ed., *A Documentary History of Art* (New York, 1957), vol. I, p. 8.

could read, Durandus believed that they would be more deeply impressed by an image than by any written description:

But Gregory saith that paintings are not to be put away because they are not to be worshipped; for paintings appear to move the mind more than descriptions: for deeds are placed before the eyes in paintings, and appear to be actually carrying on. But in description, the deed is done as it were by hearsay: which affecteth the mind less when recalled to memory. Hence it is that in churches we pay less reverence to books than to images and pictures.[32]

During the Renaissance art had often been used more with an eye to decoration than propagation of the faith. Then had come the Protestants who had very nearly denied the value of any kind of religious art. But during the Counter Reformation Catholic church-men had reaffirmed their conviction that religious images were an incitement to piety and an assistance to salvation.[33] The decisions of the Council of Trent on religious art had been revealing in this respect:

Let the bishops diligently teach that the stories of the mysteries of our Redemption, portrayed in paintings and other representations, instruct and confirm the people in the habit of remembering and in assiduously rehearsing the articles of faith; and also that sacred images are the source of great spiritual profit, not only because the people are thus reminded of the benefits and gifts bestowed upon them by Christ, but also because the miracles which God has performed by means of the Saints and their wholesome examples are set before the faithful; that they might give thanks for these things, might order their lives and manners in imitation of the Saints, and may be excited to adore and love God, and to cultivate piety.[34]

Again the arguments were similar to those which were to be employed by eighteenth-century French thinkers. Possevinus had argued in his *Tractatio de poesi et pictura*, written toward the end

---

[32]William Durandus, *Rationale Divinorum Officiorum*, Book I, transl. J. M. Neale and B. Webb as *The Symbolism of Churches and Church Ornaments* (Leeds, 1843), pp. 53–69, in Holt, *Documentary History*, vol. I, p. 123.

[33]The Counter Reformation produced numerous books defending the use of art as an instrument of propaganda. For example: Ambrosius Cartharinus, *De certa gloria invocatione ac veneratione sanctorum* (Lyons, 1542); Conradus Brunus, *De imaginibus* (Augsburg, 1548); Nicholas Hartsfield, *Dialogi sex* (1566); Nicholas Sanders, *De typica et honoraria sacrarum imaginum adoratione* (Louvain, 1569).

[34]*Canons and Decrees of the Council of Trent*, Session XXV, Tit.2.

of the sixteenth century,[35] that although art could give pleasure, its proper purpose was utility. And if religious art was to be useful it was necessary to exclude every false idea which might enter into it, thus misleading the onlooker. Above all Possevinus had wanted to get rid of the pagan divinities and other shameful images which had made their way into religious art during the Renaissance. In his view art reached its highest level when it created religious paintings so realistic that the spectators seemed to behold the events themselves. Similar views had been expressed by Paleotti in a treatise *De imaginibus sacris*, written in the same period. Visible representations, Paleotti had claimed, appeal more vividly to the minds of many men than the spoken word.[36]

In his dialogue *Il Figino*, Comanini had expressed views on art which many eighteenth-century thinkers could have supported had the arguments not been applied to religious propaganda.[37] In the first part of the dialogue one of the speakers, a patron of the fine arts, argues that the aim of painting is simply to arouse pleasure, and supports the notion of art for art's sake. A priest answers him, arguing that although painting produces pleasure by means of imitation, its real purpose is utility rather than pleasure. Art, the priest points out, has always been controlled by the state, as for instance in Egypt, Greece, and Rome, and has invariably been directed by the state toward proper goals. Since men were now in a Christian era, the Church ought to control the influence of art, and direct it toward the support of Christianity. In the end the art patron admits he has lost the argument, acknowledges that the primary purpose of painting is utility, and concedes that the aesthetic pleasure which it arouses is only of secondary interest.

The great churches which such convictions had inspired were not the only examples of art regarded as a social force. The *philosophes* and revolutionaries did not even originate the idea of employing art for a secular cause. Modern rulers had shown their appreciation of the value of images. Louis XIV had provided a

35Antonius Possevinus, *Tractatio de poesi et pictura* (Lyons, 1595), cited in Pierre Janelle, *The Catholic Reformation* (Milwaukee, 1948), pp. 198–200.

36Gabriele Paleotti, *De imaginibus sacris* (Ingolstadt, 1594), cited in Anthony Blunt, *Artistic Theory in Italy: 1450–1600* (Oxford, 1940), pp. 110 ff.

37Gregorio Comanini, *Il Figino* (Mantua, 1591), cited in Blunt, *Artistic Theory*, pp. 131–32.

recent example of how art could be used to glorify the state as personified by the king. The monarchy had made use of the Académie royale de peinture et sculpture to direct painting and sculpture toward political ends. The Académie had been used to eliminate the personal relationship of the artist with the general public and to minimize the importance of private patronage. Originally a free society with unlimited membership, the Académie had been transformed into a state institution organized on an hierarchical basis under an authoritarian directorate. Obviously the goal had been to make artists dependent on the state for status and employment. This had become especially true after 1664 when the minister of finance, Colbert, became *surintendant des bâtiments* or "Minister of Fine Arts."

As his artistic collaborator the minister of finance had favoured Charles Le Brun. *Premier peintre du roi*, director of the Académie, head of its branch in Rome, and manager of the Gobelin tapestry works, Le Brun had become virtually the art dictator of France. In a series of monumental works he devoted his talents to the idealization of Louis, whom he liked to clothe in classical garb. His "Batailles d'Alexandre," now displayed in the Louvre, for example, were meant to glorify the Sun King who in 1667 had completed a military campaign in Flanders. "It was Louis XIV," writes Plekhanov, "who was applauded in the image of Alexander."[38] Besides turning out such heroic works Le Brun had directed a vast programme of art production intended to spread the glory of the king through paintings, statues, busts, reliefs, tapestries, and medallions. Artists had been marshalled like soldiers and works of art manufactured like munitions.

Neither Louis XIV nor Colbert had much love for art as a means to aesthetic enjoyment. For both the King and his minister art had been only an instrument of government useful for enhancing the prestige of the monarchy. Nothing could make this clearer than the text of the *lettre d'ennoblissement* awarded to Le Brun for his services:

Ceux qui ont excellé dans la peinture, ont toujours esté, dans tous les temps, très favorablement traitez dans la Cour des plus grands princes

[38]Plekhanov, *Art and Social Life*, p. 153.

où non seulement leurs ouvrages ont servi à l'embellissement de leurs palais, mais encore de monuments à leur gloire, exprimant par un langage muet leurs plus belles et plus héroïques actions.[39]

Versailles was the supreme achievement of the *style Louis XIV*. Just as the medieval cathedral had served as an architectural symbol of divine revelation, so this immense palace had provided a symbol of royal grandeur. All the decoration had been consciously related to the dominating theme, the power and beneficence of Apollo, the Sun God. The statues and ornaments which embellished the palace were not placed in haphazard positions, but were all arranged around the symbol of the Sun, the emblem of Louis XIV. Some represented the fruits of the earth, some the winds, others the months of the year—all either the products or the handmaids of the Sun.[40]

In special circumstances art was used, not only to symbolize the greatness of the king, but to transmit a direct political message. On one occasion when the pope refused to give satisfaction to Louis XIV the king sent him a tapestry by Hallé representing the Doge of Genoa coming to apologize courteously at Versailles in order to dramatize the humiliation in store for those who refused to submit to the will of the king.

Although this intimate liaison between art and politics broke down in the first half of the eighteenth century, the *philosophes* and revolutionaries were keenly aware of such recent examples of how art could be given a social and political role. The notion of art as propaganda was indeed deeply rooted in the Western tradition; it had only to be resurrected, restated in more modern terms, and put to use for a new cause.

But there was another tradition deeply rooted in the West—the concept of art as an end in itself. Although the phrase *l'art pour l'art* was coined by certain nineteenth-century aesthetes, the attitude

[39]Arch. Nat., X¹ A8683, p. 319.
[40]The symbolism of the palace had been explained very early in a guide book: Laurent Morellet, *An Historical Explanation of what there is most Remarkable in that Wonder of the World the French King's House at Versailles* (London, 1684). French edition 1681.

was certainly not new. It was the Greeks who had first conceived of art as an autonomous activity whose creations could be enjoyed as pure forms. Just as they had discovered the idea of science as pure research, so also they had developed the concept of art independent of any purpose but its own, the idea of art for its own sake. They had seen that art could be enjoyed simply for its play of line and colour, its rhythm and harmony, its grace and symmetry. Because art had usually served magic or religion in most early societies, this concept of pure art had represented a revolutionary development.[41] Since classical times it had competed with the older notion of art in the service of some social goal.

During the Middle Ages the notion of art as an autonomous activity had been overshadowed by the concept of art as the handmaid of religion. Then the Italian Renaissance had witnessed a rebirth of interest in art as an end in itself. This had not meant that art was no longer used by the Church to portray its beliefs or by despots to glamorize their régimes. But it had meant that those who wrote about art seldom tried to justify it on the grounds that it was useful to diffuse ideas. Almost without exception those who wrote about art during the Italian Renaissance had cherished it as a beautiful imitation of the natural world.

Such an attitude was already clear at the beginning of the fifteenth century in the treatise *Della pittura* by Leone Battista Alberti. This artist and humanist no longer viewed art primarily as a means of evolving symbols by which to convey the religious and moral teachings of the Church. For him art is first and foremost a means of creating the most beautiful possible reproduction of the outside world according to the principles of human reason. The noblest kind of painting in his view is historical painting because it could stir the spectator deeply with its pictures of human activities. But he did not go on to suggest that historical paintings ought to choose themes likely to produce better citizens, although he believed that good citizenship was the highest virtue.[42] Apparently it was enough for art to reproduce the outer world as faithfully as possible.

[41]Hauser, *Social History of Art*, pp. 91–93.
[42]Leone Battista Alberti, *Della pittura* (1436), Eng. transl. J. R. Spencer (London, 1956), p. 77.

Leonardo da Vinci's *Trattato della pittura* revealed the same tendency to treat art as an autonomous pursuit.[43] For Leonardo the dignity of art rests in its ability to make images of natural phenomena with scientific accuracy. Apparently, in his view, art is valuable, not as a moral force in society, but simply as an exact imitation of the outer world (p. 115 ff.). Like Alberti he thought that historical painting was the highest type of painting because it requires the artist to display all his imitative skills in a single work of art. In painting historical themes, the artist has to be able to paint man as well as the setting in which he lived. A good painter also has to know how to portray the ideas in his subjects' minds by means of gestures and facial expression (pp. 341–45, 368–69). In spite of the fact that Leonardo believed painting has a far more lively effect on the mind than the written word, he seldom argued that art should be used as an educational instrument (pp. 58–59). It was enough that it should mirror the wonders of the universe.

Savonarola was one of the few in the Italian Renaissance who harked back to the medieval conception of the role of art in society. Although he burned works of art which he considered incitements to sin, he believed strongly in the good which could come from the right sort of art.[44] On more than one occasion he urged those who could not read the scriptures to contemplate the figures of Christ and his Saints represented in the churches. But this conception of art had been temporarily overshadowed by worship of the beauties of the world and of man. In his *Le Vite de' piu eccellenti pittori, scultori, et architettori*, written in the middle of the sixteenth century, Vasari had emphasized the progress made over the two preceding centuries in capturing the splendours of the visual world. According to Vasari, this progressive development had reached its height in the early sixteenth century when artists delighted the eye with the delicacy, refinement, and grace in their imitations of

[43]Leonardo da Vinci, *Trattato della pittura* (n.d.), Eng. transl. J. P. Richter, *The Literary Works of Leonardo da Vinci* (2 vols., Oxford, 1939), vol. I, pp. 30–372.

[44]Fra Girolamo Savonarola's comments on art have been brought together by G. Gruyer in *Les Illustrations des écrits de Jérôme Savonarole publiés en Italie au quinzième et au seizième siecle et les paroles de Savonarole sur l'art* (Paris, 1879); see pp. 204, 207.

nature.[45] Although in his writings he described endless religious paintings, he was interested in their aesthetic qualities rather than their influence. There was not a word about the religious significance of Michelangelo's "Last Judgment," which for him was simply "an exemplar in foreshortenings and all the other difficulties of art."[46]

Meanwhile the Renaissance had produced a new conception of the artist. Throughout ancient and medieval times painters and sculptors had been excluded from the coveted ranks of the liberal arts because their work involved manual labour. During the fifteenth and sixteenth centuries they succeeded in gaining admission to the upper circle by emphasizing the intellectual and imaginative nature of their work. As a result, a gulf had been opened up between the crafts and the "fine arts." The concept of the artist as a lonely genius pursuing a special vision had been born. It followed that the artist had to be free to follow this vision wherever it led him. Later artists sometimes surrendered this hard-won freedom in return for honour and patronage, but the Renaissance spirit continued to protest against autocratic and bureaucratic control. Bernini embodied this spirit when he attacked the slavishness of French artists under Louis XIV. "Submission," he told them, "is necessary only in matters of faith: otherwise man has complete freedom in all spheres of life."[47]

When they came to restate the idea of art as propaganda, the *philosophes*, Encyclopedists, and revolutionaries were to bring two lively Western traditions into confrontation. The notion of using art as a social weapon went back through modern statesmen and medieval churchmen to classical philosophers. But classical antiquity had also given birth to the concept of art valued for its aesthetic qualities alone, and this idea had been reborn in fifteenth-century Italy to become a vital force in the artistic life of the West. Both the art and the criticism of the early eighteenth century

[45]Giorgio Vasari, *Le Vite de' più eccellenti pittori, scultori et architettori* (Milan, 1550); English transl. Gaston de Vere (10 vols., London, 1912–15); see vol. IV, p. 80.

[46]*Ibid.*, IX, p. 130.

[47]Cited in the *New Cambridge Modern History*, vol. V, p. 162.

revealed the persistence of *l'art pour l'art*.[48] At the same time there had emerged the idea of the artist as a genius who ought to be free to follow his creative impulses. Eighteenth-century intellectuals, nurtured in the classics, heirs of the Renaissance, could scarcely be insensitive to this other tradition. Here then was a dilemma—could they direct art toward a social goal without sacrificing the artistic values and artistic freedom of the Renaissance?

[48]This was clear in the aesthetics of the Abbé du Bos, *Réflexions critiques sur la poésie et sur la peinture* (Paris, 1719). Even Saint-Yenne, for all his emphasis on noble themes, could not help at times admiring the aesthetic qualities of some of the types which he condemned.

Diderot's Views
on the Social
Function of Art

2.

*Mais il faudrait que les productions de nos
artistes eussent, comme celles des poëtes, un but
moral. C'était l'opinion de Diderot. Il semble
qu'il prévoyait déjà cette révolution qui devait,
quelque temps après sa mort, changer les
opinions, les goûts, le caractère des Français, leur
donner un gouvernement qui, bien différent de
la monarchie, s'appuie sur l'instruction, les vertus,
l'amour de la vérité, enfin sur les bonnes mœurs.*

LA DÉCADE PHILOSOPHIQUE[1]

DIDEROT EPITOMIZED the new ideas which were abroad in eighteenth-century France. Son of a staid provincial cutler, he had arrived in Paris at the age of sixteen to prepare himself at the famous college Louis le Grand for a career as a Jesuit. But the throbbing life of the metropolis so lured him that he abandoned the idea of becoming a priest, resisted family pressure to enter the legal profession, and chose the life of a bohemian. For a good many years he lived from hand to mouth, obtaining money by one expedient or another, pursuing women, reading omnivorously, and debating with his friends in the cafés of the Latin Quarter. It was there that Diderot mixed with other young men destined to make

[1]*La Décade philosophique,* an IV, vol. X, p. 210.

a name for themselves, men such as Rousseau, Condillac, and Toussaint. In 1747 he was asked to edit the translation of Chamber's *Cyclopaedia* at a salary of twelve hundred pounds a year. Diderot soon transformed this project into the production of a great new encyclopedia which would provide its readers with a comprehensive picture of modern knowledge. In his opinion such a work could help to emancipate mankind from its bondage to the past. Before he began his work on this enterprise he had been only on obscure translator; the *Encyclopédie* not only provided him with some financial security, but transformed him from a hack into one of the most eminent literary figures in France.

A few years earlier Diderot had begun to expound his views in various publications. His works reveal a steady though painful retreat from Christianity. When he had translated Shaftesbury's *Inquiry into Merit and Virtue* in 1745, he had still professed belief in a deity. His *Pensées philosophiques* of 1746 show him with more sympathy for atheistic arguments, but dissatisfied with the mechanistic explanation of life. By the time he wrote his *Lettre sur les aveugles* in 1749, a work which got him locked up for three months, he was already attracted to the idea that chance combinations of matter in motion provided the creative force in the universe, a notion he later developed into the most advanced system of materialism in the century. For the sake of morality he hesitated to dismiss God altogether, but soon he was willing to base morals on a purely human foundation. For him God was henceforth a discarded hypothesis.

But although he now embraced a godless philosophy, Diderot did retain some of the ingredients of the Christian tradition. He never lost his faith in the dignity of human life, in the value of the individual person, in the brotherhood of all men, or in the prospect of a better future for mankind. Above all he retained a sense of mission which sustained him in the face of adversity. The article "Philosophe" which he inserted in the *Encyclopédie* asserted that for a true philosopher, society ought to be a kind of divinity on earth (vol. XXV, p. 669). And in a brief satire which he later penned against excessive luxury, he summed up the goals for which he fought: "La vertu, la vertu, la sagesse, les mœurs, l'amour des enfants pour les pères, l'amour des pères pour les enfants, la tendresse du souverain pour ses sujets, celle des sujets pour le souverain, les bonnes lois, la bonne éducation, l'aisance générale: voilà, voilà, ce que j'ambitionne."[2]

In 1759 this philosopher with a mission became an art critic. In that year his friend Grimm asked him to review the biennial art salons for his *Correspondance littéraire*. For six years Grimm had been sending out reports of the latest books and news to a select list of German subscribers. These literary reports were copied out by hand and circulated through the diplomatic mails to upper class readers. On the whole the literary quality of these newsletters is remarkably high. Until his death Diderot contributed reviews of all the exhibitions in the Louvre, except when he was away travelling or was too ill to do the job. Altogether he produced nine *Salons* during the years 1759 to 1781, which have proved to be among his most popular works. These reviews display liveliness, charm, inventiveness, and a delight in his work, which make them still a joy to read.[3]

Only Grimm's correspondents and some close friends were privileged to read these spirited reviews at the time. Diderot did not want them to be widely published lest he bring down on his head the wrath of those artists whom he had criticized. However, although they reached only a small group at the time, these *Salons* are historically important. They reveal the direction in which progressive thought was moving, and allow us to observe an eighteenth-century reformer reacting to the art of his own day. At the same time they enable us to observe some inner contradictions in his attitude toward art—tensions which will take on a deeper significance when viewed from the vantage-point of the Revolution.

The *Salons* show a definite progression of thought. In his early reviews Diderot concentrated mainly on the artistic merits of the works on display. Thus in his first article in 1759 (vol. X, pp. 90 ff.), he does not suggest that there is anything wrong with the

[2]*Satire contre le luxe*, in *Œuvres complètes de Diderot*, ed. Assézat and Tourneux (20 vols., Paris, 1875–77), vol. XI, p. 94.

[3]There is a new illustrated edition of the *Salons* in preparation, of which three volumes have appeared: Diderot, *Salons*, ed. J. Seznec and J. Adhémar (Oxford, 1957–). Since the new edition is incomplete, the references here are to the volumes in the *Œuvres complètes*, vols. X, XI, and XII.

subjects which artists had chosen.[4] His criticisms are focused on weaknesses in composition and on technical deficiencies. Again, in his second review in 1761 (vol. X, pp. 107 ff.), he admires numerous paintings which had no real moral message, such as the "Portrait du Roi" by Michel Van Loo, "La Lecture" by Carle Van Loo, "Saint Germain" by Vien, "Saint André" by Deshays, "Le Soleil Couchant" by Le Bel, the "Diomède" by Doyen, the "Jeune Elève" by Drouais, and a "Bataille" by Casanove. In conclusion Diderot expresses his general satisfaction with the works on exhibit. "Jamais nous n'avons eu un plus beau salon," he exclaimed (vol. X, p. 151). "Presque aucun tableau absolument mauvais; plus de bons que de médiocres, et un grand nombre d'excellents."

As Diderot warmed to his task as art critic, he became increasingly antagonistic toward the erotic subjects favoured for art by the aristocracy of the period. His growing dislike for this frivolous art was demonstrated by his outbursts against the works of Boucher. Coming to Boucher's "La Bergerie" in his review for 1763, Diderot lashed out at the decadent art which the popular painter was producing (vol. X, pp. 160 ff.). This artist was the ruination of all the young students of painting. Scarcely had they learned how to manipulate a brush and hold a palette, than they laboured at entwining garlands around infants, at painting chubby pink posteriors, and at rushing headlong into all sorts of extravagances. In his *Salon* for 1765, Diderot was even more damning in his attack on the kind of art produced by Boucher (vol. X, pp. 233 ff.). Commenting on the twelve pastoral paintings which the artist had on display, he could scarcely control his indignation:

Je ne sais que dire de cet homme-ci. La dégradation du goût, de la couleur, de la composition, des caractères, de l'expression, du dessin, a suivi pas à pas la dépravation des mœurs. Que voulez-vous que cet artiste jette sur la toile? Ce qu'il a dans l'imagination; et que peut avoir dans l'imagination un homme qui passe sa vie avec des prostituées du plus bas étage? (vol. X, p. 256)

Diderot claimed that Boucher had degenerated to the point where he was no longer really an artist. And it was precisely at that moment that he became first painter to the king. Boucher revealed by his works that he had never understood truth and was a

[4]See his general conclusion about the exhibit, vol. X, p. 103.

stranger to innocence. His paintings demonstrated that he had never known nature, at least not the nature which moved the heart of an unspoiled child or a sensitive woman. His productions were too full of affectation and his nudes were too decked out with rouge, pompons, beauty spots, and other tricks of the powder room. Above all Diderot could not tolerate all the innumerable little infants with which the artist strewed his canvases. "Dans toute cette innombrable famille," complained Diderot (vol. X, p. 257), "vous n'en trouverez pas un à employer aux actions réelles de la vie, à étudier sa leçon, à lire, à écrire, à tiller du chanvre. Ce sont des natures romanesques, idéales, de petits bâtards de Bacchus et de Silène."

The paintings of Baudouin likewise aroused the indignation of the *philosophe* who looked upon them as examples of art consecrated to a harmful purpose (vol. X, pp. 332–36). "Greuze s'est fait peintre, prédicateur des bonnes mœurs; Baudouin, peintre, prédicateur des mauvaises," claimed Diderot; "Greuze peintre de famille et d'honnêtes gens, Baudouin peintre de petites-maisons et de libertins. . . ." Among the works which the artist had on display in 1765 was one entitled "Le Confessional" which shows a group of young girls come to confess their various sins, only to be disturbed suddenly by two lewd young men who bear down upon them. The priest is shown leaping out of the confessional box to chastise the young rascals, one of whom is about to tell the old priest what he thinks of him. In the background the artist had depicted some young monkeys who obviously think the whole scene is quite amusing. In another painting entitled "L'Espérance déçue" a cavalier is portrayed stretched out on a couch looking rather reluctant to bestir himself. A scantily dressed girl stands nearby eyeing her companion in an annoyed manner as if to ask whether this is all he can do. In still another work, "La Fille querellée par sa mère," the artist had depicted a scene in a cellar where a mother has obviously interrupted some interesting activity. In the foreground the mother, flushed with anger, is shown confronting her daughter. The daughter, who has not found time to readjust her dress, stands weeping in front of a pile of freshly cut straw. In the background a corpulent lad, obviously hurrying to pull up his trousers, tries to escape up the cellar stairs. Diderot could see the humour in such themes, but he thought that art should serve some nobler purpose. "Quand il n'en coûte aucun sacrifice à l'art," he observed, "ne vaut-il pas mieux mettre la vertu que le vice en scène?" (vol. X, p. 336).[5]

Diderot became exasperated by the number of artists who devoted their talents to mythological themes which had no relevancy to real life. For instance, in his *Salon* for 1767 he attacked a little trifle by La Grenée entitled "L'Amour rémouleur" which depicted a cupid sharpening an arrow while one helper keeps the grindstone wet and another turns the wheel. Diderot rebuked artists who wasted their time on such subjects. "Les peintres se jettent dans cette mythologie," he lamented (vol. XI, pp. 56–57); "ils perdent le goût des événements naturels de la vie; et il ne sort plus de leurs pinceaux que des scènes indécentes, folles, extravagantes, idéales, ou tout au moins vides d'intérêt. . . ." What interest did he have in the sinful adventures of Jupiter, Venus, Hercules, Hebe, Ganymede, or any of the other divinities from ancient myths? Would not a painting satirizing contemporary customs or dealing with modern history appeal much more than pagan stories?

Many of the artists who displayed their paintings at the biennial exhibitions still drew their subjects from Christian traditions. For example in the exhibition of 1765 Carle Van Loo presented seven "Esquisses de la vie de Saint Grégoire"; La Grenée displayed "L'Apothéose de Saint Louis"; Deshays, "La Conversion de Saint Paul"; Briard, "La Résurrection de Jésus-Christ"; Brenet, "Le Baptême de Jésus-Christ par Saint Jean"; Monnet, "Jésus-Christ expirant sur la Croix"; and Taraval, "L'Apothéose de Saint Augustin." In the essay which Diderot added to his review of this exhibition (vol. X, p. 492), he complained that Christianity was a miserable religion which was dominated by stupid bigots and which had been established by blood and murder. Such an abominable creed forced artists to paint cruel scenes and disgusting butchery. Again in his *Salon* for 1767 Diderot argued that art could be useful only if it was not used to depict heinous scenes of fanaticism which poisoned men's minds with prejudices of the most dangerous sort. Christian themes, like mythological subjects, perverted the true purpose of art (vol. XI, p. 217). "Si tous les tableaux de martyrs, que nos grands maîtres ont si sublimement peints, passaient à une

[5]He attacked Baudouin again in the *Salon de 1767*, vol. XI, p. 190.

postérité reculée, pour qui nous prendrait-elle?" Diderot asked in his *Pensées détachées sur la peinture*; "Pour des bêtes féroces ou des anthropophages."[6]

The *Salons* also give us a deeper insight into the kind of art which Diderot thought would incline men toward the good. Greuze was the artist whose canvases came nearest to filling his conception of the social function of art. In his review of the exhibition in 1763 (vol. X. p. 208), Diderot waxed enthusiastic over "Piété filiale" in which Greuze had painted an old paralytic stretched out on a couch surrounded by his children and grandchildren who are all eager to wait upon his needs. Diderot thought it was an admirable example of moral painting. For too long, painting had been consecrated to debauchery and vice. Painting ought to converge with dramatic art in order to chastise men and lead them to virtue. "Courage, mon ami Greuze," exclaimed the *philosophe*, "fais de la morale en peinture, et fais-en toujours comme cela!" On the right of the paralytic one of his daughters is depicted raising his head and adjusting his pillow more comfortably. In front of him on the same side, his son-in-law has come to serve him some food, while listening sympathetically to what he says. A young boy brings the old man a drink while other children of various ages press forward to help him. Diderot liked everything about the painting, most of all its idealization of the virtues of family life.

Again in the *Salon* of 1765 it was the contributions of Greuze which won the most admiration from the reviewer. "Voici votre peintre et le mien," announced Diderot (vol. X, p. 341), "le premier qui se soit avisé, parmi nous, de donner des mœurs à l'art, et d'enchaîner des événements d'après lesquels il serait facile de faire un roman." This time it was a series of sketches by the genre painter which won his praises. One of these drawings conveyed its moral message in a negative fashion. Entitled "Le Fils ingrat," it depicts a young man who had decided to leave home to join the army just at the time when he was most needed to assist his parents in their old age. Not content to forsake his old father and mother, he has come back to the poverty-stricken cottage to make additional demands on them. This rebellious son is shown in the centre of the picture, impetuous and fiery, taunting his aged parents. The feeble

[6]*Œuvres*, vol. XII, p. 83.

father is enraged at this insolence but is restrained in his chair by one of his daughters. The mother, distraught over what is happening, clings to her son who is trying to free himself by kicking her aside. A sister also hangs on to the rebel, trying in vain to make him realize what he is doing. Even a young brother, pulling on the rebel's arm, seeks to restrain him. Diderot thought that this sketch was admirable in every way.

Clearly the next sketch, which he thought even more inspiring, was intended as a sequel to the previous work. Entitled "Le Fils puni," it portrays a young man returning from war just at the moment when his old father has passed away. On his return the son has found everything in the house transformed so that it now typified poverty, sadness, and distress. The light coming through a small window is just sufficient to reveal the face of the dead father who is stretched out on a dilapidated bed without a mattress of any kind. The eldest daughter has collapsed on a chair beside the bed, holding a crucifix in one hand; with the other, she holds her head in despair over her father's death. One grandchild tries to hide himself in the daughter's skirts, while another has raised his arms in alarm as the meaning of what has happened dawns on him. The poor mother is near the door, obviously overcome with grief and barely able to stand. She eyes the son, now returned wounded from his adventures, with a look which seems to demand that he consider the misery that he has caused. The wayward son, clearly shocked at the spectacle before him, his head bent in contrition on his breast, beats his brow with his fist. "Quelle leçon pour les pères et pour les enfants!" commented Diderot (vol. X, p. 356).

Diderot's favourite, however, of this series was "La Mère bien-aimée," which presented a domestic scene set in a low-ceilinged room in a country home. On the right a mother reclines on a long couch surrounded by at least six children. The smallest child is shown under her arm, two others hang one on either side of her, a fourth clambers up the back of her chair to kiss her brow, a fifth bites his cheek, and a sixth hangs his head on his chest, evidently not content with his role. The mother's face radiates tender joy with just a suggestion of the weariness natural to anyone with so many children. In the background, the grandmother sits in an armchair with her back to the fireplace, enjoying the domestic spectacle. In the foreground yet another tiny tot plays with a little cart. On the left the husband enters the cottage on his return from the hunt, throwing open his arms and tossing his head back in mirth, obviously proud of having produced such a merry family. Diderot thought that this sentimentalized view of family life conveyed a useful lesson (vol. X, p. 354). "Cela est excellent, et pour le talent, et pour les mœurs," he pronounced. "Cela prêche la population et peint très-pathétiquement le bonheur et le prix inestimables de la paix domestique."

From time to time Diderot liked to suggest compositions which he thought could be rendered successfully on canvas. Usually these had a definite moral tone. For instance, when he was asked how an artist might portray a woman completely nude without offending decency, he suggested a composition entitled "Le Modèle honnête." As he imagined it, the painting would depict a young girl sitting completely naked on a chair beside a heap of ragged clothes which would reveal her destitution. The girl would be sitting supporting her head with one hand, her eyes lowered in modesty, two tears rolling down her pretty cheeks. Her other hand would be resting on the shoulder of her mother, who would be shown hiding her head in her hands and dressed in clothes that would leave no doubt as to her dire poverty. Touched by this distress, the artist would be portrayed letting his palette drop in order to contemplate the scene in front of him. Such a suggestion for a painting indicates the sort of sentimental theme which Diderot liked better than something like Boucher's "Vénus sortant du bain." Despite his own personal sensuality Diderot preferred a canvas idealizing innocence, decency, and modesty.[7]

Other themes which he proposed also dramatized a social lesson of some kind. For example, in order to idealize peace Diderot suggested a painting of Mars, dressed in armour, his loins girt about with a sword, and his noble head held high and proud. At his side would be Venus in all her many charms, smiling up at the warrior enchantingly, and pointing to his headpiece which would be lying on the ground. A pair of pigeons would be nesting in the helmet,

---

[7]*Salon de 1767, Œuvres,* vol. XI, p. 74. Baudouin did his version of this theme for the Salon of 1769 but Diderot told him, "Croyez-moi, abandonnez ces sortes de sujets à Greuze." *Ibid.,* p. 425.

the mother bird sitting on her eggs in a straw nest, the male perched on the visor, standing guard.[8] In his study of *Diderot and the Encyclopedists*, Morley was to critize the *philosophe* for failing to remember that the classical gods were dead forever. Morley thought that if Diderot could have seen Landseer's "Peace," with its children playing at the mouth of a slumbering gun, he would have been the first to cry out how much nearer this came to the spirit of his aesthetics than did classical divinities.[9] Perhaps Morley was right, but the point remains Diderot wanted a theme which would symbolize the benefits of peace.

In order to idealize patriotism, Diderot suggested, in the same review (vol. XI, p. 75), a painting of the death of Turenne. Under a pall of fiery smoke issuing from a besieged fortress in the rear, there would be represented a group of four, made up of the dead marshal and the aides who are preparing to carry his body away. One aide, with his arms under the marshal's legs, would be turning away his head because he is unable to bear the tragic sight in front of him. Another, holding up the marshal's shoulders, would be depicted overcome with grief. A third, apparently less shaken, would be about to help lift the legs of the dead hero. A little further to the rear, an equerry with tears rolling down his cheeks, would grasp the bridle of his leader's piebald horse. The main attention, however, would be focused on M. de Saint-Hilaire and his son, who together would occupy the foreground of the painting. The son would be portrayed holding his father's shattered arm, which would be covered in a tattered and blood-stained sleeve. Saint-Hilaire, pointing to the body of the dead marshal, would be saying to his son, "Ce n'est pas sur moi, mon fils, qu'il faut pleurer, c'est sur la perte que la France fait par la mort de cet homme."

The exhibitions did not display many works which fulfilled Diderot's idea of the true purpose of art. In his *Essai sur la peinture*, he renewed his appeal to artists to transform the biennial exhibits into schools of virtue. Diderot thought that a wicked man who

[8]*Salon de 1767*, vol. XI, p. 74. Vien treated this theme in a painting displayed in 1769. La Grenée, to whom Diderot had suggested the idea in the first place, exhibited his version in 1771, but the *philosophe* thought the painting failed to convey the allegory effectively. See vol. XI, pp. 471 ff.

[9]John Morley, *Diderot and the Encyclopedists* (London, 1878), vol. H, pp. 86–87.

wandered into an exhibit ought to be afraid to face the accusing canvases on the wall. A man who harboured some vicious deed deep in his heart would be chastened by works of art; he would find himself sitting in the culprit's seat and would be forced to support his own conviction. In Diderot's opinion it was the duty of artists to perpetuate the memory of noble deeds, to vindicate virtue and stigmatize vice, and to strike fear in the hearts of tyrants. Artists ought to anticipate the verdicts of posterity, or if that was more than they dared, they should at least transmit the judgments of history:

Renverse sur les peuples fanatiques l'ignominie dont ils ont prétendu couvrir ceux qui les instruisaient et qui leur disaient la vérité. Étale-moi les scènes sanglantes du fanatisme. Apprends aux souverains et aux peuples ce qu'ils ont à espérer de ces prédicateurs sacrés du mensonge. Pourquoi ne veux-tu pas t'asseoir aussi parmi les précepteurs du genre humain, les consolateurs des maux de la vie, les vengeurs du crime, les rémunérateurs de la vertu?[10]

A brief look at Diderot's theory of art is essential if we are to understand why he felt that art could assist the philosopher in his social mission. In his opinion the human mind derived pleasure from the perception of harmonious relationships, wherever they might be found. In a letter to Mlle de la Chaux, written in 1751, he outlined this concept of beauty which he had been working out gradually over a period of years. Taste, he argued, consisted in the perception of *rapports.* "Un beau tableau, un poëme, une belle musique, ne nous plaisent que par les rapports que nous y remarquons."[11] Later, in his article "Beau" in the *Encyclopédie,* we find this aesthetic theory more fully developed. In his opinion man was not born with any innate idea of beauty, but he did possess the faculties of feeling and thinking. As the necessities of life forced man to exercise his faculties he became conscious of order and arrangement in the world. And whenever man discovered such harmonious connections he experienced a sense of beauty.[12] Soon man himself was creating objects endowed with order and symmetry, thus giving birth to the fine arts.

[10]*Essai sur la peinture, Œuvres,* vol. X, pp. 502–503.
[11]*Œuvres,* vol. I, pp. 405–406.
[12]"Beau," *Encyclopédie,* in *Œuvres,* vol. X, pp. 24–27.

Such an aesthetic theory, emphasizing harmonious relationships, might well have suggested some abstract form of art, but this was furthest from Diderot's mind. He insisted on a profound realism. The artist must refer back constantly to the natural world from which he had derived his sense of arrangement and order in the first place. If he did not ground his art on the natural world it would represent only the fleeting taste of a particular society rather than the fundamental nature of things. It was absolutely essential for the artist to return to nature in order to overcome the many artificial forces—conventions, customs, prejudices, superstitions, and changing circumstances—which constantly distorted man's understanding of the world around him. The artist had to penetrate beyond the passing taste of his age to the fundamental realities of nature if his work was to have a lasting value (vol. X, pp. 35–40).

When Diderot insisted on realism he was not thinking merely of the beauties of the physical world. Because the artist also dealt with human relationships, it was essential for him to have a clear conception of the fundamental character of man. He had to realize that one of the most important elements in the human make-up was the penchant for order which had been impressed on man's mind by the orderliness of nature.[13] Virtue was simply this sense of order extended to the moral world. His *goût de l'ordre* led man toward the good except when he was distracted by some unruly passion. This taste for order leading to virtue was reinforced by man's capacity to sympathize with his fellow men. Diderot believed that a man never completely lost his love of virtue no matter how wicked he became. In his *Entretiens sur le Fils naturel* the philosopher contended that goodness was far more deeply rooted in mankind than wickedness, "et, qu'en général, il reste plus de bonté dans l'âme d'un méchant, que de méchanceté dans l'âme des bons."[14] Such was the truth about man which the artist had to embody in his work if he was to imitate nature in the deepest sense.

It was in his discussions of drama that Diderot first worked out the ideas on the role of the artist which he later applied to painting and sculpture. In *De la poésie dramatique*, completed in 1758, he argued that the artist would never excite his fellow men if he was

---

[13]See *Entretiens sur le Fils naturel*, completed in 1757, in *Œuvres*, vol. VII, p. 127, where Diderot defines virtue as "le goût de l'ordre dans les choses morales."
[14]*Ibid.*, vol. VII, p. 128.

incapable of deep emotion himself. And what could move men more deeply than the two most powerful forces in nature, truth and virtue? The artist could not even depict vice powerfully unless he realized how much it ran counter to public welfare and individual happiness.[15] He would be distorting reality if he did not show that virtue alone could bring happiness. Consequently by the very nature of his work, the artist was inevitably committed to moral comment. Diderot's own dramas, *Le Fils naturel* and *Le Père de Famille*, sought to convey a moral message by glorifying private virtues and domestic life. In his view the highest function of the artist was to show his contemporaries how much they had departed from the ideal revealed by nature. Every society needed works of art because ". . . tout peuple a des préjugés à détruire, des vices à poursuivre, des ridicules à décrier. . . ." (vol. VII, p. 369)

Diderot thought that art was extremely valuable because it could convey its message to the human heart much more directly than language ever could. In his remarkable *Lettre sur les sourds*, completed in 1751, he argued that language could never reflect actual impressions which occurred in the soul. Language had to analyse and decompose sensations into signs and symbols which were useful but which nevertheless disintegrated and distorted the actual processes of the soul. In contrast, the arts could appeal to the soul in the same way as events in the real world, that is, through the senses rather than the mind. Admittedly, language might be improved so that it would speak more directly to the soul, but since it dissected reality it could never appeal as directly as the arts, which could communicate actual sensations.[16] Each of the arts—music, poetry, drama, and painting—had its own method of transmitting sensation, but painting possessed one of the most effective means of conveying emotions to the soul. True, the painter was restricted to a single instant, but Diderot argued that this was offset by the fact that "c'est la chose même que le peintre montre; les expressions du musicien et du poëte n'en sont que les hiéroglyphes." (vol. I, pp. 387-8)

Art could be an effective instrument of progress because it would not have to change human nature but only revitalize that sense of virtue implanted in the human heart. "Ce sont les misérables

[15]*De la poésie dramatique*, in *Œuvres*, vol. VII, p. 389-90.
[16]*Lettre sur les sourds*, in *Œuvres*, vol. I, pp. 369-74.

conventions qui pervertissent l'homme, et non la nature humaine qu'il faut accuser," wrote the *philosophe*. "En effet, qu'est-ce qui nous affecte comme le récit d'une action généreuse?"[17] A work of art which portrayed the consequences of virtue or vice would never become chimerical because it would embody eternal truths about man. In everyday life men would be quick to recognize the types which they saw depicted in such art. This was why statues portraying virtuous men were valuable even though the names on the pedestals might change in successive generations. Elsewhere Diderot suggested that such statues ought to be raised up in public squares and gardens so that they might invite the public to virtue from atop those pedestals which at present exposed the debauches of pagan gods.[18]

In real life selfish interests often prevented men from sympathizing with virtuous deeds, but in front of a work of art the spectator could admire virtuous acts without any risk to himself. In such a situation the spectator played two roles: imaginatively he became the man of virtue struggling against the forces of evil, while at the same time he remained a spectator safe from any threat to himself.[19] Before a work of art, even a wicked man could be quickened into admiration for virtue. Diderot felt that this identification with virtuous actions, even in such an indirect manner, would ultimately promote the practice of virtue in real life. For him this psychological phenomenon meant that the fine arts could be extremely useful:

O quel bien il en reviendrait aux hommes, si tous les arts d'imitation se proposaient un objet commun, et concouraient un jour avec les lois pour nous faire aimer la vertu et haïr le vice! C'est au philosophe à les y inviter; c'est à lui à s'adresser au poëte, au peintre, au musicien, et à leur crier avec force: Hommes de génie, pourquoi le ciel vous a-t-il doués? S'il en est entendu, bientôt les images de la débauche ne couvriront plus les murs de nos palais; nos voix ne seront plus des organes du crime; et le goût et les mœurs y gagneront.[20]

[17]*De la poésie dramatique, Œuvres*, vol. VII, p. 312. Diderot, like Rousseau, affirmed the essential goodness of nature, including human nature.
[18]The article "Encyclopédie," *Œuvres*, vol. XIV, pp. 487–88.
[19]Diderot mentioned this psychological theory about art in various works. One of the best examples is in his *Réfutation de l'ouvrage d'Helvétius, Œuvres*, vol. II, pp. 391–92; also the *Salon de 1767*, vol. XI, pp. 118–19.
[20]*De la poésie dramatique, Œuvres*, vol. VII, pp. 312–13.

Awareness that the Church had also used art as a means of propaganda confirmed Diderot in his belief in the utility of art. In his *Salon* for 1765 he argued that images played a vital role in the task of impressing religious beliefs on the minds of the masses. To his way of thinking a painting in a church was a kind of preacher, only clearer, more striking, more intelligible, more on the level of the ordinary man, than the priest. The priest could only speak to the ear, which was often closed to what he had to say, whereas a painting could appeal to the eye in the same way that nature herself had in teaching man most of what he knew. Diderot went so far as to claim that iconoclasts who wanted to get rid of religious images unwittingly made themselves allies of philosophy, which was the enemy of superstition. Suppress all these palpable religious symbols, and soon everything which was left would be reduced to metaphysical balderdash with as many different interpretations as there were heads. Abolish all religious images, and soon men would no longer agree with each other, but would slit each other's throats over the simplest essentials of their creed. In fact, religious works of art were so persuasive that they would have to be destroyed if truth was to triumph. "Mon ami," wrote Diderot, "si nous aimons mieux la vérité que les beaux-arts, prions Dieu pour les iconoclastes." (vol. X, p. 391)

Repeatedly Diderot reiterated his belief in the educational capacity of art. In his *Essai sur la peinture*, an appendix to his review of 1765, he contended that artists ought to take up the cause of the unfortunate (vol. X, p. 502). In his *Pensées détachées sur la peinture*, intended as a sequel to his art reviews, he argued that artists ought to associate themselves with philosophers in conveying important maxims to the masses.[21] In his *Plan d'une université pour le gouvernement de Russie*, written between 1775 and 1776, he argued that, even if the fine arts were not absolutely essential for social existence, once they appeared they had to be used for moral purposes lest they corrupt society.[22] And in his *Essai sur les règnes de Claude et Néron*, written during 1778–82, he rebuked Seneca

---

[21]*Pensées détachées sur la peinture, la sculpture, l'architecture, et la poésie pour servir de suite aux salons*, in *Œuvres*, vol. XII, pp. 83–86.

[22]*Plan d'une université pour le gouvernement de Russie ou d'une éducation publique dans toutes les sciences*, in *Œuvres*, vol. III, p. 469.

for having questioned whether the arts had any real value in comparison with philosophy:

Que Sénèque pousse son énumération aussi loin qu'il voudra, je persisterai dans la même réponse, et je lui dirai, d'après mon expérience, d'après l'expérience des bons et des méchants, que l'imitation d'une action vertueuse par la peinture, la sculpture, l'éloquence, la poésie et la musique, nous touche, nous enflamme, nous élève, nous porte au bien, nous indigne contre le vice aussi violemment que les leçons les plus insinuantes, les plus vigoureuses, les plus démonstratives de la philosophie. Exposons les tableaux de la vertu, et il se trouvera des copistes. L'espèce d'exhortation qui s'adresse à l'âme par l'entremise des sens, outre sa permanence, est plus à la portée du commun des hommes. Le peuple se sert mieux de ses yeux que de son entendement. Les images prêchent, prêchent sans cesse, et ne blessent point l'amour-propre.[23]

Diderot was not entirely consistent in his attitude toward art. Despite his contention that art ought to serve a social function, his *Salons* revealed that he was able to wax enthusiastic about art simply because of its beauty. Still life paintings which bore no moral message often evoked his highest praises. His reaction to the works displayed by Chardin in the *Salon* for 1763 was one of enthusiasm for purely aesthetic qualities. The *philosophe* was very much taken with still life paintings which the artist had submitted depicting wine bottles, bread, fruit, and plants. He was delighted by the way the artist had painted a porcelain vase which looked like the thing itself, olives which appeared to swim in liquid, biscuits which seemed ready to eat, oranges waiting to have the juice pressed out of them, and wine ready to be drunk. Here was an artist who really understood the harmony of colour and the reflection of light. "O Chardin!" exclaimed Diderot, "ce n'est pas du blanc, du rouge, du noir que tu broies sur ta palette : c'est la substance même des objets, c'est l'air et la lumière que tu prends à la pointe de ton pinceau et que tu attaches sur la toile."[24]

---

[23]*Essai sur les règnes de Claude et de Néron et sur la vie et les écrits de Sénèque pour servir d'introduction à la lecture de ce philosophe*, in *Œuvres*, vol. III, pp. 259–60.
[24]*Ibid.*, vol. X, pp. 194, 195. See his enthusiastic comments on Chardin in subsequent exhibitions: *Salon de 1765, ibid.*, pp. 299 ff.; *Salon de 1767, ibid.*, vol. XI, pp. 97 ff.; *Salon de 1769, ibid.*, pp. 408 ff., and the *Salon de 1771, ibid.*, pp. 481–82. In his *Essai sur la peinture*, Diderot demonstrated his enthusiasm for the different effects of colour and of shading in the works of a master painter. See his ideas on colour (*ibid.*, vol. X, pp. 468 ff.) and on shading (*ibid.*, pp. 474 ff.).

His great admiration for certain landscape paintings was further evidence of his love of art apart from any social value it might have. In the *Salon* for 1767 he paid a long tribute to Vernet for the landscapes which the artist had placed on display. He supposed himself unable to visit the exhibition that year, and imagined that he was visiting a country house set amid lovely scenery not far from the sea (vol. XI, pp. 98 ff.). Then he described long walks which he took through the countryside, observing all the beauties of nature at various times during the day and under different atmospheric conditions. On these daily walks he engaged in a number of dialogues with an abbé, tutor of the children at the country house, on the workings of the universe and the nature of art. Only at the very end of his account of his stay in the country did he reveal that these walks were wholly imaginary and that the scenes which he had described were really inspired by the landscapes which had been exhibited by Vernet. Diderot applauded these paintings because the artist seemed able to recreate all the aspects of nature in her different moods. "Que ne fait-il pas avec excellence!" exclaimed the *philosophe* (vol. XI, p. 140).[25] Here was the critic who had argued that all art was silent unless it conveyed some *grande idée morale*, praising a landscape painter solely for his miraculous use of colour and shading. Clearly Diderot was still haunted by the spirit of the Renaissance.

One might argue that still life paintings and landscapes were the proper sphere of art for the sake of art because they were not concerned with human actions. But we find Diderot often carried away by those same classical paintings which he condemned so vehemently on other occasions. For example, in the exhibition of 1771 he was attracted to a painting entitled "Jupiter, sous la forme de Diane, séduit Calistro" by La Grenée. Despite the fact that the painting conveyed no moral lesson, he was won over by the ingenious composition, the perfect drawing, the lively style, and the realistic colouring. The figure of Diana pleased him most of all because it seemed to be made of actual flesh, ready to be laid hold of, to be handled, and to be kissed (vol. XI, p. 473).

Diderot's reaction to religious art provides the best evidence of

---

[25]See his praise for Vernet in other reviews: *Salon de 1763, Œuvres*, vol. X, pp. 200–204; *Salon de 1769, ibid.*, vol. XI, pp. 415–17; and the *Salon de 1771, ibid.*, pp. 482–83.

his role as art critic transcending his mission as *philosophe*. The *Salons* reveal many instances in which the skill of the artist overcame his distaste for the religious message which the work of art conveyed. In his review of the exhibition of 1765 (vol. X, pp. 247 ff.) he lauded the seven "Esquisses pour la Chapelle de Saint-Grégoire aux Invalides" by Carle Van Loo. The sketches, which were really paintings in themselves, depicted the saint selling his worldly goods, bringing an end to a plague by his intercessions, converting a woman heretic, turning down papal office, receiving homage from his clergy, and ascending into heaven. Diderot was very impressed with these unfinished sketches, despite the fact that they portrayed episodes from the life of Saint Gregory. He praised the skill with which the painter had composed his scenes, his artistry in rendering the various characters, his ability to capture different light effects, and his technique in painting varied colour tones. Again, in his review of the exhibition of 1771, to cite just one more example among many, Diderot commended La Grenée for his painting entitled "Saint Germain donne à Sainte Geneviève une médaille où est empreinte l'image de la Croix" because the composition was laid out well, the drawing was skilful, the touch was dextrous, and the colouring very pleasing (vol. XI, p. 468). Diderot had argued that he who loved truth more than the fine arts would have to pray for some iconoclasts. In his own response to religious paintings, the lover of the fine arts most often won out over the iconoclast.

On some occasions we even find Diderot defending Christianity as a source of artistic inspiration. In the third canto of a poem about "La Peinture," Le Mierre had let loose his rage against the atrocities depicted in Christian art. Diderot objected to this attack on religious art. Had the poet suggested other subjects equally as interesting as these religious ones, Diderot would not have feared for the destruction of Christian art. However, he was reluctant to see the precious masterpieces of many artists condemned in such a casual fashion. Admittedly, some scenes were too horrible to be contemplated, but many scenes of martyrdom provided themes which could only be dealt with by great masters. No theme demanded such great artistry, no subject made possible greater expression, than the image of a man rising above the terrors which beset him. And from a religious point of view these men torn to bits were suited to follow in the steps of a God who had been nailed to a tree.[26] In making such a defence of Christian themes Diderot was obviously thinking as an art critic rather than as an ideologist. As a *philosophe* he himself had complained of the disgusting butchery which "cet abominable Christianisme" had forced artists to depict.

In the *Salon* for 1767 Diderot even admitted that the sort of actions which gave birth to great art might not be conducive to happiness in real life. He suggested that, just as there was a particular morality belonging to each species, so perhaps there was a different morality for different individuals, or at least for different kinds of individuals. Perhaps there was a morality peculiar to artists or to art, and this morality might well be the reverse of common morality. In fact those deeds which caused misery in real life might inspire great art:

Oui, mon ami, j'ai bien peur que l'homme n'aille droit au malheur par la voie qui conduit l'imitateur de la nature au sublime. Se jeter dans les extrêmes, voilà la règle du poëte. Garder en tout un juste milieu, voilà la règle du bonheur. Il ne faut point faire de poésie dans la vie. Les héros, les amants romanesques, les grands patriotes, les magistrats inflexibles, les apôtres de religion, les philosophes à toute outrance, tous ces rares et divins insensés font de la poésie dans la vie, de là leur malheur. Ce sont eux qui fournissent après leur mort aux grands tableaux. Ils sont excellents à peindre. Il est d'expérience que la nature condamne au malheur celui à qui elle a départi le génie, et celle qu'elle a douée de la beauté; c'est que ce sont des êtres poétiques.[27]

Diderot offered no plan by which the arts could be diverted from frivolous activities to serious goals. Certainly he was much clearer about what caused the decadence of contemporary art than he was about how to remedy the situation. In his introductory remarks to the *Salon* for 1767 he outlined what he considered some of the basic reasons for the lamentable state of art at that time. One difficulty was that artists were forced to consider the tastes of their patrons rather than the interests of the nation as a whole. Another problem stemmed from the influence of pretentious connoisseurs

---

[26]*Sur la peinture, poëme en trois chants par M. Le Mierre, 1769, Œuvres*, vol. XIII, pp. 91–92.
[27]*Salon de 1767*, vol. XI, pp. 124–25.

who set themselves up as arbiters of artistic taste. But the basic malady sprang from certain cultural conditions which prevented the arts from attaining perfection. There was the contemporary preoccupation with prettiness which forced the artist to compromise himself because people would not tolerate serious subjects. There was above all that vicious form of luxury which corrupted artistic talent: "N'oubliez pas parmi les obstacles à la perfection et à la durée des beaux-arts," he warned, "je ne dis pas la richesse d'un peuple, mais ce luxe qui dégrade les grands talents, en les assujettissant à de petits ouvrages, et les grands sujets en les réduisant à la bambochade." For proof Diderot pointed to "La Vérité," "La Vertu," "La Justice," and "La Religion" adapted by La Grenée for the boudoir of a financier (vol. XI, p. 8).

Later in the same *Salon* Diderot again discussed the influence of luxury on the fine arts because he felt that the problem was very important. As things stood, he thought that the whole question was hopelessly confused. Men realized the fine arts owed their birth to the growth of wealth. However, men also observed that the very force which produced the arts and led them to perfection ended up by degrading and destroying them. As a result of these observations, thinkers had divided into rival parties. Some lauded luxury because it gave birth to the fine arts and raised them into full flower. Others attacked luxury because it subjugated the arts and led them into degradation. Still another group used luxury and its consequences in order to decry the fine arts themselves. Diderot thought that this last group represented one of the most absurd viewpoints (vol. XI, p. 85). Perhaps in making such a comment he was thinking of Rousseau's argument in his *Discours sur les sciences et les arts*.

Diderot sought to solve this problem by distinguishing between two different kinds of luxury. In his view there was a beneficial variety of luxury which was based upon the general prosperity of the nation and especially on the success of agriculture. In a society where agriculture was encouraged instead of being handicapped by onerous levies there would be a general increase in wealth throughout the nation. He thought that such prosperity would encourage all the various arts without corrupting or debasing them. The second kind of luxury created wealth for a small minority by burdening agriculture with oppressive taxes. Thus, while a small fraction of the nation squandered wealth, the majority of the nation languished in poverty. In such a society, usurers flourished, and lured dissipated monarchs into burdensome loans. Under such conditions education had no general frame of reference and no public purpose. Luxury of this harmful variety was no more than a fatal veneer which covered up the almost universal misery lying underneath. It was this vicious sort of luxury which degraded and destroyed the fine arts (vol. XI, pp. 86–87).

Oppressed by these pernicious aspects of luxury, the arts had to live on the scum which arose from miserable social conditions. Either the arts had to abandon themselves to the destitute masses who sought to gain the influence and prestige of wealth by inferior productions of every sort; or they had to subordinate themselves to the caprices of a handful of bored rich men whose taste was just as corrupt as their morals. Under such perverted social conditions the exhausted nation brought forth no great enterprises, no outstanding works, nothing which would sustain the spirit and elevate the soul. In such disjointed times no great artists were born, or if they were, they had to debase themselves to escape starvation. Then it was that there were a hundred little easel paintings for every historical painting. Then it was that mediocre artists multiplied, and the nation was glutted with them. Diderot concluded that there were thus two sorts of luxury, one born of wealth and general prosperity, the other of ostentation and widespread misery. The first sort was just as favourable to the fine arts as the second was injurious (vol. XI, pp. 88–89).

Diderot developed this theme in a small fragment entitled *Satire contre le luxe* (vol. XI, pp. 89 ff.). In this brief dialogue he argued that contemporary society suffered from the pernicious type of luxury in which everything could be obtained with money whereas nothing could be gained through merit alone. In what was supposed to be the most civilized country on earth, a handful of embezzlers paraded their wealth ostentatiously while most of the nation grovelled in poverty. Even the leading families were often ruined in an attempt to emulate the ostentation of the rich financiers. Men married in order to acquire wealth, with the result that their wives sought satisfaction elsewhere. By imitating the upper classes, others sank into the same kind of debauchery. In such a society a great amount of art was produced but it was corrupted by the *mores* surrounding it. "Oui," said Diderot, "beaucoup d'ouvrages, et beaucoup d'ouvrages médiocres. Si les mœurs sont corrompues, croyez-vous que le goût puisse rester pur? Non, non, cela ne se peut; et si vous le croyez, c'est que vous ignorez l'effet de la vertu sur les beaux-arts."

All these comments on luxury suggested that art reflected the social conditions of the period. Art was decadent because it mirrored a corrupt and maladjusted environment. Such a theory implied that art could never regain its dignity and purity without a basic reconstruction of society. But Diderot argued that art itself ought to become an instrument of social change. The problem was to convert art from a medium which reflected social conditions into a force which could help to change society. It was not clear how this could be done, so long as the artist had to bow to the demands of his patron and had to conform to the taste of his age. In the end Diderot could offer no real plan by which the arts could be diverted from frivolous activities into an instrument of enlightenment.

Despite the contradictions and unsolved problems implicit in his thought, Diderot expressed the aesthetic tendencies of his time. Folkierski has called him "un esprit qui ramasse en lui, comme en une lentille, les mille rayons de la pensée du siècle, et les projette en un faisceau de lumière claire."[28] Certainly in emphasizing the social utility of art he voiced the conviction of most of the philosophic party. Voltaire repeatedly emphasized the didactic possibilities of art, although he had little to say about the plastic arts.[29] Marmontel stressed the need for *un but moral* for the arts to such an extent that his biographer has accused him of neglecting aesthetic values.[30] And d'Holbach argued that the various arts ought to act in unison to propagate the secular moral code which he hoped would one day replace Christianity and other religions.[31] But perhaps the best place to analyse the aesthetic trends of the age is in the great *Encyclopédie*, the central organ of eighteenth century liberal thinkers.

[28]W. Folkierski, *Entre le classicisme et le romantisme, étude sur les esthéticiens du XVIII*e *siècle* (Cracow, 1925), p. 335.
[29]Voltaire, *Œuvres complètes*, ed. Moland (Paris, 1877), vol. II, pp. 544–45, III, p. 373.
[30]S. Lenel, *Marmontel, un homme de lettres au XVIII*e *siècle* (Paris, 1902), p. 370.
[31]D'Holbach, *La Morale Universelle*, vol. II, pp. 228–41.

The Encyclopedia on the Utility of Art

3.

De tous les ouvrages de l'art, ceux-là ont, sans contredit, l'utilité la plus importante, qui gravent dans notre esprit des notions, des vérités, des maximes, des sentimens propres à nous rendre plus parfaits, et à former en nous les caractères dont nous ne saurions manquer sans perdre de notre prix soit en qualité d'hommes, soit en qualité de citoyens.

L'ENCYCLOPÉDIE[1]

THE YEAR 1747 was destined to become a landmark in Western intellectual history. In that year the publisher Le Breton asked Diderot to edit the translation of Chamber's *Cyclopaedia* which was already under way. As Diderot reviewed the work which had previously been done, he came to the conclusion that the plan was incomplete and disjointed. What was needed was a new work, surveying the whole of human knowledge, in which each subject would be treated by a specialist and the articles would be co-ordinated by a system of classification. This imaginative scheme impressed the publisher, and it was decided to produce a work consisting of eight volumes of text plus two of illustrations. Thus the great project was launched which turned out to be, not only

[1]*Encyclopédie*, vol. III, p. 500. Some editions read "avantages" instead of "ouvrages."

one of the most influential works of the century, but a model for all later encyclopedias.

In the following years Diderot tried to attract the best collaborators he could find. As an assistant editor, he already had the outstanding mathematician d'Alembert. Some other eminent personalities were persuaded to contribute: Voltaire wrote more than forty articles on a variety of subjects before his enthusiasm waned; Buffon wrote an important article on nature; and Montesquieu ground out an article on taste. Other able men were recruited: Daubenton to write on biology, La Condamine on physics, Malouin on chemistry, Rousseau on music, Blondel on architecture, Cahusac on the dance, Yvon on logic and morality, and Turgot on philosophy and economics—to name only a few. Jaucourt, a tireless worker, compiled hundreds of articles. Despite the assistance of such men, a tremendous burden still rested on the chief editor, who had to plan the work, line up contributors, revise manuscripts, and of course write many articles himself. The project turned out to be even more formidable than Diderot had envisaged: in the end there were seventeen volumes of text containing close to twenty million words.

The *Encyclopédie* was no mere compendium of factual information. Like the encyclopedias produced by some religious groups and certain totalitarian states, it embodied a world view and a social programme. It provided radical thinkers with an ideal medium for undermining traditional beliefs and disseminating progressive ideas. Although differences emerged as the work progressed, most of the contributors shared basic assumptions and were animated by a common spirit. On the whole they believed in the superiority of reason over authority and the efficacy of science to solve human problems; they all saw a need to create a secular basis for morality, and were optimistic about the possibility of terrestrial progress. Diderot's article "Encyclopédie" reveals the faith which inspired him and his fellow workers through all their tribulations—the confidence that men would be both happier and more virtuous once they were better informed.

Because it embodied a message opposed to tradition and authority, the *Encyclopédie* was exposed to attack from the beginning. After the appearance of the first two volumes in 1751–52, Church officials were successful in having the work halted. Thanks however to Malesherbes, the government's director of publications, and Mme de Pompadour, work was eventually allowed to continue until the appearance of the seventh volume in 1757. Then a number of incidents, including the attempted assassination of Louis XV and the condemnation of *De l'esprit* by Helvétius, made the government more responsive to the complaints of the clergy. In 1759 the privilege to publish was revoked and the whole work was condemned by Pope Clement XIII. Nevertheless the enterprise continued secretly with the connivance of some government officials until the end of 1765, when the final ten volumes of text were completed. Then one last ruse was necessary: subscribers were informed that the last volumes had been published at Neufchâtel in Switzerland but were available in Paris.

Diderot continued to edit the volumes of plates until they were completed with the appearance of the eleventh in 1772, but he refused to have anything to do with the five supplementary volumes—four of text and one of plates—which were added during 1766 and 1777. These additional tomes were brought out by the publisher Panckoucke and two associates, who announced that they would incorporate new discoveries and fill in gaps in the original edition. The fact that Diderot had nothing to do with these volumes is no reason to ignore them. The additions were faithful to the original spirit of the *Encyclopédie* and in later editions they formed an integral part of the text. The articles on art in the supplementary volumes elaborated and amplified the stand taken in the earlier volumes and from a historical standpoint are obviously important.

Within a decade of its completion, the *Encyclopédie* appeared in a number of new editions. The cost of a complete set still restricted purchase to men of means, such as nobles, magistrates, merchants, abbots, lawyers, and doctors, but this group included most of those who participated in the intellectual life of the nation. Those who could not buy a set could always consult a copy owned by a friend or go to a reading room. L'*Encyclopédie*, concluded the literary historian Brunetière, ". . . est la grande affaire du temps, le but où tendait tout ce qui l'a précédée, l'origine de tout ce qui l'a suivie, et conséquemment le vrai centre d'une histoire des idées au XVIIIe siècle."[2]

Throughout the *Encyclopédie* there was a marked emphasis on utility. This was already evident in the celebrated *Discours préliminaire* with which d'Alembert introduced the first volume. Here he tried to show that society had arisen when men banded together to satisfy their needs more effectively. Because of the advantages which society offered, he exhorted men to render it as useful as possible by binding themselves together even more closely than they had in the past.[3] D'Alembert thus established what was to be one of the key ideas of the whole work—the concept of social utility. Assuming that society had originated to satisfy the needs of natural man, the Encyclopedists proceeded to try to deduce its functions from its origins. All social institutions and activities tended to be judged according to their ability to satisfy basic human needs.

In discussing political institutions, for instance, the contributors repeatedly applied the utilitarian test. Although they accepted monarchy, they rejected the claim that its power rested solely on divine right. In their view legitimate power was conferred in a contract by which the king agreed to work within the framework of certain fundamental laws for the common good of his subjects.[4] "La puissance qui vient du consentement des peuples," said the Editor in the article "Autorité politique," "suppose nécessairement des conditions qui en rendent l'usage légitime, utile à la société, avantageux à la république, et qui la fixent et la restreignent entre des limites . . ." (vol. IV, p. 121). In general the contributors did not fear strong monarchical power provided that it demonstrated its *utilité publique* by reforming abuses, improving social conditions, combatting superstition, and spreading enlightenment.

[2]Ferdinand Brunetière, *L'Evolution des genres dans l'histoire de la littérature* (Paris, 1890), vol. I, p. 210.
[3]Jean Le Rond d'Alembert, *Discours préliminaire de l'Encyclopédie* (Paris, A. Hatier, n.d.), pp. 9–10.
[4]René Hubert, *Les Sciences sociales dans l'Encyclopédie* (Paris, 1923), pp. 215 ff.

In developing their ethical theories, the contributors again favoured attitudes which they considered useful to society. Christian morality was attacked because, among other reasons, it distracted man from interest in society and emphasized eternal salvation rather than social improvement. The Encyclopedists promoted a system of morality which would help to make man's terrestrial existence as happy as possible. Because they thought that he could solve his problems best through social co-operation, they gave first place in their hierarchy of values to those which they considered most useful to society—labour, justice, toleration, benevolence, and patriotism. In their ethical doctrines they thus anticipated the utilitarian philosophers of the nineteenth century.

The criterion of social utility likewise shaped discussion of education in the *Encyclopédie*. The contributors were united in the view that education ought to be controlled by the state in order to mould desirable citizens. Such was the opinion of Rousseau in the article "Economie politique" (vol. XI, p. 807), of d'Alembert in the article "Collège" (vol. VIII, p. 494), of Faiquet in the article "Etudes" (vol. XIII, p. 304), and Diderot in the article "Législateur" (vol. XIX, p. 769). The Editor looked on education as a potential instrument for attaching citizens to their motherland, for moulding a national character, for cultivating social virtues, and for arousing motives useful to the state. It was in order to reform education in this direction that the contributors wanted modern languages, recent history, civic morality, and experimental science to replace the present curriculum of the Jesuit colleges which was based on a study of the classics.

This preoccupation with utility was perhaps best revealed in the amount of space devoted to science and technology in the *Encyclopédie*. The contributors were disciples of Francis Bacon and his vision of the New Atlantis, where science would endow man with ever-increasing power over nature. They saw in applied science the possibility of eliminating conditions where even in France many people barely subsisted and one-half of the population died before they were fifteen. They were interested in pure science primarily because it was the key to technological progress and social improvement. In discussing the "Arts méchaniques" (vol. III, p. 481), the Editor called for co-operation between workers and intellectuals to improve methods of production. The *Encyclopédie* featured long articles on various crafts and agricultural methods which almost amounted to technical manuals, and the same enthusiasm for technology was revealed in the eleven volumes of plates.

This emphasis on utility threatened the prestige which the visual arts had enjoyed since the fifteenth and sixteenth centuries. The arguments employed by artists to improve their status had all been based on the alleged inferiority of the mechanical compared with the liberal arts. This disdain for the mechanical arts rested on the tradition that there was something ignoble about manual labour. Artists had never argued that their creations ought to be honoured because of their practical value: they had simply assumed that imaginative productions had an excellence far beyond objects of mere practical use. Now for the Encyclopedists the test of value was whether or not an activity contributed to social improvement. No longer could the superiority of the fine arts over practical crafts be taken for granted.

This shift in values was already apparent in the *Discours préliminaire*, where d'Alembert challenged the assumption that the liberal arts were superior to the mechanical. The distinction seemed to have arisen because men who prided themselves in their intelligence liked to look down on those who worked with their hands. D'Alembert stated that this contempt for manual crafts was unjust because, in general, these occupations were much more useful than the vaunted liberal arts. Having questioned the traditional pre-eminence of the liberal arts, he then subdivided them into the more useful ones such as grammar or ethics, and those which were merely pleasant, such as painting or poetry.[5] Thus ranked according to utility, the *arts d'agrément* tended to lose status.

Granted the above, if the prestige of the fine arts was to be re-established on a firm basis, it was imperative to demonstrate that they were not merely pleasant luxury products but indispensable social instruments. As the later volumes of the *Encyclopédie* appeared, there was an increasing emphasis on the valuable

[5] D'Alembert, *Discours préliminaire*, pp. 30–33.

service which the fine arts could render as a means of diffusing ideas; and by the time the supplementary volumes were published, this had become the major theme in articles on the fine arts. In developing this theme, the editors drew very heavily on a recent treatise entitled *Allgemeine Theorie der Schönen Künste* by the Swiss thinker Johann Sulzer.[6] Evidently this work attracted them because the author had based the dignity of the fine arts on their capacity to impress ideas on the human mind.

This attempt to demonstrate the utility of the fine arts was already evident in the later volumes edited by Diderot. For example in his article "Peinture" Jaucourt pointed out that this art could be used to spread ideas (vol. XV, pp. 119 ff.). The article admitted that this had not been the original object of painting. Nature seemed to invite men to imitate the objects which she had placed before their eyes. One had therefore to classify painting among those products whose end was pure pleasure, because this art had no connection with the basic necessities of life. Poetry likewise had originally had no other goal than to give pleasure. Later on, *la vertu* borrowed the charms of these two arts in order to create a more vivid impression on the mind. Virtue sought to enhance the worth of painting and poetry by giving them a moral purpose. Thus, having made it clear that moral teaching was not the original end of painting, the article proceeded to show that this art had always been used to convey ideas to the masses.

Painting was admirably suited to influence the mind, according to the article. Admittedly poetry spoke directly to the mind, whereas painting had to reach the consciousness through the eyes. But painting probably had a more lasting impact because it operated on the mind through the senses in the same way as nature herself. Painting beguiled the viewer's eyes by a magic that made him aware of objects which were far distant or which no longer existed at all. The impact of painting was on everyone: the ignorant, the connoisseurs, even artists themselves. No one could approach a well-executed canvas without being arrested by surprise and held there enjoying the marvel. Quintilian had cited cases where prosecutors before a tribunal had used paintings of the crimes in order to incite

[6]Johann Georg Sulzer, *Allgemeine Theorie der Schönen Künste* (2 vols., Leipsig, 1771–74).

the indignation of the judges against the guilty. Saint Gregory had told the story of a prostitute who was awakened to serious thought when she happened to encounter the portrait of a philosopher famous for the transformation in his way of life. On the other hand, harmful paintings could just as well corrupt the heart or ignite undesirable passions in the breast. Because of this influence which images could have on the human mind, those who had governed throughout history had always used paintings and statues so as to inspire the sort of religious or political sentiments which they wished their subjects to hold.

The article "Sculpture" by Falconet, a well-known sculptor and friend of Diderot, presented a similar argument (vol. XXX, p. 448). In his view the value of sculpture lay in the moral influence which it could exercise. Like history, sculpture was a durable record of what men had done. It could warn its viewers of the worst horrors which men had committed, as well as remind them of the noble deeds which men had performed. Considering sculpture from a moral viewpoint, its most worthy objective was to perpetuate the memory of illustrious men, and thus to provide models of virtue for mankind. Falconet suggested that these models were likely to be all the more effectual because the heroes were no longer alive to arouse the jealousy of their fellow men. "Nous avons le portrait de Socrate et nous le vénérons," the article pointed out; "Qui sait si nous aurions le courage d'aimer Socrate vivant parmi nous?" The sculptor was therefore open to censure or praise, depending on whether or not he treated moral themes or licentious ones.

The article "Luxe" (vol. XX, pp. 544 ff.)[7] had considerable to say about the use which could be made of the fine arts in an enlightened state compared with their misuse in a disordered society. In a maladjusted state, in which excessive wealth could be acquired without effort, the rich sought to forget their uselessness and to dispel their boredom in an endless round of frivolity. In such a decadent society the fine arts were forced to defile themselves by serving superstition and debauchery. But in a well-ordered state the various arts would treat subjects which would be useful in estab-

[7]Saint-Lambert later claimed this article, but it seems to have been written in close collaboration with Diderot, to whom it is often assigned.

lishing morality. Under a wise administration the fine arts would be valued as an assistance in spreading enlightenment:

... tous les états sentiront le prix des beaux-arts et en jouiront; mais alors ces beaux-arts ramènent encore l'esprit des citoyens aux sentimens patriotiques et aux véritables vertus : ils ne sont pas seulement pour eux des objets de dissipation, ils leur présentent des leçons et des modèles. Des hommes riches dont l'âme est élevée élèvent l'âme des artistes; ils ne leur demandent pas une Galatée maniérée, de petits Daphnis, une Madeleine, un Jérôme; mais ils leur proposent de représenter Saint-Hilaire blessé dangereusement, qui montre à son fils le grand Turenne perdu pour la patrie. (vol. XX, p. 555)

This attempt to prove the social value of art was carried much further in the supplementary volumes which had been added to the *Encyclopédie* by 1777. One of the most important additions was a very long article entitled "Beaux-arts" (vol. III, pp. 484 ff.) based on material from Sulzer. It began with speculation about how the fine arts had arisen in the first place. They had originated, it suggested, in the attempt to beautify useful objects. The first man to join the word *beaux* to the word *arts* had understood that their essence was to marry the charming to the useful, and to beautify the objects which the mechanical arts had produced. The fine arts had arisen simply from the tendency which men had to embellish everything around them. A man built himself some place in which to live before he thought of making it more attractive. The shepherd who first tried to give a more elegant turn to his crook, and to decorate it with some carving, was the originator of sculpture. The savage who first thought of adding some proportion and order to his hut was the founder of the art of architecture. These were the feeble beginnings from which the human mind gradually developed the various fine arts.

Such an account of the fine arts seemed to imply that they were originally merely attempts to create things which would appear pleasant to the eye of the beholder and hence much less important than the practical arts. However, the article warned that one should not confine the true purpose of the fine arts within such a narrow sphere. In order to appreciate the ultimate value of the fine arts they had to be considered, not as they were in their infancy, but as they were in their full maturity. "La première question qui se présente ici," the article argued, "c'est donc de rechercher quelle utilité l'homme peut se promettre des beaux-arts considérés dans toute l'étendue de leur essence, et dans l'état de perfection dont ils sont susceptibles" (vol. III, p. 485).

Nature, the original artist, had revealed how the fine arts could be useful. First of all she had demonstrated that beauty could make human beings more civilized by arousing tender passions within them. Art could exploit beauty in a similar way to elevate the emotions and create a sense of order in the mind. In fact society could scarcely exist without this refining influence of the arts. The cynics of classical times had protested quite properly against abuse of the arts, but they had also failed to appreciate what the arts had accomplished. The article ridiculed Diogenes for his preposterous idea of returning to a pure state of nature. Only if Athens and Corinth had been submerged in the sea could the influence of the fine arts have been destroyed—and then the philosopher would have been forced to live among the barbarous Scythians. It even mocked Rousseau, "meilleur Diogène qui vit parmi les Grecs modernes," because he too had attacked the fine arts without stopping to consider what he owed to them.

So far the article had been trying to determine what could be considered the most widespread result of all the fine arts together. It concluded that their most general result was a refinement of that moral sense which was known as *le goût du beau*, and this influence alone demonstrated their social value. "Ce premier service que les beaux-arts nous rendent est si important, que quand il seroit le seul, nous devrions encore par reconnaissance élever des temples et ériger des autels aux muses" (vol. III, p. 489). A nation which possessed this taste for beauty would, on the whole, be made up of better men than nations where good taste had as yet not made its influence felt.

This civilizing role was only part of the service which the fine arts could render to society. Nature had revealed another way in which they could prove useful. Like a tender mother she had embellished those things which were most necessary for men and had rendered unattractive those things which were useless or harmful. In the same way, the fine arts could attract men to virtue or repel them from vice. *Les beaux-arts* were admirably suited for this purpose because their very essence consisted of imposing a certain form on a subject in order to make it more arresting. These arts aimed at creating a lively impact, at impressing the mind, and at touching the heart. Even when treating a melancholy theme, a painting could charm the eye with beautiful form, pleasing contrasts of light and shade, and the brilliant lustre of colour. By such means the fine arts, like sirens whose appeal was irresistible, forced men to submit to their influence.

This power which the fine arts exercised over the mind had, however, to be directed toward some higher end. Without an exalted purpose the arts would be no more than dangerous seductresses. Only the weak-minded failed to see that everything in the universe had a decided bent toward perfection. Yet there were artists who imagined that they had fulfilled their function when they had done nothing more than tickle sensual desires. Although only a few paragraphs before the article had defended the arts on the grounds of their refining influence alone, it now argued that they were dangerous unless they served morality more directly. Without a specific moral message the arts did not deserve respect from the wise man or protection from government. But guided by an enlightened government they could become the main instruments of human happiness.

The article had begun by asking what utility could be expected from the fine arts in their most perfect state. Now it was clear that *les beaux-arts* were to justify their existence by serving as educational tools:

Il faut à une nation, pour être heureuse, de bonnes lois relatives à son étendue, et adaptées au sol et au climat: mais ces lois, qui sont l'ouvrage de l'entendement, ne suffisent pas, il faut encore que chaque citoyen ait continuellement sous les yeux, de la manière la plus propre à le frapper vivement, certaines maximes fondamentales, certaines notions directrices qui soient comme la base du caractère national, qui le maintiennent et l'empêchent de s'altérer. De plus, dans les conjonctures critiques où tantôt l'inertie, tantôt les passions s'opposent au devoir, il est nécessaire qu'on ait en main des moyens propres à donner à ce devoir de nouveaux attraits; et voilà deux services qu'on peut se promettre des beaux-arts. Ils ont mille occasions de réveiller en nous ces maximes fondamentales, et de les y graver d'une manière ineffaçable; eux seuls, après nous avoir insensiblement préparés à des sentiments délicats, peuvent dans les moments de crise faire une douce violence à nos cœurs, et nous enchaîner par une sorte de plaisir aux devoirs les plus pénibles; eux seuls possèdent le secret, quoique diversement, et chacun à sa manière, de présenter avec tous les appas que l'on peut imaginer, les vertus, les sentiments d'un cœur honnête, et les actes de bienfaisance que la circonstance exige. Quelle âme un peu sensible pourroit leur résister alors?   (vol. III, p. 489)

The Encyclopedists were thus keenly aware of how important it was to appeal to the emotions in guiding human behaviour. Philosophy could show man the way to happiness, but, the article conceded, it could not fill him with the zeal to overcome all the difficulties which beset that way. Philosophy ought therefore to consider the fine arts as auxiliary troops whose assistance was indispensable. If a prince would reveal to an artist his plans for leading his people to a realization of their real interests, then that artist, like a second Orpheus, could guide them even against their will by a pleasant sort of compulsion. By smoothing their way and sprinkling it with flowers, the artist could compel the people to perform zealously everything necessary for their happiness. For this to become possible all that was needed was for the philosopher to provide the artist with maxims, the legislator to guide him with laws, and the humanitarian to provide him with projects.

The article did not try to hide the fact that the fine arts could also be harmful. Like the tree in the Garden of Eden the arts bore the fruits of both good and evil. They could deprave the man who used them carelessly. But even a refined sensuality could have disastrous consequences whenever it was not constantly directed by reason. The extravagances of extremists in both religion and politics, the flights of imagination by members of fanatical sects, were the products of sensuality free from the reins of reason. At bottom, of course, it was the same sensuality which motivated heroes and fools, saints and scoundrels. Consequently when the power of the fine arts fell into base hands a good medicine became a fatal poison. When the arts were misused vice received the attractive appearance of virtue and in a drunken stupor man was seduced into the arms of evil. The state ought therefore to encourage the arts and diffuse their influence among all the classes of society, but, because of the abuses to which the arts were subject, it ought also to supervise their use in the interests of utility.

The idea of art as propaganda thus led to the notion of some sort of state supervision of the arts. Assuming that good taste led to moral refinement, the article argued, a wise government should not permit any artist to contaminate the taste of his fellow citizens. No artist should be allowed to practise unless he gave proof of sound judgment and right intentions as well as artistic skill. The government ought to make sure that all works of art bore the imprint of good taste in the same way that it checked to see that money was sound. The astute magistrate would also make use of the fine arts in order to ensure that every public festivity, every solemn ceremony, and even every domestic fête contributed to a common goal. Since the arts could have such a powerful influence it was important to direct their use toward the happiness of mankind. And because the arts were to serve as educational instruments it was essential that their impact should be widespread:

Ensuite, puisque les beaux-arts doivent, selon leur essence et leur nature, servir de moyens pour accroître et assurer le bonheur des hommes, il est, en second lieu, nécessaire qu'ils pénètrent jusqu'à l'humble cabane du moindre des citoyens; il faut que le soin d'en diriger l'usage et d'en déterminer l'emploi entre dans le système politique, et soit un des objets essentiels de l'administration de l'état: il faut donc aussi que l'on consacre à cet objet une partie des trésors que l'industrie et l'épargne d'un peuple laborieux fournit chaque année au souverain pour subvenir aux dépenses publiques. (vol. III, p. 491)

Eighteenth-century thinkers liked to bolster philosophical arguments by appealing to history—for them history was philosophy teaching by examples. The "Beaux-arts" article did not claim that any society had ever made full use of the arts as a means of bringing truth alive and rendering virtue appealing, but it maintained that the Greeks had come close to this ideal. They had regarded the various arts as instruments suitable for shaping morality and supporting the teachings of philosophy. Poetry, drama, music, and the plastic arts had all been used to impress moral concepts and the love of noble deeds on the minds of citizens in a pleasant way. It was because the Greeks had realized how much the various arts could contribute to the public good that artists of classical times were given such high honours and granted extraordinary financial support by the government.

The Etruscans had also taken great pains to see that the fine arts had a useful moral influence. Even though very little was known about the political arrangements in this nation, the numerous remains of their works of art showed clearly how closely they had tied the arts to all the functions of private life. On looking at these monuments, one could visualize how amongst the Etruscans the lowest citizen could not look around him without the fine arts reminding him of his gods and his heroes. However, the *Encyclopédie* article continued, as the sentiment of public good became weaker, as rulers substituted their personal interests for public welfare, and as covetousness along with a taste for luxury enfeebled character, the fine arts ceased to serve the good of the state. They became the arts of extravagance and soon lost the consciousness of their proper dignity.

The article argued that there was a useful lesson to be gained for the eighteenth century in examining the enormous abuses which had resulted from this process of artistic degeneration. The Athenians had begun to abandon themselves to the pleasures of the various arts, and those arts which had been used to incite patriotic vigour in the breasts of citizens now served only to nourish idleness and to smother all interest in the general good. Great men hired artists in the same way they hired cooks, and the arts which had once provided salutary remedies for the soul now only served up perfumes. Such was the condition of the arts when the Romans built up their empire in the ancient world, and that is why the arts had the same character in Rome. Those who had seized power in Rome employed these mercenary artists to make tyranny pleasant and thus to help consolidate their power. The inevitable consequence of this sort of politics was not only that the arts were diverted from their proper functions, but that they lost their previous aesthetic perfection. From that time on, according to the *Encyclopédie*, the arts declined unconsciously until they finally fell into that state of degradation in which they had stagnated for so many centuries.

The article disagreed with those writers who implied that during the Middle Ages the practice of the arts had disappeared altogether. This was clearly contradicted by history which proved that throughout the whole medieval period there were artists at work. The arts did not disappear, but they gradually withered until they had lost most of their former beauty. In the twelfth century and the period following, said the *Encyclopédie*, society became so depraved that the fine arts were put to shameful use. In books of devotion, in religious buildings, and around pulpits subjects were depicted that one would be shocked to come across even in places devoted to debauchery. The only compensation was that such abuses lost most of their unhappy influence because medieval works of art were absolutely devoid of artistic merit. Gradually, however, the arts recovered their skill in Italy by the sixteenth century and spread throughout the rest of Europe.

Late classical and medieval art thus revealed the dangers which threatened society when the arts were misused, and according to the *Encyclopédie*, the same pattern was recurring in contemporary Europe. Art no longer served any purpose other than to assist luxury and ostentation. It would be difficult to prove that any of the modern patrons of the fine arts were motivated by any real awareness of their true value. When an artist did succeed in creating a useful work, it had to be the product of his personal genius rather than the intention of his patrons. One had only to look at the thoughtless choice of subjects in order to realize that men had lost the proper conception of the utility of the fine arts. Whether a painter chose some inane subject from mythology or some useful theme did not seem to matter so long as the picture was well done. The same was even true of paintings in the churches which sometimes presented pious myths which were more shocking to sound reason than pagan fables.

According to the *Encyclopédie*, it was not a lack of technical skill in the arts which was the source of the trouble. The modern artist had all the skills necessary to achieve the splendour of classical times. The trouble was that for a long time the artist had not been directed toward his proper goal, but had been hired only to gratify the demands of sensual pleasure. Now the artist was looked upon as a kind of artisan whose only role was to distract the great and rescue the idle rich from the boredom which pursued them. Thus it was not the fault of the artists that the fine arts were degraded. They could not raise the arts to a higher purpose without the assistance of wise legislation, calculated to lift them from their debasement and to recall them to their grand destination. For a long time they had known no other vocation than to amuse the great. What they now needed was to be redirected:

... qu'au contraire l'artiste soit appellé, non dans le cabinet du prince, où celui-ci n'est qu'un homme privé, mais au pié du trône pour y recevoir des commissions tout aussi intéressantes que celles qu'on y donne aux chefs de l'armée, de la justice, ou de la police: que le plan général du législateur embrasse les grandes vues de porter le peuple à l'obéissance envers les loix, et à la pratique des vertus sociales par le ministère des beaux-arts, on verra bien vite toutes les forces du génie se déployer pour remplir ce grand objet; on pourra s'attendre à voir renaître des chefs-d'œuvre, et des chefs-d'œuvre vraisemblablement supérieurs à ceux de l'antiquité. (vol. III, p. 497)

It should be emphasized that when the Encyclopédists spoke of the fine arts—*les beaux-arts*—they were using the word in its widest sense to include drama, opera, and music, as well as painting, sculpture, and engraving. What they were advocating, therefore, was the total mobilization of all the means of impressing ideas on the human mind. According to the article we have been following, the only way to appeal to the soul was through the senses, but the methods of doing this varied because there were a number of different senses. Touch, taste, and smell were perhaps the most powerful senses, but they were of little interest to the fine arts because they concerned man only as an animal. It was a higher sensuality which alone could serve to elevate the character of man by involving the mind and soul; this involvement took place in drama, opera, music, and the plastic arts. Here the great principle was to be to make sure that all the parts of the work of art contributed to make the most favourable impression possible on the viewer's imagination so as to engrave the message indelibly on his mind. The fine arts could not achieve this impact without beauty, regularity, and good taste, but in addition they had to select subjects calculated to improve the mind and heart.

This emphasis on utility recurred constantly in the supplementary volumes of the *Encyclopédie*. The articles "Agréable," "Belle Nature," "Bonté," "Esthétique," and "Expression," mostly culled from Sulzer, all proposed union of *l'agréable à l'utile*.[8] The article

8"Agréable," *Encyclopédie*, vol. I, pp. 656–57; "Belle Nature," vol. XXII, p. 757 f.; "Bonté," vol. V, pp. 274–76; "Esthétique," vol. XIII, p. 90 f.; "Expression," vol. XIII, pp. 681–82.

"Esthétique" advocated a new science not unlike what we would call motivational research. Because the fine arts attained control over the emotions by stimulating pleasant or unpleasant sensations, an exhaustive investigation was needed to show how various objects aroused those feelings. This research would reveal the ways in which the greatest possible utility could be culled from the enjoyment of the fine arts—"utilité qui ne tend pas à moins qu'à remplir les vues de la philosophie et de la morale" (vol. XIII, p. 92).

A modern reader might conclude that art which was forever preaching would become rather tedious after a time. The *Encyclopédie* argued the opposite in an article entitled "Intéressant," in which it contended that only art with a social message could move deeply. A thing became interesting, according to this article, when it excited a feeling of involvement in the spectator, when it aroused desires, initiated projects, excited fears, or evoked hopes. An artist could not really arouse this inner activity, this sense of involvement, without giving a moral and social content to his work. He had to realize that there were more interesting subjects than a pretty landscape or a gentle Zephyr, that to evoke a deep response he would have to treat serious social themes which could excite humanity. His task would be incomplete unless he used the interest which he aroused to improve the soul by directing it toward justice and virtue. "Cela prouve encore," the article concluded, "que tout grand artiste doit être philosophe et honnête homme" (vol. XVIII, p. 916).

The Encyclopedists who had begun by questioning the utility of *les arts d'agrément* in comparison with more practical crafts, had thus ended up by making social utility the basis for their defence of the fine arts. They could esteem these arts because they could impress on the human mind those social virtues—labour, justice, toleration, benevolence, patriotism and so on—which the eighteenth century cherished. Like the church thinkers before them the Encyclopedists came to value the fine arts mainly as potential instruments of propaganda. Both the churchmen and the eighteenth century philosophers believed that they had to present their teachings in a striking fashion which would make an indelible impression on the mind. But the Encyclopedists had even higher hopes for the arts in the service of a religion. The churchmen had believed that the arts were a valuable aid to their cause, but they placed their real faith in the sacraments and divine redemption. The Encyclopedists thought that the arts themselves, conveying the conclusions of enlightened thought, could redeem man by making him more humane and benevolent.

Despite its emphasis on utility, nevertheless, the *Encyclopédie* was not entirely consistent in its attitude toward art. Various articles revealed an enthusiasm for aesthetic values entirely apart from any consideration of social utility. For example, the articles on classical painting certainly did not develop the theme suggested in the article "Peinture," of how painting had been used in different periods to impress religious and political ideas on the minds of men.[9] Instead the articles praised classical artists for their achievements in design, shading, colouring, perspective, expression, composition, and other purely artistic matters, rather than for any useful function which they performed in society. One might have expected that an article in the *Encyclopédie* would have been especially interested in the decline of classical painting because of the chance it offered to draw moral conclusions. But the articles even mentioned Pliny's moral condemnation of the painting of his century without exploiting such an opportunity to discuss the proper use of art.

Again in the articles on modern painting the *Encyclopédie* had nothing to say about the use to which painting had been put by the Church and other patrons following its rebirth in the fourteenth and fifteenth centuries.[10] Artists before the middle of the fifteenth century were credited with making great progress in copying nature, and were criticized only for their lack of skill in portraying the nude body in action, in rendering light and shade, in aerial perspective or the elegant contours of drapery. Enthusiasm for the work of sixteenth-century artists was likewise based on purely aesthetic criteria: the charm, the grace, the originality, and the poetic expressiveness of their paintings. At times the standard of social utility seems to have been abandoned altogether: "Le plus grand peintre pour nous," said Jaucourt writing about the Venetian school, "est celui dont les ouvrages nous font le plus de plaisir, comme le dit fort bien l'abbé du Bos" (vol. XI, pp. 796–97).

9"Peinture antique," vol. XXV, pp. 121–25; "Peinture des Grecs," pp. 125–27; "Peinture des Romains," pp. 127–34. Articles by Jaucourt.
10"Peinture moderne," vol. XXV, pp. 135–37; "Ecole Lombard," vol. XI, pp. 786–92; "Ecole Vénitienne," vol. XI, p. 795 ff. All articles by Jaucourt.

The *Encyclopédie* blamed the subsequent decline of Italian art on a gradual deterioration of artistic talent rather than on any misuse of art. According to the article "Peinture moderne" (vol. XXV, p. 134), the Florentine and Venetian schools had simply lost their creative vitality in sixty to eighty years, whereas the Roman school had managed to sustain its output somewhat longer thanks to an influx of foreign artists. In his article on schools of painting (vol. XI, p. 802) d'Alembert too failed to find any moral reason for artistic stagnation in contemporary Italy. He suggested that art seemed to flower and decline for no apparent reason: in producing talent, nature opened new mines capriciously from time to time, only to close them down later for several centuries. Here d'Alembert, who idealized utility, had not a word to say about the social influence of art.

Falconet's article on "Sculpture" had asserted that the value of this art lay in its potential moral influence, but the two articles on the history of sculpture did not examine what this influence had been in various periods. Once again the discussions concentrated on purely artistic developments with almost no mention of the use or misuse of sculpture in different societies. Although "Sculpture antique" (vol. XXX, p. 452) stated that degeneration of classical sculpture was connected with loss of political liberty, it failed to elaborate. "Sculpture moderne" (vol. XXX, p. 456–58) lamented the condition of sculpture in contemporary France without claiming that this was caused by lack of some high moral or political purpose. Jaucourt called on the king to revive sculpture by a series of great projects but he did not suggest that these works be used to arouse patriotic sentiments or teach social virtues.

The contributors demonstrated repeatedly that they could appreciate art simply for its play of line and colour, for its rhythm and harmony, for its pleasing imitation of nature. In numerous articles they revealed their interest in the intrinsic value of artistic techniques—for example, the articles on shading, draperies, elegance, grace, harmony, and a host of others.[11] Often they put aside the notion of utility to discuss the aesthetic pleasure which a work of art could produce. There was an obvious tension in their attitude

[11] "Clair-obsur," vol. VIII, p. 204; "Draperies," *ibid.*, vol. XI, p. 368; "Elégance," *ibid.*, vol. XII, p. 71; "Grâce," *ibid.*, vol. XVI, p. 418; "Harmonie," *ibid.*, vol. XVII, p. 84; "Lumières," *ibid.*, vol. XX, p. 468.

toward art: in spite of all their emphasis on social utility, as heirs of fifteenth-century Italy they were still susceptible to art for its own sake.

The *Encyclopédie* failed to offer any workable plan for transforming the fine arts into instruments of enlightenment. It blamed the misuse of art on social maladjustment without showing how artists could rise above their environment to help regenerate mankind. The various arts simply mirrored the state of society in which they were produced. Such was the thesis of the long article on "Luxe" which contended that artistic decadence was the product of general social dislocation (vol. XX, pp. 544 ff.). Luxury was absolved from the charge of corrupting society and the arts. Since luxury was simply the use of wealth to make existence more pleasant, it was not evil in itself. It was misgovernment and maladministration rather than luxury which undermined moral vigour and polluted the fine arts.

Extreme inequality, which was often blamed on luxury, was really caused by over-taxation of certain groups, exclusive privileges granted to other classes, or over-emphasis on certain kinds of production. When extreme wealth had been acquired without effort, those who controlled this wealth forfeited social approval; they lost the sense of how to use their riches virtuously and sought to forget their uselessness in frivolous pleasure. If the government gave the rich tasks to accomplish, if it honoured them only for serving the nation, then they would not have to abuse themselves in indolence. Disordered luxury, however, left men with no other occupation than to attempt to dispel boredom; it forced them to turn from one pleasure to another without ever being satisfied, until in a torrent of amusements their souls became incapable of appreciating the grand and the beautiful. Their petty tastes preferred the insignificant, the droll, the ridiculous, the affected. They patronized those who flattered their vices and their bad taste (vol. XX, pp. 552–53).

Such degeneration was not the inevitable result of luxury or the arts which it encouraged. Under a wise and vigorous government it was possible to have all the advantages of luxury without these abuses. Such a government would consider the economic interests of the agricultural workers and the artisans of the cities. With wealth better distributed, these classes would support the institutions of the country, and there would be fewer idle rich pursuing frivolous pleasures in the capital. The middle class, uncorrupted by the great, would be the source of enlightenment which would spread down to the people and rise up to the great as well. Honour and position would be given to those who performed real services to the state rather than to those privileged by birth; the great would not be tempted therefore to lose their capacity for enlightenment in the pursuit of puerile pleasures. Consequently, the solution to the problem of the misuse of the fine arts went back to the problem of good government in general. "Ranimons encore en nous l'amour de la patrie, de l'ordre, des loix," declared the *Encyclopédie*; "et les beaux-arts cesseront de se profaner, en se dévouant à la superstition et au libertinage; ils choisiront des sujets utiles aux mœurs, et ils les traiteront avec force et avec noblesse" (vol. XX, p. 556).

All this discussion skirted the central problem of how to convert the arts into instruments of propaganda. This was a problem which was never really faced: nowhere did the contributors furnish any plan for transforming the arts from reflections of their environment into instruments of social change. Nor was it clear how the artist could be directed toward useful themes without cramping his creative impulses. The articles "Génie" by Diderot, "Enthousiasme" by Cahusac, and "Verve" by Jaucourt all depicted the artist as an individual endowed with extraordinary ardour and sensibility. Such a spirit was not to be fettered with rules and regulations. "Les règles et les loix du goût donneroient des entraves au génie," wrote Diderot; "il les brise pour voler au sublime, au pathétique, au grand" (vol. XV, p. 977). This was the conception of the artist as a free spirit which had emerged back in the fifteenth and early sixteenth centuries. It was not at all clear how this conception could be combined with the dictates of propaganda. Again there was an obvious tension in the *Encyclopédie*, a tension between the still vigorous Renaissance tradition and the rising emphasis on social utility.

4.

*Toutes ces divinités païennes, aussi absurdes que
scandaleuses, n'occupoient plus des pinceaux
précieux, désormais destinés au soin de
transmettre à l'avenir les faits les plus
importans: on entendoit par ce mot ceux qui
donnoient une plus noble idée de l'homme,
comme la clémence, la générosité, le dévouement,
le courage, le mépris de la mollesse.*

MERCIER, *L'An 2440*[1]

FOR SUCCESS dynastic autocracy requires one thing which heredity cannot guarantee: a succession of intelligent and vigorous rulers. Louis XV, who at the age of five had followed his great-grandfather to the throne of France in 1715, was intelligent enough, but he lacked the vigour to direct a system which concentrated power in the person of the king. After he had come of age he allowed his former tutor, the aged Cardinal Fleury, to rule for seventeen years, and when he finally began to direct affairs himself at the age of thirty-three, he had grown accustomed to yielding to those who were more intelligent or more forceful than himself. He wished for

[1]Louis-Sébastien Mercier, *L'An 2440: rêve s'il en fût jamais* (Amsterdam, 1770). References here are to the definitive edition (3 vols., Paris, 1786). See vol. II, p. 61, for the quotation.

the welfare of his people, but never exerted his will sufficiently to bring about the necessary innovations. He exhibited a marked distaste for work, he lacked self-confidence and was afraid to stand up to his ministers. "C'est le vide qui règne," was the acid pronouncement of the Marquis d'Argenson.

In the absence of an energetic prince the machine of state might have been directed by a powerful minister as it had been in the days of Richelieu. But the example of the Sun King, who had insisted on being master himself, militated against appointment of a prime minister to exercise power in the name of the king. Unfortunately Louis XV could only be aroused by court intrigue, ministerial feuds, and diplomatic machinations; internal administration failed to interest him. The unending round of court ceremony, the royal ballet which his predecessor had performed so faithfully, also wearied him. He sought relief in two main distractions—hunting animals and pursuing women. In both cases the king was provided with a seemingly inexhaustible supply.

Art reflected this loss of dynamism at the centre. Louis XV did nothing to turn art into an instrument to glorify his reign. *Louis le Grand* had supervised artistic activities and on occasion had even dictated subjects himself. His successor did not seem to care what was commissioned in his name or what artists were doing. He neither selected his court painter nor laid out any programme for him. He simply let the artistic administration which he had inherited from the Sun King run on its own momentum without royal guidance. As Pierre Marcel has pointed out, the phrase "style Louis XV" refers to art produced in a certain period, not to influences which the king had brought to bear on it.[2] No longer was art consciously directed to celebrate the grandeur of the monarchy.

During the middle of the century, Mme de Pompadour came close to making herself minister of fine arts in France. This vivacious little beauty had exploited her attractions to marry into the circle of financiers who waxed rich collecting indirect taxes. Then through a distant relative who worked at court, she managed to meet the king who was captivated by her charm and wit. In 1745 she abandoned her husband to become the titled mistress of the

[2]"Les peintres et la vie politique en France au XVIIIᵉ siècle," *Revue du dix-huitième siècle*, no. 4 (1913), p. 349.

King. After five or six years she ceased to share the royal bed, but she remained the confidante and companion of the king for another fifteen years. The royal favourite was a woman of genuine taste who took a real interest in the artists of the day. With access to the King's purse she was able to make herself chief patroness of the fine arts.

At times this *maîtresse en titre* seems to have understood the role which art had played under Louis XIV. She had schemes for new buildings and parks which would perpetuate the memory of the King and his mistress. She also glimpsed how art might be used to idealize the deeds of the monarch. For example, she ordered Vien to do a drawing celebrating the victory at Fontenoy: it showed the King dressed as a Roman emperor standing on a chariot with the dauphin at his side, while overhead hovered the figure of Victory. Mme de Pompadour herself did an engraving of this theme as well as one symbolizing the prelude to the peace of Aix-la-Chapelle: Peace and Victory were shown wrangling over the King who had turned his gaze from the battlefield to view the crops pushing upwards. On another occasion she depicted Louis XV as Apollo, god of the arts, crowning the guiding spirits of painting and sculpture.[3]

But Mme de Pompadour, whose power rested on her ability to amuse and distract the King, was hardly the person to direct art toward serious goals. She summoned most of the outstanding painters and sculptors of the day to portray her charms in various poses and settings. When she commissioned works other than portraits, she favoured light-hearted themes rendered in a delicately sensuous style. Small wonder then that she made Boucher her favourite artist: he seemed to have been born to idealize her reign and celebrate her way of life. She gave him commissions for easel paintings. She gave him the task of dashing off erotic scenes which might excite the sensuality of a satiated monarch. It was largely through her efforts that Boucher became the chief court painter in 1765, the year after her death. This artist, as we have already seen, was not likely to turn out heroic allegories on the model of Le Brun. Thus, despite her occasional glimpses of *l'art politique*, Mme de Pompadour failed to guide art toward any great projects similar to those of Louis XIV.

[3]*Ibid.*, pp. 354–55.

Although the court continued to prefer art dedicated to pleasure rather than politics, there was a growing demand for didactic art after the middle of the century. The *philosophes* and Encyclopedists led the way, but many others lent their support to the idea that art ought to instruct. In his utopian novel, *L'An 2440*, Mercier argued that the visual arts should be used to transmit enlightened moral precepts to the masses. Among the art critics, whose writings became more prolific with each successive exhibition, there emerged a group which called on painters and sculptors to treat moral and patriotic themes. At the same time the art ministers and the officials who dispensed royal patronage and supervised the Academy also began to favour a type of art quite different from that commissioned in the first half of the century.

Official efforts to direct art away from petty themes began when the uncle of Mme de Pompadour, Lenormant de Tournehem, became *Directeur général des bâtiments*. As his assistant, Tournehem chose Charles Coypel who became *premier peintre du roi* and director of the Academy. During his years in office, Tournehem attempted to encourage historical painting which had declined steadily in popularity because of the demand for more decorative art. He cut the price for portraits and increased the rate for historical paintings. To improve the calibre of the historical genre he created a special committee, composed mostly of historical painters, to judge paintings submitted to the exhibitions at the Louvre. At the same time the Academy was furnished with a respectable library where artists could study history and the classics.[4] Tournehem did not talk of giving art a moral content, but he did initiate the reaction against the petty manner which had dominated the work of the previous generation.

Tournehem died in 1751 after more than five years of vigorous activity directed toward reviving the historical genre. He was immediately replaced by his nephew, the brother of Mme de Pompadour, who a few years later became the Marquis de Marigny. For two years before assuming control of the ministry of fine arts he had toured Italy, accompanied by the designer Cochin, the architect

---

[4]Jean Locquin, *La Peinture d'histoire en France de 1747 à 1785: étude sur l'évolution des idées artistiques dans la seconde moitié du XVIIIᵉ siècle* (Paris, 1912), pp. 2–10.

Soufflot, and the Abbé Leblanc. As Cochin explained later in his book *Voyage d'Italie*, the purpose of this grand tour was "acquérir les connaissances nécessaires pour servir dignement un grand roi dans la Direction des Monuments qui doivent immortaliser la gloire de son règne."[5] This tour convinced the future minister that France had wandered from the grand style. His experience turned him into an opponent of what he called *la chicorée moderne*. Yet as Locquin has noted, there is a striking dichotomy in Marigny's attitude toward art. As a private collector he exhibited a taste for the erotic *petite manière*; among his own paintings were Boucher's "Une jeune femme couchée sur le ventre"; Van Loo's "Jupiter en satyre suprenant Antiope endormie"; Pierre's "Io sous les caresses d'un nuage"; and Natoire's "Léda s'abandonnant au cygne." Marigny had over nineteen paintings by Boucher, fourteen by Van Loo, and seven by Natoire. But as the royal official in charge of commissions he favoured the graver and more idealistic historical genre.[6]

During most of his career as minister of fine arts Marigny was assisted by Charles Cochin who was permanent secretary of the Academy. Cochin was a friend of some of the *philosophes*, especially of Diderot and Marmontel, and an exponent of the idea that art ought to instruct.[7] In 1764 he found a favourable opportunity to guide historical painting in that direction. Marigny had put him in charge of completing the decoration of the Château de Choisy. Up until this time the rooms of the château had been decorated with landscapes, hunting scenes, and light mythological themes. But the Seven Years' War had just ended and Cochin thought it could draw a moral. In a letter to Marigny he suggested a series of paintings which he thought would be more appropriate than conventional subjects. In his opinion, men had given too much praise to military exploits which only contributed to the destruction of mankind. Would it not sometimes be better to represent those generous and humanitarian deeds by which good kings brought happiness to their subjects? Therefore he proposed a

[5]Charles-Nicolas Cochin, *Voyage d'Italie* (Paris, 2 vols., 1758), vol. I, dedication to Marigny.
[6]Locquin, *La Peinture d'histoire en France*, pp. 16–17.
[7]*Ibid.*, pp. 19–20.

sequence celebrating the beneficent deeds of Augustus, Trajan, Titus, and Marcus Aurelius ". . . que le Roy, en voyant célébrer leur vertus, reconnoisse quelques-unes de celles qui le rendent si cher à son peuple."[8]

Apparently Cochin hoped not only to flatter Louis XV, but to inspire him with noble thoughts through scenes selected from classical history. A picture of Augustus closing the doors of the temple of Janus would express the peaceful intentions of the King. A view of Titus standing before the ruins of Jerusalem and cursing the factions which had forced him to reduce it to such a state would recapture the humane sentiments which Louis had felt after the battle of Fontenoy. Trajan stopping to render justice to a poor woman while he was hurrying to a campaign would provide a subject full of humanity. Marcus Aurelius showing extreme concern for his people during a period of famine and pestilence would not only provide artistic possibilities, but would illustrate the spirit of a king who deserved the adoration of his subjects. For other parts of the hall Cochin suggested figures personifying the same virtues as these large murals.

Marigny replied that he was enchanted by these subjects, but he wondered whether Cochin might not find some happier incident from the life of Titus.[9] Cochin replied that he had combed Suetonius and Josephus for some other subject from the reign of Titus, but apart from his military achievements, which were out of keeping with the purpose of the paintings, all that could be found were some humanitarian enactments and some wise aphorisms which could not be portrayed in paint. In the end Cochin came up with a subject which he thought would make a striking painting and would also illustrate the humanity of the emperor: Titus releasing forty thousand of the prisoners who had been brought to him as slaves following the capture of Jerusalem. Cochin also suggested that the efforts of the emperor to extinguish the fire set by his soldiers in the temple might provide some additional subjects. "C'est tout ce que j'ay pu trouver," the secretary of the

[8]Abel-François Poisson, Marquis de Marigny, *Correspondance de M. de Marigny avec Coypel, Lépicié et Cochin,* ed. M. Marc Furcy-Raynaud, in *Nouvelles archives de l'art françois,* 3e série, vols. XIX–XX, 1903–1904 (Paris, 1904–1905); quotation from vol. XIX, pp. 324–25.

[9]*Ibid.,* pp. 326–27.

Academy lamented; "les historiens, malheureusement, sont moins attentifs à relever les actions qui font honneur à l'humanité que celles qui la font gémir."[10]

Cochin indeed envisaged a whole series devoted to portraying the humanity of ancient rulers. He did not find it easy to choose subjects which served exactly the same purpose as the first four which he had proposed, either because benevolent deeds were rare, or because he could only recall a few. However, he did manage to find a number of noble themes not unlike the earlier selections he had chosen: the Consul Quintus returning to a besieged town the boys who had been handed over to him by a traitorous schoolmaster; Furius Camillus coming to the aid of Rome even though it had banished him unjustly; Lucius Albinus piously descending from his chariot along with his family in order to make room for the Vestal Virgins who were fleeing Rome; Lycurgus wounded in a riot provoked by his Laws; and Solon making the Athenians swear to observe the code he was presenting to them.[11] To fill the spaces between these murals and over the doors, Cochin suggested figures representing Mercy, Justice, Benevolence, and Generosity.

This preference for subjects which illustrated some civic virtue represented a significant shift in the official attitude toward art, although only the original themes from the lives of Augustus, Trajan, Marcus Aurelius, and Titus were actually executed. Unfortunately Louis XV was not anxious to be surrounded by moral lessons on every wall. Indeed after two years Cochin was forced to order the four paintings replaced with works by Boucher. But the idea of moral themes did not die. Boucher was unable to complete the paintings for the Château de Choisy before his death in 1771. Pierre, who had just succeeded Cochin, took up again the project for a series of paintings embodying moral ideals.[12] Writing to Marigny, Pierre pointed out that there were already panel-friezes by Lagrenée representing Justice, Mercy, Benevolence, and Generosity and suggested that these themes be continued with a sequence of scenes depicting heroic deeds and virtuous actions— Courage: Cloelia crossing the Tiber with her companions; Vigilance: Semiramis leaving her toilette to crush Babylon; Filial Devotion: Coriolanus pacified by his mother's tears; Humanity: Glaucias,

[10]*Ibid.*, pp. 330–31.   [11]*Ibid.*, pp. 331–32.
[12]Locquin, *La Peinture d'histoire en France*, pp. 25–26.

FRANÇOIS BOUCHER, LA TOILETTE DE VÉNUS
(Musée du Louvre, Archives Photographiques)

JEAN-BAPTISTE GREUZE, *LE FILS PUNI*
(Musée du Louvre, Archives Photographiques)

JACQUES-LOUIS DAVID, *LE SERMENT DES HORACES*
(Musée du Louvre, Archives Photographiques)

FRANÇOIS-ANDRÉ VINCENT
LE PRÉSIDENT MOLÉ ARRÊTÉ PAR LES FACTIEUX
(Salle des Conférences, Chambre des Députés, Archives Photographiques)

PIERRE PRUD'HON, *LE TRIOMPHE DE LA RÉVOLUTION*
(Musée Carnavalet, Photo Bulloz)

ANTOINE VESTIER
LATUDE MONTRANT DES DÉMOLISSEURS DE LA BASTILLE
(Musée Carnavalet, Photo Bulloz)

JACQUES BERTAUX, PRISE D'ASSAUT DES TUILERIES
(Musée de Versailles, Photo Giraudon)

LOUIS LÉOPOLD BOILLY, LE TRIOMPHE DE MARAT
(Musée de Versailles, Photo Giraudon)

JEAN-JACQUES-FRANÇOIS LE BARBIER
LE DÉVOUEMENT HÉROÏQUE DE DESILLES
(*Musée de Beaux-Arts, Nancy, Photo Lott*)

JACQUES-PHILIPPE CARESME
DERNIÈRES PAROLES DE JOSEPH CHALIER
(*Département des Estampes, Bibliothèque Nationale*)

CHARLES THEVENIN, *AUGEREAU AU PONT D'ARCOLE*
(Musée de Versailles, Photo Réunion des Musées Nationaux)

king of Illyria, welcoming the child Pyrrhus. Pierre, like Cochin, evidently preferred noble subjects to light-hearted ones. But this time morality was to be made more palatable for Louis XV. "Ces quatre sujets, dans lesquels il entre beaucoup de femmes," wrote Pierre, "seroient susceptibles d'agrément et d'expression. . . ."[13]

As secretary of the Academy Cochin supported historical painting with as many commissions as possible. Still he usually commissioned painters to treat lighter themes than those which he had suggested for the Château de Choisy. For the Château de Bellevue he ordered themes from the Iliad, from the Metamorphoses, and from various classical myths.[14] But when it seemed possible, he also injected some of the newer philosophy. For instance, when he ordered the decoration for the Petit Trianon he commissioned four great paintings which praised the practical arts, especially agriculture.[15] Thus, during their terms of office Cochin, Pierre, and Marigny all strove to encourage historical painting, although during much of that period they were seriously handicapped by lack of funds.

Marigny retired in 1773 and the Comte d'Angiviller was appointed *Directeur général des bâtiments* the following year. The ascension of Louis XVI to the throne, followed by the reforming ministry of Turgot, and later that of Necker, opened a favourable period for historical painting. Royal assistance to the historical genre was to reach its peak under d'Angiviller.[16] Shortly after his appointment, the new minister of fine arts wrote a letter to the Academy disclosing the philosophy which was going to guide in his administration. Echoing the opinion of the *philosophes*, he declared that the true function of art was to combat vice and preach virtue. He urged artists to choose their subjects carefully, and announced a plan aimed at redirecting art toward worthy themes. Each year he would commission four or five historical paintings with a moral impact, whose subjects would include incidents from French history:

. . . il [le Roi] verra avec un intérest [*sic*] particulier les Peintres de son Académie retracer les actions et les faits honorables à la nation.

---

[13]Marigny, *Correspondance*, vol. XIX, p. 244.
[14]Locquin, *La Peinture d'histoire en France*, p. 27.
[15]Marigny, *Correspondance*, vol. XX, pp. 138–41.
[16]Locquin, *La Peinture d'histoire en France*, p. 49.

Quel plus digne emploi pour les Arts que cette espèce d'association à la législation des mœurs. En voyant ces images déjà antiques, nos neveux rougiront peut-être, au milieu de tant de titres, de se trouver si peu de pairs.[17]

D'Angiviller set out at once to put his plans into effect. In June, 1775, he selected the painter Durameau to do four canvases for the Gobelin factory which needed designs for their tapestries. The arts minister thought that the style of this artist was well suited for the purpose he had in mind. "J'ai considéré d'ailleurs," d'Angiviller wrote to Pierre, "que pour rendre ses talens à la fois intéressans et pour la nation et pour les mœurs, rien ne conviendrait mieux que de les faire servir à représenter des traits célèbres et des actions nobles et vertueuses de notre histoire."[18] The letter proceeds to list the four subjects selected: the City of Randan honouring the valour and virtue of the Constable du Guesclin; the Chevalier Bayard returning his prisoner to her mother and giving her a dowry; the President Molé seized by rebels; and the assassins of Coligny falling to their knees as they are overcome with respect. D'Angiviller remarked that he thought this series of paintings would be all the more interesting because up until then men had been unaware of the possibilities which their own history offered art.

After eighteen months of meditation and conversation with Pierre, d'Angiviller drew up another project, this one consisting of eight paintings, six dealing with ancient history and two with French history. All the subjects to be painted by various artists had been carefully chosen to illustrate religious devotion, honest work, selflessness, steadfastness, or patriotism. There would be such scenes as Cleobis and Biton helping Oxen to pull the priestess to the temple in time for the sacrifice; Cimon throwing open his house so that the people could share his stores; Cressinus defending himself against the accusation of magic by displaying his agricultural implements in good repair; Fabricius turning down the gifts offered him by the envoys of Pyrrhus; Portia swearing to die with Brutus

[17]A. de C. Montaiglon, ed., *Procès-verbaux de l'Académie royale de peinture et de sculpture, 1648 à 1793* (10 vols., Paris, 1875–1909), vol. VIII, p. 176.

[18]Charles Claude de la Billarderie, Comte d'Angiviller, *Correspondance de M. d'Angiviller avec Pierre*, ed. M. Marc Furcy-Raynaud in the *Nouvelles archives de l'art français* 3e série, vols. XXI–XXII (Paris, 1905–1906), quotation from vol. XXI, pp. 42–43.

should the plot against Caesar prove disastrous; and du Guesclin honoured for his virtue.[19] The critic for the *Mémoires secrets* commended the new Director for curtailing the number of portraits on display. "On l'a remplacée par des tableaux d'histoire du premier genre; et dans ceux commandés par le Roi, on a remarqué avec satisfaction que beaucoup de sujets étoient choisis dans nos Annales."[20]

The commissions for the next Salon had a similar intention: d'Angiviller called them *une suite de vertus*.[21] Among the eight canvases were to be scenes of Regulus leaving Rome to subdue Carthage in spite of the tears of his family and the regrets of his fellow citizens; Metellus saved from the death sentence by the intercession of his son who had been named a judge by Augustus; the Indian philosopher Calanus burning himself in defiance of Alexander and his army; Agrippina debarking at Brindisi carrying the remains of her husband Germanicus who had died in Syria; and the courageous deed of Eustache de Saint-Pierre and his five compatriots during the siege of Calais.[22] Perhaps Diderot would not have approved of all these themes—he was too ill to write reviews of this or the preceding Salon—but it was significant that art was being used to idealize sacrifice for the state and magnanimity of soul. Significant too was the fact that once again some subjects had been included from the history of France.

François Vincent's "Molé arrêté par les factieux de la Fronde," one of the subjects from French history commissioned by d'Angiviller for the Salon of 1779, illustrates the sort of work favoured by this minister of fine arts. Mathieu Molé had been first president of the powerful Paris *parlement* when political turbulence erupted during the minority of Louis XIV. Without yielding the rights of the high tribunal over which he presided, Molé had attempted to play a conciliatory role among the rival factions. In the popular tumult known as the Day of the Barricades, August 26, 1648, he had sought out the Queen and Cardinal Mazarin to demand the release of prisoners whose arrest had sparked the outbreak. Braving

[19]Locquin, *La Peinture d'histoire en France*, p. 51.
[20]L. P. de Bachaumont and others, *Mémoires secrets pour servir à l'histoire de la république des lettres depuis 1762 jusqu'à nos jours*, vol. XI, p. 4.
[21]D'Angiviller, *Correspondance*, vol. XXI, p. 167.
[22]Locquin, *La Peinture d'histoire en France*, p. 52.

the threats of the Parisian mob, he had eventually won release of the captives. This was only one of several occasions on which he displayed remarkable bravery in his attempts to act as peace-maker. For his efforts the Queen had rewarded him with the post of Keeper of the Seals. Vincent's great canvas which now hangs in the National Assembly shows Molé, calm and dignified, defying the wild-eyed rioters around him. The artist has turned his hero into a symbol of stability and devotion to the state in a period of disorder.

Henceforth up until the Revolution the royal commissions for each exhibition included eight or more historical paintings with either classical or modern themes. Like the *philosophes*, d'Angiviller was convinced of the moral and political value of the fine arts. Not only did he direct painting toward moral subjects which would do honour to the monarchy, but at the same time he put sculpture to work honouring some of the great men in French history. For the Salon of 1781 he commissioned statues of the Duc de Montausier, "un homme de cour qui a donné l'exemple d'une vertu austère au milieu de la corruption"; Pascal, "un philosophe qui a éclairé la nation et l'humanité par ses écrits"; the Maréchal de Tourville, "un général de mer illustre par ses victoires"; and the Maréchal de Catinat, "un général de terre non moins recommandable pas ses talens militaires que par son désintéressement, son humanité, et son esprit philosophique."[23] Sculptured likenesses of such men were features at each of the exhibitions before the Revolution.

Neither Louis XV nor his successor gave any impulsion to art comparable to that given by the Sun King; nevertheless their art officials did strive to guide art toward noble themes which would be fitting emanations from the throne. In 1791 when the deputy Barère attacked d'Angiviller as an incompetent official, the painter Duplessis was able to claim that the minister had given art a patriotic purpose.[24] Official preference for didactic historical themes also assisted the emergence of the neoclassical style which made headway against rococo after the middle of the century. Royal patronage, combined with the stimulus of excavations at Pompeii

23 D'Angiviller, *Correspondance*, vol. XXI, pp. 264–65.
24 Joseph Siffrède Duplessis, *Lettre à M. Barère de Vieusac, député à l'Assemblée nationale, par M. Duplessis, peintre du roi* (28 mai, 1791).

and Herculaneum, the popularization of classical culture by the
archaeologist Winckelmann and the painter Mengs, and the appearance of richly illustrated tomes on archaeology, encouraged the
evolution of the new style which combined classicism with realism.

David's "Serment des Horaces," which caused a stir at the Salon
of 1785, marked the triumph of neoclassicism over rococo. According to Roman legend, Rome and Alba had once agreed that the
outcome of a war between them should depend on a combat
between three champions selected by each side. By chance the
task fell on the Horatii brothers for Rome and the Curiatii brothers
for Alba. On a huge canvas David depicted the three Roman warriors, their hands raised in salute, swearing on swords held high by
their father to win or die for their native land. David's austere and
theatrical manner was ideal for conveying a lesson in civic virtue.
By guiding art toward such heroic themes, government officials
had unwittingly helped to forge a potential revolutionary weapon
for the bourgeoisie.

While the art ministers sought to redirect art, the critics began to
call for moral and patriotic themes. Some of the pamphleteers
merely complained about the decline in historical painting without
offering any remedy, but others invited artists to revive historical
painting by portraying memorable deeds or national events. For
example, in 1769 the author of the *Lettre sur les peintures, gravures
et sculptures exposées cette année au Louvre* contended that artists
ought to choose interesting national themes, instead of searching
classical history for obscure subjects.[25] "Est-ce que notre histoire,"
he asked, "ne fourmille pas d'événemens aussi illustres à représenter
que l'histoire romaine?"[26] Were he a member of the Academy, he
would suggest that all the paintings submitted for admission should

[25]There is a large collection of reviews in the Collection Deloynes in the
Bibliothèque Nationale in France. For an index to this valuable collection see
George Duplessis, *Catalogue de la collection des pièces sur les beaux-arts . . .
recueillie par M. Deloynes* (Paris, 1881).

[26]Daudé de Jossan, *Lettre sur les peintures, gravures, et sculptures qui ont été
exposées cette année au Louvre, par M. Raphaël à M. Jérosme* (Paris, 1769),
Deloynes, vol. IX, Item 123, p. 27. For other demands for national themes see
Jean Restout, *Essai sur les principes de la peinture* (Paris, 1755), p. 43; Reboul,
Essai sur les mœurs des temps (Paris, 1768), p. 109; *Journal Encyclopédique*,
vol. II (September, 1761), p. 59; *Année Littéraire*, 1779, vol. VII, pp. 37 and
56.

deal with events in the history of France. Soon the nation would possess a collection of patriotic works which could distinguish public buildings and gardens.

In a critique entitled *Dialogues sur la peinture* published in a revised edition in 1773, three speakers discussed art as a means of communicating moral lessons. Fabretti, who represented a Roman priest in the dialogue, complained about the number of trivial still life paintings on display. All these pipes and flagons of beer did not speak to his soul as could the great themes of historical painting. He remarked that history and the Church Fathers were full of lessons which could lead a man to virtue if they were depicted in good taste. Lyttleton, another of the speakers, replied that he would leave sacred matters to the priest. He thought that classical literature and history provided the best lessons for paintings to treat. "Pour moi," he told the priest, "je ne vous rappellerai que la prophane antiquité qui regardoit avec raison les artistes comme les plus utiles précepteurs du genre humain."[27]

The *Lettres pittoresques à l'occasion des tableaux exposés au Salon en 1777* reviewed the exhibition in which had been displayed the great series of didactic paintings commissioned by d'Angiviller. The critic was lavish in his praise of the new minister and the scheme of putting artists to work on national themes. Historical painting was about to be revived after being allowed to languish too long. The author concluded his letters on the exhibition by lauding the idea of portraying great ministers, magistrates, and philosophers who could serve as models for their fellow men. He admired the sculptures of Sully, Descartes, Fénelon, and the Chancelier de l'Hôpital, not because they were good art, but because they taught him to love his country, to respect its laws, and to live a life of virtue. "Tous contribuent à me rendre meilleur," wrote the critic. "Tous font rejaillir sur moi quelques rayons de la gloire nationale et je me félicite d'être français."[28]

The critique entitled *La Muette qui parle au Salon de 1781* began with some interesting reflections on the role of art in society.

[27]*Dialogues sur la peinture*, 2e édition enrichie par notes (Paris, 1773); *Deloynes*, vol. X, Item 147, p. 118.
[28]*Lettres pittoresques à l'occasion des tableaux exposés au Salon en 1777*; *Deloynes*, vol. X, Item 190, p. 48.

The author was convinced that the historical genre was the highest form of painting because it could make the dead breathe and thus could move the human heart. But for this very reason historical painting had to be used with care. It was essential that it portray moral and national subjects. The artist had to choose worthy themes which would have the greatest appeal for the spectator. "A mérite égal de deux sujets, l'un national, l'autre étranger, le national nous intéressera davantage."[29] This critic rebuked Lépicié for choosing a subject devoid of national interest such as Fabius Dorso carrying his household gods. On the other hand he lauded Ménageot's painting of Leonardo da Vinci expiring in the arms of Francis I, Beaufort's representation of the death of the Chevalier Bayard, and Le Barbier's depiction of Jeanne Hachette and other women helping to throw back the enemy at Beauvais. The critic did admire some of the portraits and landscapes on display, but it was the *scènes nobles et héroïques* which he thought were the glory of the exhibition.

In 1783 one critic commended the minister of fine arts for commissioning paintings and sculptures intended to inspire virtue.[30] Another critic, the author of *La Morte de trois mille ans au Sallon*, criticized some of the paintings because they provided no practical lesson for the spectator. He disapproved of Lépicié's canvas showing Mattathias immolating an unfortunate fellow who had sacrificed to an idol. Such a painting came close to fanaticism and offered no useful instruction. Nor was there any lesson for Frenchmen in La Grenée's painting of a young Indian woman about to burn herself alive along with her husband's corpse. "J'aime mieux," said the critic, "qu'on choisisse des sujets nationaux."[31] Consequently he admired Berthélemy's version of Marcel being struck down just as he was about to betray Paris to the King of Navarre, Le Barbier's picture of the reconciliation of Henry IV and Sully, and a canvas showing the virtuous president de Harlay repelling an attempt by the Duc de Guise to corrupt him.

[29]*La Muette qui parle au Salon de 1781* (Amsterdam, 1781); *Deloynes*, vol. XII, Item 257, p. 6. According to A. A. Barbier, *Dictionnaire des ouvrages anonymes* (4 vols., 3e édition, Paris, 1882) this work is by R. M. Lesuire.
[30]*Le Véridique au Sallon* (Athènes, 1783), *Deloynes*, vol. XIII, Item 298, p. 32.
[31]*La Morte de trois mille ans au Sallon de 1783*; *Deloynes*, vol. XIII, Item 286, p. 11. Barbier also credits this pamphlet to R. M. Lesuire.

An even more interesting example of the changing attitude toward art was a review of the same exhibition entitled *Observations générales sur le Sallon de 1783 et sur l'état des arts en France*. The critic complained that for some time trivial works had dominated the exhibition, but he was pleased to see that the minister of fine arts was restoring the dignity of painting and sculpture. "Les moyens que M. le Comte d'Angiviller a imaginés pour cela," the author asserted, "ne pouvaient être ni mieux combinés ni plus sûrs."[32] Later in his review this critic pointed out that lack of interest in great public buildings was further evidence of the extent to which the political importance of the arts had been ignored. The government ought to present monuments to the people which would leave a lasting and useful impression on their minds. In classical times men had understood the political utility of the buildings and monuments with which they decorated their cities. The author called on the government to erect arches, fountains, and other kinds of public monuments which would honour their sovereigns, acts of virtue, and men of outstanding talent. Never before would the arts have received such splendid encouragement.

Such appeals for national themes became extremely common.[33] They coincided with numerous proposals for a national educational programme which would produce citizens devoted to the state. Despite this nationalistic trend, some art critics continued to defend the value of subjects drawn from the classics. In 1785 the author of *L'Aristarque moderne au Sallon* came to the defence of classical themes. The basis on which he justified these subjects is worth noting. He valued historical painting for much the same reason that the *philosophes* prized the study of history—that it served to convey object lessons. "Une leçon de morale tirée de l'histoire moderne," wrote the modern Aristarchus, "n'est pas plus propre à réformer le cœur, à faire aimer la vertu, que si elle nous étoit transmise par l'histoire grecque ou romaine."[34]

[32]*Observations générales sur le Sallon de 1783 et sur l'état des arts en France* (Paris, 1783); *Deloynes*, vol. XIII, Item 299, p. 31.
[33]Some appealed for national themes explicitly, for instance, the Marquis de Villette in the *Journal de Paris*, MS copy in *Deloynes*, vol. XIV, Item 350. Others simply revealed a preference for national subjects in their critiques; e.g., *Lettre d'un amateur de Paris à un amateur de province sur le Sallon de Peinture de 1787*; *Deloynes*, vol. XV, Item 381.
[34]*L'Aristarque moderne au Sallon* (Paris, 1785).

The reaction against rococo was now in full swing. Attacks on the art of Boucher and his disciples were numerous. For instance a critic who called himself "L'Ami des artistes au Salon" was convinced that after a period of brilliance under Louis XIV painting and the kindred arts had become frivolous and decadent. Painting especially had lost its force and elevation. "Dans la peinture," this critic complained, "on a négligé l'histoire pour se livrer au genre. C'est moins le génie qui manque aux artistes que les mœurs du temps dont ils suivent l'impulsion : partout où l'amour de la patrie aura peu d'influence on s'intéressera peu aux actions et aux traits de ses héros."[35] In the last Salon before the Revolution this critic admired paintings with a noble theme such as La Grenée's scene of Darius' satrap refusing to bend his knee before Alexander. But the critic wanted the conqueror portrayed in a hideous rage in order to impress the lesson more forcefully on the spectator. David's painting of the death of Socrates likewise won the critic's favour because it depicted a worthy deed which served as an example to others. However, this pamphleteer, like so many others, would have preferred to see more national themes. In a supplement to his review he appealed to artists to fill themselves with patriotism.[36]

This demand for didactic art was also expressed in proposals for public monuments. One citizen proposed to arouse patriotism by transforming the side of the Louvre next to the Seine into a gallery of famous Frenchmen.[37] Another wrote a lengthy discourse on the use of public works of art in the past with a view to convincing the government of their political importance.[38] And yet another proposed that inscriptions be in French so that monuments would

[35]L'Ami des artistes au Sallon: réflexions sur l'origine et le progrès des arts, sur leur état actuel en France, et sur les tableaux exposés au Louvre par ordre du Roi (Paris, 1787), Deloynes, vol. XV, Item 379, p. 16. According to Barbier this author was M. L. A. R. Robin.
[36]L'Ami des artistes au Sallon précédé de quelques observations sur l'état des arts en Angleterre (n.d.); Deloynes, vol. XV, Item 380, p. 3. For another attack on rococo, see Discours sur l'origine, le progrès et l'état actuel de la peinture en France, contenant des notices sur les principaux artistes de l'Académie (Paris, 1785); Deloynes, vol. XIV, Item 325.
[37]Maille Dussausoy, Le Citoyen désintéressé, ou diverses idées patriotiques concernant quelques établissemens et embellissemens utiles à la ville de Paris (2 vols., Paris, 1767–68), passim.
[38]C-F. Abbé de Lubersac de Livron, Discours sur les monumens publics de tous les âges et de tous les peuples connus, suivi d'une description de monument projeté à gloire de Louis XVI et de la France. . . . (Paris, 1775), passim.

convey their message to the people. He thought it would be much better if the inscription below the statue of Henry IV on Pont Neuf read:

Henri Quatre Vainqueur et Père
de ses Sujets, s'occupait de leur
bonheur, lorsqu'il tomba sous
le poignard du Fanatisme
l'an 1610

In reading such an inscription in French an ordinary man would be moved by memory of the king and horrified by the atrocities caused by fanaticism. At present he would find the Latin inscription unintelligible and would pass by with no other impression than that of having seen a man on horseback.[39]

The social utility of art was also the overriding consideration in a treatise entitled *Sur la peinture* published in 1782.[40] Its author, who identified himself only as "Paul," revealed his basic viewpoint at the very beginning when he argued that any occupation had to justify its existence by demonstrating its value to society. Like so many eighteenth-century thinkers, he went back to primitive times to prove his point. He contended that in early societies, when men were struggling to survive, every occupation had to contribute to the welfare of the species. A useless profession was a dangerous one. In a simple agrarian society, where the main duties of people were to help one another and to ward off the enemy, the man who wanted to be a painter had to explain his motives. The author imagined such a painter, accused of leaving others to raise food and look after defence, justifying his work (pp. 11–16). He tells his fellow citizens that the state needs his spirituality more than it needs his physical strength. By his spirituality he can summon men to noble actions, can transmit the traits of their wise elders, can fill youth with filial devotion, and in general can consecrate virtue with moving images. "Toujours bon, comme toujours patriote," this painter promises (p. 21), "je n'opérerai que par des vues d'utilité;

[39]Andrien-Jean-Baptiste Le Roi, *Examen de la question: si les inscriptions doivent être en langue nationale* (Amsterdam, 1783), pp. 32–33.

[40]*Sur la peinture, ouvrage succinct qui peut éclairer les artistes sur la fin originelle de l'art, et aider les citoyens dans l'idée qu'ils doivent se faire de son état actuel en France* (La Haye, 1782).

et mes ouvrages ne seront que l'exemple du bien, l'évidence de ses agréments, et la facilité de s'y asservir."

Repeatedly throughout his little essay the author complained that contemporary artists had failed to live up to the pact which they had made with society (pp. 27–34). They had become accomplices to crime. Only a handful of them had enough pride to refuse to work for vicious prodigals. In their pursuit of financial gain painters were even willing to portray lewd prostitutes. The essayist wanted artists to rise above their environment and take up their original task of instructing their fellow men (p. 64). But he did not make it very clear how artists were to accomplish this feat. Like so many others who exhorted artists to give moral lessons, he did not explain how the artist was to escape from the economic necessities of the market. Apparently artists were simply to purify their ranks and improve the moral tone of their profession:

Il n'y a seulement qu'à remettre de garde le civisme, la vérité, la justice aux portes des Lycées; qu'à empêcher les Praticiens de devenir hommes du monde, que n'admettre dans les corporations des membres invulnérables au vice, sourds à tous autres mots qu'à ces deux, *Vertu*, *Patrie*; pour qui l'argent et les dehors du luxe ne soient d'aucun attrait; alors bons sujets, Citoyens, fidèles à la nature . . . . (p. 84)

Often utopian novels reveal the aspirations of progressive groups at a particular moment in history much as dreams may disclose the longings of an individual. Certainly Mercier's *L'An 2440* provides an insight into many aspects of the French Enlightenment. The author was a young bourgeois intellectual who had set out in search of literary fame in Paris. An attempt at heroic verse having failed, he decided to affect a profound disdain for poetry. After a short stint as a teacher in the provinces, he returned to the capital to earn his living writing stories, doing translations, and experimenting with sentimental dramas. His novel, which appeared in 1770, revealed that he had been absorbing ideas from most of the reformers of the century. Since the book was a telling indictment against the government, it was banned, but the author was not molested. In the early years of the Revolution, before his enthusiasm had been soured by the Terror and imprisonment, he boasted that his work had anticipated many of the changes that were taking place and had in fact helped to bring them about.[41]

The book opens with the author encountering an elderly Englishman who dislikes Paris with its unhealthy streets, its sickly children, and its dissolute manners. Mercier tries in vain to answer these criticisms and then falls asleep—to sleep nearly seven hundred years. When he finally awakes he is surprised to find that Paris has been transformed into a clean city with broad avenues and orderly traffic. The Louvre has been completed and a great space has been created for public celebrations. The Hôtel-Dieu has been replaced with new hospitals and the Bastille has been torn down. And he finds the people are now decorous and sensibly dressed.

Mercier finds the changes in government even more amazing. The government is still monarchical because centralized authority is essential in a large state and because sound administration is easier to obtain under a single ruler. However, monarchical government has been purged of all its former abuses. All citizens enjoy equal rights and all harmful privileges have been removed. The estates of the kingdom meet every two years to legislate, but while they are not sitting the king and the senate carry on the administration. The king now conforms to the ideal of the philosopher-king who is both virtuous and wise. He and his ministers devote all their attention to combatting ostentation on the one hand and poverty on the other. Taxation is no longer a burden because the state does not waste money and because citizens do not resent taxes which are used for public welfare. Furthermore the complex and incoherent laws of the eighteenth century have been simplified and codified. Law is now based on the clear and distinct teachings of nature. Under this enlightened régime the people prosper and are contented.

Society has been reformed along the lines advocated by Rousseau. Mercier observes that there are no longer extremes of wealth and poverty, that hard work and frugality now provide enough for everyone, and that wasteful and harmful products have been abolished. He notes that there is a greater simplicity in dress and food, that virtue dominates conversation and human relations, and

[41]De *Jean-Jacques Rousseau considéré comme l'un des premiers auteurs de la Révolution* (2 vols., Paris, 1791), vol. I, p. 61.

that men are governed by principles rather than by passions or selfish ambitions. Social utility is now accorded the highest praise. Society honours those who cultivate a field, build a house, bear a child, or perform some other useful service. Consequently, all the professions strive to contribute to the welfare of the community.

All these astonishing changes have been brought about by an educational programme which employs every possible method of diffusing moral lessons. Education extends far beyond the schools. For instance, religious institutions provide one of the principal means by which the state propagates civic virtues. Religion is now purified of all its former fanaticism and restored to its natural simplicity. The believer is taught simply to love God and to love his neighbour. Church ceremony is reduced to the singing of hymns and listening to moral exhortations. The clergy have given up their unnatural vows, forsaken their dogmatic subtleties, and turned simply to teaching men their moral duty. Anyone who rejects belief in God is re-educated, and incurable unbelievers are banished. Obviously in this society religion is valued primarily as an instrument for shaping social behaviour.

Literature shares in this educational programme. In the ideal society which Mercier envisages enlightened morality has invaded every aspect of life including drama, poetry, and other forms of literature. Conducted to a play, the author discovers that theatres have become instruments for disseminating moral truths. "C'est le gouvernement qui les entretient," he recounts; "car on en a fait une école publique de morale et de goût. On a compris toute l'influence que l'ascendant du génie peut avoir sur des âmes sensibles" (vol. I, pp. 281–82). Poetry is not banished from this utopia as it had been in the *Republic* of Plato, but it is now devoted to celebrating those deeds which do honour to humanity, and no longer serves frivolity and immorality. Nurtured on models of courage and virtue, children form a sound standard of nobility and value the hammer more than the diadem. Authors who produce dangerous works are subjected to re-education by public censors until they see the light. State officials prescribe what is worth keeping in public libraries. Frivolous works are destroyed and theological tomes are kept under glass.

In this rational society the arts are valued because of their utility. Classical literature and history are proscribed because they do not meet this test. Because history is a tangle of crimes and follies historical writing is discouraged lest it damage the morals of the young. But men of letters are honoured because their persuasive power makes them valuable to the state. The government relies on them to disseminate the idea that the highest good is to contribute to the welfare of society. "C'est à eux," reports Mercier, "que l'Etat a confié le soin de développer ce principe des vertus" (vol. I, p. 374). The *Académie française* has survived, but it has been completely transformed. The academicians are not only the great writers of their day, but the guardians of public morality meeting in a kind of secret conclave. Literature thus exercises a kind of tutelary power over society and shares the same educational function as religion (vol. II, pp. 1–25). Like religion, it propagates the principles of *la foi morale* which was the foundation of the good society.

The visual arts likewise disseminated enlightened morality. Entering the Salon of the future, Mercier found the arts flourishing, but completely transformed in nature and purpose. "J'entrai dans de vastes sallons garnis des tableaux des plus grands maîtres," he recorded. "Chacun donnoit l'équivalent d'un livre moral et instructif" (vol. II, p. 59). There was not a trace of the mythological themes which had been portrayed endlessly in former centuries. Gone too were the scurrilous sort of paintings which fawning artists had produced to deify monarchs. In a footnote Mercier explains that at Versailles the image of Louis XIV, with a lightning bolt in his hand, enthroned on azure clouds like a thundering god, had aroused a scornful pity for Le Brun. But in the utopian society the arts are forbidden to lie. No longer are there any of those gross connoisseurs who, with their money in hand, used to dictate to genius. Genius is free, at liberty to follow its own laws, and no longer forced to debase itself (vol. II, p. 61).

In the Salon of the year 2440 there are no longer paintings of bloody battles, no more pictures of the shameful debaucheries of classical gods, and of course no more canvases of monarchs surrounded by precisely those virtues which they lacked. Only those works are exhibited which are capable of inspiring sentiments of grandeur and virtue (p. 61). Most important is a series of paintings immortalizing the nobility of soul which certain rulers had revealed in the past—Henry IV feeding the city which he had been besieging; Sully slowly counting a sum of money which his master had reserved for his pleasures; Louis XIV on his deathbed confessing, "J'ai trop aimé la guerre"; Trajan tearing his clothes to pieces in order to bind the sores of a poor wretch; Marcus Aurelius on a hurried expedition dismounting from his horse in order to accept a petition from a penniless woman; Titus having bread and medicines distributed to the people; Saint-Hilaire with his hand upraised showing his weeping son the body of Turenne lying in the dust; and the generous Fabre taking the irons of the galley slave in place of his father.

There are no sombre or grievous scenes on display in this Salon of the future. Vile courtiers no longer mock at painters who try to convey a moral lesson. Instead men are grateful that painters have assembled pictures of all the sublime traits of human nature based on episodes from history. "Ils avaient sagement pensé que rien ne seroit plus utile," commented Mercier. "Tous les arts avoient fait, pour ainsi dire, une admirable conspiration en faveur de l'humanité" (vol. II, p. 62). Through this alliance the arts have illuminated the sacred image of virtue, making her more attractive than ever. With her features always embellished, these pictures of virtue provide a form of public instruction, just as effective as it is touching. All these paintings capture the eye of the spectator by their subject-matter and also by their masterly execution. Painters have learned how to combine the style of the Italians with the colouring of the Flemish, and nature seems to be reproduced as though in a mirror. Virtuous men rejoice at the sight of these paintings. Culpable individuals, however, are afraid to look at them for fear that the inanimate figure might begin to speak and accuse the guilty.

In this utopian society the whole system of educating artists and judging their works has been changed. In the art schools of the capital each student is apprenticed to several masters so that he does not have to conform to one of them. In addition the artist is free from the tyranny which parasitical patrons had once exercised over the arts. "Autant ces arts étoient dangereux dans mon siècle, parce qu'ils favorisoient le luxe, le faste, la cupidité, et la débauche," comments Mercier, "autant ils étoient devenus utiles, parce qu'ils n'étoient employés qu'à inspirer des leçons de vertus, et à donner à la ville cette majesté . . . qui élève l'âme des citoyens" (vol. II, p. 65). Paintings are now judged in public contests which are open to everyone, including foreigners. Usually the best painting wins the acclaim of the people. This new system of artistic education and public competition frees the artist from the despotism of the master and the patron. We observe, however, that this new system does not give the artist the freedom to choose his own subject; the government decides each year on four subjects which artists are to treat for the contest.

Mercier next enters a special room of the Salon of 2440 where huge allegorical paintings ridicule the vices of past centuries—the ignorance of the Middle Ages, the excesses of fanaticism, the follies of mysticism, the foolishness of trial by combat, and various other foibles. The author lingers before the painting illustrating the character of the eighteenth century. The century is represented by a woman whose lovely head is weighted down with the most extravagant ornaments and jewellery. Her eyes are lively, yet her smile is somewhat forced. Her expression is seductive, though it is not truthful. In each hand she grasps two long ribbons which seem to be ornamental, but actually hide chains which bind her tightly. Nevertheless she is left enough room to frisk about, thus disguising her bondage. Running his eye over her magnificent robe, Mercier discovers that at the bottom it is torn and dirty: like the prostitute who roams the street, she is as hideous in her extremities as she is alluring on top. Through holes in her dress one can also see that she is trying to hide thin little waifs who, wailing, feed on a morsel of black bread. In the background of the painting one can glimpse magnificent châteaux set amid poorly cultivated fields filled with miserable peasants (vol. II, pp. 72–73).

After examining a few more of these allegorical canvases, Mercier proceeds into the room where works of sculpture are displayed. He finds that sculpture has also been completely transformed in nature and outlook. It is no longer compelled to prostitute itself by portraying scoundrels as despicable as the subjects which they commissioned. Artists living on government pensions are able to use their skills to praise merit and virtue. Unlike the Salons of the eighteenth century, busts of vile tax farmers are not ranged alongside the king whom they robbed. In this ideal society the sculptor portrays only those whose nobility and virtue warrant public recognition. Mercier sums up the change (vol. II, p. 78):

Il étoit expressément defendu de sculpter des sujets qui ne disoient rien à l'âme; par conséquent on ne gâtoit point de beaux marbres ou d'autres matières aussi précieuses.

Tous ces sujets licencieux qui bordent nos cheminées, étoient sévèrement bannis. Les honnêtes gens ne concevoient rien à notre législation, lorsqu'ils lisoient dans notre histoire que, dans un siècle où l'on prononçoit si fréquemment le nom de religion et de mœurs, des pères de famille étaloient des scènes de débauche aux yeux de leurs enfans, sous prétexte que c'étoient des chef-d'œuvres [*sic*]. . . .

Passing into the last gallery, Mercier comes upon a huge collection of drawings and prints. Engraving is here being used to reproduce and propagate all the masterpieces of painting and sculpture, and by this means it is possible for everyone to have a copy which rivals the original. All the citizens are able to decorate their walls with scenes which present examples of virtue and heroism. Mercier was obviously aware that, if art was to serve as an effective instrument of propaganda, it was not enough to expose didactic paintings and statues in the Salon: these works must penetrate into the home of the common man. Engraving could multiply copies, and Mercier considered that it was just as useful as typography as a means of public instruction (vol. II, p. 84).

In this visionary society of the year 2440 public monuments also convey lessons to the masses. Mercier is led to an immense monument which had recently been completed. In the centre there stands a huge figure whose noble features clearly show that she represents humanity. Around this central figure are statues of women on their knees expressing anguish and remorse. These women symbolize the various nations asking humanity to forgive the wounds they had inflicted on her. Spain, for example, is portrayed in marble the colour of blood because she had committed so many atrocities and had enslaved millions (vol. I, pp. 190–93). Mercier notices yet another figure on a magnificent pedestal. It is the image of a coloured man, his head bare, his arms extended, a proud look in his eye. Around him lie the pieces of twenty broken sceptres. On the pedestal Mercier reads "Au vengeur du nouveau monde" (vol. I, pp. 194–96).

Later, in the *Tableau de Paris*, written just before the Revolution, Mercier was to complain that in the French capital there were no eloquent monuments conveying a message to the people.[42] Evidently Mercier wanted all art forms to be utilized to disseminate the civic faith which was to be the basis of the ideal society.

The coming of the French Revolution would provide scant support for the intellectual historian who might be tempted to declare that ideas rule the world. Eighteenth-century social critics may have undermined confidence in existing institutions, but they did not preach revolt. Revolution sprang from the interplay of a variety of causes—the failure of Louis XVI to stand by his reforming ministers, the bankruptcy of the government following intervention in the American rebellion, the aristocratic obstruction which forced the king to summon the Estates General, the ambitions of a burgeoning middle class, the discontent among the peasants, and the crop failures and unemployment which incited the lower classes on the eve of the cataclysm. Nor does the abstract and idealistic spirit of eighteenth-century thought explain the extremes of the Revolution once it got under way. Modern scholars have shown that it was the insurrections by the lower classes, especially uprisings of urban mobs protesting high prices and food scarcity, which drove the revolution to the left. No competent historian would now dare to suggest that ideas alone explain the behaviour of Robespierre and his colleagues during the Terror.

Nevertheless it would be absurd to neglect the role of ideas. The attacks of the *philosophes* on existing institutions provided both the ideological justification for revolt and the inspiration for many of the changes which were to take place. It is doubtful whether the middle-class leaders of the Revolution would have exhibited the same assurance had the intellectuals not convinced them that history and reason were on their side. Both the so-called moderates of the early Revolution and the Jacobin leaders later were to hold that faith in the possibility of progress which had been aroused by

[42]*Tableau de Paris* (12 vols., Amsterdam, 1782–88), vol. I, p. 111.

pre-revolutionary thinkers. Moreover the American Revolution not only exposed the financial weakness of the government but also dramatized the fact that the theories of the philosophers could be realized here and now. Discontent alone does not breed revolt —there must be hope as well.

Discussion of art before 1789 provides a striking example of the intellectual origins of the programme of the Revolution. The advocates of didactic art created a blueprint for the educational programme of the Jacobins at the height of the Revolution. But those who called for propaganda in art left the revolutionaries problems as well as a programme. The appeal for didactic art had by no means obliterated interest in art as an end in itself. Nor had the proponents of utilitarian art any practical scheme for transforming art production. Exhortation alone was unlikely to overcome the pressures of the art market. In the *Encyclopédie* there had been a hint of the need for government control and direction of artistic production. Mercier carried this suggestion much further: in his utopia the state would control artistic production, dispense patronage, select subjects, and proscribe anti-social themes. Yet Mercier still paid lip-service to the ideal of artistic fredom. Already one can glimpse the problem of artistic freedom versus government regulation which emerged during the Revolution.

Revolutionary Plans to Mobilize the Fine Arts

5.

*Qu'ils seroient coupables les artistes profanateurs
qui prostitueroient leurs talens à offrir des images
contrerévolutionnaires, qui oublieroient que leur
première qualité essentielle est d'être philosophe;
leur premier devoir est de choisir des sujets qui
tendent à instruire, à régénérer les mœurs, à inspirer
l'amour de la patrie, et l'enthousiasme de la liberté.*
JACQUES LEBRUN, *La Société
populaire et républicaine des arts.*[1]

THE OPENING YEARS of the French Revolution have often been depicted as a moderate phase in contrast with the radicalism which later gained ascendancy during the Terror. Admittedly the original leaders of the Revolution were compelled by peasant uprisings and urban revolts to take more extreme measures than they had first contemplated, but from the very beginning they were determined to root out many existing institutions in order to begin afresh. The men who transformed the Estates General into the Constituent Assembly were inspired by a radical notion derived from the *philosophes* and the recent American example—the idea of a people, represented in a special convention, who would in a

---

[1]Athanase Détournelle, *Aux armes et aux arts! Peinture, sculpture, architecture, gravure. Journal de la Société républicaine des arts séant au Louvre* (Paris, n.d.), p. 192.

sense revert to the state of nature in order to set up new institutions of government. This exercise of the sovereign will of the people intensified the hope for a better world which had first been kindled by news of the American Revolution. In 1789 there were already some who dreamt of creating a perfect society surpassing even that of the Americans.

It was thus the alleged moderates of the Constituent Assembly who demolished the institutions of the Old Régime and announced an entirely new order. In the Déclaration des droits de l'homme et du citoyen they affirmed the sovereignty of the people, conferred equal rights on all citizens, proclaimed the rule of law, and guaranteed liberty of thought. They also destroyed the remnants of the manorial system, swept away the historic provinces with all their variations, created a national church largely beyond papal control, transformed the king from an absolute monarch into a first magistrate, and set up a government based on broad popular participation. The men who wrought these sweeping political and social changes realized that they would have to create new habits of thought as well. From all sides came plans for a national educational system which would produce citizens loyal to the newborn régime.

In this atmosphere of destruction and renewal it was natural that men should take up the proposal that art ought to serve a social purpose. At the very moment when the Third Estate was transforming itself into a Constituent Assembly and calling on the other Estates to join it, the *Mercure de France* was predicting that in the new society the arts would help to attract men to novel ideas.[2] The Salon of 1789 opened in the Louvre just a few days before the proclamation of the Rights of Man. Only about ten works had any direct relevance to the Revolution: scenes of the Estates General, a portrait of Bailly, a bust of Necker, and various items related to July 14—a likeness of a soldier who was first to gain entrance to the Bastille, a portrait of Latude who had been imprisoned there, and a view of the prison-fortress being demolished.[3] Several critics of the exhibition urged artists to take up revolutionary themes capable of stirring men's hearts.[4]

[2]*Mercure de France*, no. 25, le 20 juin 1789, pp. 115–16.
[3]*Livret*, nos. 6, 36, 99, 111, 199, 124, 324–25, and 327 (1789).
[4]*Vérités agréables, ou le Salon vu en beau* (Paris, 1789); *Deloynes*, vol. XVI, no. 415. *Le Spectateur français au Salon de 1789; Deloynes*, vol. XVI, no. 424.

"Les préjugés vont s'éteindre," exclaimed one critic; "les vertus et les arts vont renaître."[5]

The next three years brought a flood of suggestions for monumental works of art devoted to the Revolution—public squares decorated with statues of Revolutionary leaders, representations of various civic virtues for each ward of the capital, huge allegorical figures symbolizing the blessings of liberty, immense altars embellished with Revolutionary scenes, and great galleries transformed into political sanctuaries.[6] Typical of these proposals was one describing a monument to Mirabeau. Death was to be depicted holding a scythe in one hand and beckoning the hero to the grave with the other. Mirabeau, wearing a civic crown, was to pull Despotism and Fanaticism with him into the tomb. Despotism was to be decked out like a medieval knight, trampling underfoot a book entitled *Les Droits des nations*. Fanaticism was to appear as a wild-eyed Dominican monk, holding a crucifix in one hand and a dagger in the other. In the background France would be seen trying with one hand to hold her hero back from the abyss, and pointing with the other to the constitution. "Homme, qui que tu sois," the inscription was to read, "honore Mirabeau. Il entraîne avec lui les tyrans au tombeau."[7]

Quatremère de Quincy, an amateur archaeologist and art critic who later served on the Committee of Public Instruction set up by the Legislative Assembly, supported the idea of art as propaganda in a series of long essays published in 1791. Quatremère conceded that in the past the arts had served tyrants, but he was confident that once they had been purified by a free government they would stimulate love of virtue and liberty. It was up to the legislators

[5]*Les Elèves au Salon, ou L'Amphigouri* (Paris, 1789); *Deloynes*, vol. XVI, no. 416.

[6]H. J. Jansen, *Projet tendant à conserver les arts en France, en immortalisant les événements patriotiques et les citoyens illustrés* (Paris, 1791); A-G. Kersaint, *Discours sur les monuments publics prononcé au conseil du département de Paris le 15 décembre 1791* (Paris, 1792); le Chevalier de Mopinot, *Proposition d'un monument à élever dans la capitale de France pour transmettre aux races futures l'époque de l'heureuse révolution* . . . (Paris, 1790); B. Poyet, *Mémoire sur la nécessité d'entreprendre de grands travaux publics* . . . (s. 1, 1790); Sobre le jeune, *Projet d'un monument à élever dans le champ de la Fédération* (Paris, n.d.); and a scheme presented to the sections of Paris by various citizens, *Projet d'utilité et d'embellissement pour Paris* (1790).

[7]F. N. Benoît-Lamotte, "Projet de Monument à la gloire de Mirabeau," *Mercure de France*, no. 18, le 4 juin 1791, pp. 39–40.

to guide the fine arts. He suggested that all the departments throughout the nation submit lists of men they had produced who embodied the virtues of good citizenship. The National Assembly would then screen these lists to produce an inexhaustible source of patriotic subjects for artists working in various genres.[8] This idea of turning the arts into instruments of public education inspired newspaper articles, an occasional poem, and even a play, *L'Artiste patriote*, by Dupuis.[9]

At the same time leaders in the National Assembly called on artists to devote their talents to serving the Revolution. In June 1790 a group of artists petitioned the deputies in an attempt to preserve the four supporting figures which the Assembly had ordered removed from the base of the statue of Louis XIV on the Place des Victoires. The statue represented the monarch, on foot, being crowned by Victory. Around its base were four slaves in chains symbolizing enemies whom the monarch had crushed. The artists agreed with the Assembly that slaves in fetters were certainly not suited to the new order, but they hoped to save the figures which had been created by the sculptor Desjardins. In their petition they suggested that the figures should be placed in a public square without the chains and other signs of servility which encumbered them. The area in which they would be displayed could be marked by bronze tablets giving the history of the figures and the decree of the Assembly ordering their removal. In reply the president of the Assembly, Le Peletier, welcomed the artists, but warned them that in future they would have to devote themselves to national themes: "C'est à des sujets nationaux que vous consacrerez vos talens; par-là vous saurez expier les antiques erreurs de la flatterie."[10]

[8]A-C. Quatremère de Quincy, *Considérations sur les arts du dessin en France, suivies d'un plan d'Académie, ou d'Ecole publique, et d'un système d'encouragements* (Paris, 1791), pp. 52–55, 163. Quatremère clarified his ideas in two more long essays published the same year.

[9]Jean-Baptiste Claude Robin, "Plan pour la formation d'une société des arts du dessin a Paris," *Tribut de la Société nationale des Neuf Sœurs*, le 14 avril 1791, pp. 215–24. For a poem of sorts, Dom François Ferlus, "Sur l'education publique," *Mercure de France*, le 22 mai 1790, pp. 118–28; Amable-Joseph Dupuis, *L'Artiste patriote, comédie en cinq actes et en vers* (Paris, 1791).

[10]J. Mavidal and E. Laurent *et al.*, eds., *Archives parlementaires de 1787 à 1860: recueil complet des débats législatifs*, 1ère série, 1789–99 (Paris, 1867–), hereafter cited as *Arch. parl.* See vol. XVI, p. 541; *Le Moniteur universel*

In August 1791 government spokesmen repeated their demand for revolutionary art when the Commune des arts, formed the previous autumn in opposition to the Academy, sent a deputation to the Assembly to ask for the right to exhibit without preference at the forthcoming Salon.[11] In the past the right to exhibit at the biennial exhibition had been restricted to the academicians and their associates. The deputation argued that all artists ought to be able to show their work because privileged corporations had no place under the new Constitution. As current president of the Assembly, Beauharnais supported this plea, but reminded artists that they would have to serve the state.[12] Again in September when some young artists presented a proposal for a monument commemorating the work of the Assembly, Vernier, who was presiding, praised them for recalling art to its original function of creating public symbols.[13]

When the Legislative Assembly met under the new Constitution in the autumn of 1791, the deputies continued to exhort artists to dedicate their talents to the Revolution. Before dissolution the Constituent Assembly had set up a jury, composed of members of the Academy plus twenty non-members, to distribute one hundred thousand pounds of prize money for works exhibited at the recent Salon. A group of artists who resented the power of the Academy sent a delegation to the Legislative Assembly demanding equal representation on the jury. Replying on behalf of the Assembly, Pierre Vergniaud told the artists that as yet they had given no indication what sort of painting they intended to produce. Pointing to the use to which the fine arts had been put in classical times, he assured them that the Assembly would support artists whose work reflected the glorious events of the Revolution.

Sans doute que, brûlant de l'amour de la patrie, avide de la liberté et de la gloire, le cœur encore palpitant des mouvemens qu'imprima la révolution, l'artiste heureux avec un ciseau créateur, ou un pinceau

(hereafter cited as *Moniteur*), le 30 juin 1790, no. 181, p. 737. It is interesting to note that the statues of the slaves in chains eventually ended up in the Musée des monuments.

11*Addresse à l'Assemblée nationale par la Commune des arts qui ont le dessin pour base*, le 9 août 1791; *Deloynes*, vol. LIII, Item 1508.

12*Arch. parl.*, vol. XXIX, p. 306; *Moniteur*, le 11 août 1791, no. 223, pp. 921–22.

13*Arch. parl.*, vol. XXX, p. 232; *Moniteur*, le 8 septembre 1791, no. 251, p. 1044.

magique, va reproduire, pour les générations futures, le plus mémorable des événemens, et les hommes qui, par leur courage ou leur sagesse, l'ont préparé et consommé. Croyez, Messieurs, que l'Assemblée Nationale encouragera de toutes ses forces des arts qui, par un si bel emploi, peuvent exciter aux grandes actions, et contribuer ainsi au bonheur du genre humain.[14]

The idea of art as revolutionary propaganda had indeed become so familiar that it was ridiculed by one pamphleteer who suggested some themes of his own. Perhaps the deputies could commission a painting representing all the massacres which had occurred during the Revolution, a work which could be dedicated to the memory of St. Bartholemew. Or perhaps the representatives could order a painting of Barnave, Le Chapelier, Robespierre, Talleyrand, Lameth, Pétion and others of their like being conducted to the underworld by Charon, to form part of a series of naval paintings by Vernet. A painting could be commissioned depicting Voltaire, brought back to life by the National Assembly, tearing up various parts of the Constitution which were not to his liking. Rousseau could also be portrayed emerging from the tomb with the Rights of Man in his hand, swearing revenge on those who had violated his works and saying, "Mon Père! Pardonne-leur, car ils ne savent ce qu'ils font."[15]

Despite all these proposals for revolutionary art, very little was actually accomplished. The Salon of 1791 featured more political paintings than the preceding one, but they still constituted only a small fraction of the works on exhibit. Mme Guyard had done a series of portraits of such outstanding members of the Constituent Assembly as Talleyrand, Beauharnais, d'Aiguillon, Robespierre, and the brothers Lameth. The miniaturist, Joseph Boze, who had been a favourite of Marie Antoinette, had done a portrait of Robespierre as well as a painting of Mirabeau telling the King's representative, "Nous ne quitterons nos places que par la force des baïonnettes." Several allegories dealt with the fall of the Bastille, and another with the granting of liberty to the monastic orders. Finally, David had displayed the drawing for a painting of the Tennis Court Oath which the Jacobin Club of Paris had

[14]*Arch. parl.*, vol. XXXIV, pp. 281–82; *Moniteur*, le 20 octobre 1791, no. 293, p. 1220.
[15]*Tableaux de commande par les députés pour servir de suite à ceux du Salon* (Paris, n.d.); *Deloynes*, vol. XVII, Item 446.

commissioned the previous autumn. In addition, sculptors, en-
gravers, and architects had displayed about two dozen items related
to the Revolution.[16] Several reviews of this Salon reminded artists
that they ought to turn out more works with a moral or political
message.[17] One critic, who believed that an artist should be a
philosophe, complained that most artists still ignored the proper
goal of their profession.[18]

During this initial phase of the Revolution deliberate efforts to
redirect art were also very limited. The one notable project resulted
from a proposal on April 3, 1791, by the executive of the Department of Paris as to how the grief over the death of Mirabeau might
be turned into a lesson for posterity. Rochefoucauld, the spokesman
for the Department, reminded the Constituent Assembly that
ancient peoples had used special monuments to keep alive the
memories of their heroes, and proposed creation of a similar cult in
France by converting the new church of Sainte-Geneviève into
a national shrine ". . . que le temple de la religion devienne le
temple de la patrie; que la tombe d'un grand homme devienne
l'autel de la liberté." The Department suggested that the edifice
should bear a huge inscription: AUX GRANDS HOMMES, LA PATRIE
RECONNAISSANTE.[19]

The Constituent Assembly placed Quatremère de Quincy in
charge of converting the neoclassical church into the Panthéon.
Quatremère expected the shrine to stimulate youths to emulate
the virtues, patriotism, and public service of those honoured there.[20]
During the following years a team of sculptors and craftsmen
removed Christian imagery and replaced it with revolutionary
iconography. On the pediment a low relief by Moitte depicting
"La Patrie couronnant les vertus civiques" replaced one by Coustou
representing "Le Triomphe de la Foi." Later during the Convention
huge plaster figures and low reliefs were erected around the

[16]*Livret*, 1791, nos. 10, 40, 67, 81, 132, 135, 183, 239, 242, 301, 312, 315,
390, 426, 427, 456, 508, 514, 516, 519, 527, 534, 542, 553, 557, 560, 562,
611, and 753.
[17]*Nouvelle critique impartiale des tableaux du Salon par une société d'artistes*
no. 1 (Paris, 1791); *Deloynes*, vol. XVII, Item 443.
[18]*Lettres analytiques, critiques, et philosophiques sur les tableaux du Salon*
(Paris, 1791); *Deloynes*, vol. XVII, Item 441, pp. 8-9.
[19]*Arch. parl.*, XXIV, pp. 536f., *Moniteur*, le 4 avril 1791, no. 94, pp.
385-86.
[20]A-C. Quatremère de Quincy, *Rapport sur l'édifice dit de Sainte-Geneviève*,

peristyle illustrating various political maxims. And on the ceilings inside images honouring Philosophy, Patriotism, and the Arts effaced scriptural themes.[21] These revolutionary decorations survived through the Napoleonic era until they in turn became victims of iconoclasm following the Restoration.

Numerous revolutionary prints and busts appeared in shop windows, but as yet there was no concerted effort to direct artistic output. Apart from inauguration of the Panthéon, the Constituent Assembly made only a few limited efforts to put art to work for the Revolution. In December 1790 the Assembly called for a statue of Rousseau to serve as a model for Frenchmen, but neither that Assembly nor its successor managed to work out acceptable rules for a contest to get the project under way.[22] Early in 1791 the deputies commissioned Le Barbier to do a painting of Captain Desilles who had lost his life trying to halt a mutiny at Nancy.[23] Events moved faster than the canvas. As the Revolution turned leftward Desilles came to be looked on as a reactionary who had tried to suppress a popular uprising, but Le Barbier kept working on his painting. He did not finish it until after the execution of Robespierre nor exhibit it until 1796.

In the autumn of 1791, in one of its final sessions, the Constituent Assembly requested the King to have his portrait done depicting him receiving the Constitution and showing it to his son.[24] "Le but de ce tableau," declared the *Journal de Paris*, "est de transmettre l'image du Roi et de son bon fils dans un instant qui doit rappeller aux bons citoyens l'éternelle alliance de la liberté et de la monarchie."[25] In March 1792 several newspapers reported that Madame Guyard had been commissioned to do a copy to hang in the legislature, and David another for the council chamber.[26] It seems unlikely that at this time an ardent Jacobin like David would have been willing to paint a portrait of the King. In any

---

fait au Directoire du département de Paris (Paris, 1791). Quatremère issued several other reports on the progress of the project.

[21]There is a detailed description of the decoration of the Pantheon as left by the Revolution in Joachim Le Breton, *Rapport à l'Empereur et Roi sur les beaux-arts depuis les vingt dernières années* (Paris, 1808).

[22]*Arch. parl.*, vol. XXI, pp. 619–20; vol. XXIX, pp. 755–57.

[23]*Ibid.*, vol. XXII, pp. 564–65. *Moniteur*, le 31 janvier 1791, no. 31, p. 128.

[24]*Ibid.*, vol. XXXI, p. 546; *Moniteur*, le 1 octobre 1791, no. 274, p. 1142.

[25]*Journal de Paris*, le 18 mars, 1792, Supp. no. 31, p. 2.

[26]*Folies d'un mois*, 5e mois, no. 7, s.d., p. 4; *Petites affiches de Paris*, le 9 mars 1792; *Révolution de Paris*, le 24 mars 1792, no. 141, pp. 548–49.

case, neither painting seems to have been completed. The eternal alliance between liberty and monarchy proved too brief.

Meanwhile, the Jacobin Club of Paris commissioned David to portray the Tennis Court Oath, hoping to finance the project by selling subscriptions for small engravings of the canvas.[27] When this plan failed, the Legislative Assembly agreed to pay the bill, but by that time the artist was engaged in other activities and the work was never completed.[28] Later, on April 13, 1791, the Club sponsored a contest for a bust to perpetuate the memory of Mirabeau. After six months of delay and a quarrel with the celebrated sculptor Houdon, the Club gave the prize to a deaf-mute named Desenne.[29] Meanwhile, other clubs had inaugurated busts of Mirabeau and similar idols. Such limited projects, however, scarcely amounted to a serious programme of visual propaganda.

Thus, while the demand for revolutionary art mounted during the first three years of the Revolution, the limited attempts to put the idea into practice were ineffectual. The Legislative Assembly repeatedly called on artists to treat revolutionary themes, but it did little else to prod them into action. Early in 1792 it finally set up a jury of twenty academicians and an equal number of non-academicians to judge the art exhibited at the Salon the previous autumn. Eventually this jury awarded prizes to twenty-eight painters, only one of whom had produced an historical painting in any way connected with the Revolution.[30] Only after the Revolution entered its most extreme phase was the pressure on artists really intensified in an attempt to conscript the fine arts in support of revolutionary ideals.

The system of constitutional monarchy devised by the Constituent Assembly was intended as a permanent government for France: it only survived for ten months. Constitutional monarchy could scarcely endure where the King did not rally popular support

---

[27]F. A. Aulard, ed., *La Société des Jacobins: recueil de documents pour l'histoire du Club des Jacobins* (6 vols., Paris, 1889–1907), vol. I, pp. 330–35.
[28]*Arch. parl.*, vol. XXXI, p. 438.
[29]Aulard, *Jacobins*, vol. II, pp. 315, 389, 474, 481, 488, 509; vol. III, pp. 62, 110, 119–20. Jean Antoine Houdon, *Copie de la lettre de M. Houdon à M. le Président de la Société des Amis de la Constitution* (Paris, 1791).
[30]M. Furcy-Renaud, ed., *Procès-verbaux des assemblées du jury élu par les artistes exposants au Salon de 1791* (Paris, 1906).

or even inspire trust. His attempted flight even before the constitution was approved weakened the régime from the start. Also the lower middle class and the wage-earners had few concrete results to show for their support of the Revolution through the first three years. Disorder had brought in its wake widespread unemployment and serious inflation. Radical leaders appeared who wanted to get rid of the monarchy and carry the Revolution a stage further. But it was the declaration of war on Austria which finally overturned the throne. Louis XVI and Marie Antoinette could not hide the fact that they sympathized with the enemy who threatened to overrun the country. On August 10, 1792, just four months after the outbreak of war, a Paris mob set up a revolutionary commune and stormed the palace.

The overthrow of the monarchy did not halt the leftward movement of the Revolution. At first the Convention, which had been elected to draw up another constitution, was swayed by the Girondins. These revolutionaries, named after the department from which their foremost speakers came, were men of substance who had succeeded in law, administration, or the liberal professions. Brissot, Vergniaud, Gensonné, Guadet, Barbaroux, and Buzot were among their chief spokesmen. Unfortunately for them, they sympathized more with the rights of property than with the grievances of the Parisian masses. Fearing dictatorship centred in the capital, they shrank from creating a strong war government which would save France from defeat. They also lost favour by trying, in vain, to save the deposed King from the death sentence. At last in June 1793, under pressure from an organized mob, the Convention expelled the Girondins and later ordered their arrest.

Control now fell into the hands of the Jacobins, who sat together on the high benches to the left of the rostrum and were nicknamed the "Mountain." These resolute republicans also believed in private property and free enterprise, but were more willing than the Girondins to countenance emergency measures in order to get rid of counter-revolutionaries, repel invasion, and stabilize the economy. The Convention gradually concentrated authority in the hands of twelve of the Jacobins, the members of the Committee of Public Safety—Barère, Billaud-Varenne, Carnot, Collot d'Herbois, Couthon, Hérault, Lindet, Prieur of the Côte d'Or, Prieur of the Marne,

Robespierre, Saint-André, and Saint-Just. This formidable committee ruled France in the name of the Convention for almost a year beginning in the summer of 1793. It hoped to control the anarchic violence of the Parisian extremists, but it did yield to their demand "de mettre la terreur à l'ordre du jour."

As the Revolution developed more ferment new faith took shape, complete with liturgical trappings. The Jacobin Clubs throughout France employed for their gatherings a ritual and a vocabulary not unlike that of the traditional church. They had their patriotic prayers, republican hymns, civic altars, purification rites, communal feasts, trees of liberty which substituted for crosses, processions complete with images of revolutionary martyrs, and even occasionally consecrated burial grounds reserved for the faithful. Their meetings resounded with talk of sin, heresy, salvation, regeneration, and holiness. The word holy constantly recurred—*la sainte patrie, la sainte liberté* or *la sainte Constitution*. Jacobins considered themselves members of an elect group struggling to convert those not in a state of grace and to establish the republican heaven on earth.

The Jacobin heaven envisaged by Robespierre and his supporters was a democratic republic where men would live in equality and work together for the common good. This republican paradise obviously could not be attained simply by an alteration in political machinery: it would require a moral transformation—"régénération" was the word many republicans used. To accomplish this regeneration it was necessary to convert the masses to the new republican gospel. Louis Portiez, a member of the Committee of Public Instruction, told the Convention that it was imperative to plant the seeds of civic virtues in the hearts of the coming generation. The primary schools would be the principal means of impressing civic notions on the mind of the public, but to succeed in its mission the government would have to employ all the various arts instead of driving them from the Republic.[31]

In the republican brave new world art was to propagate "la vertu." There were two main varieties of virtue which radical republicans wished to encourage, one sort grand and heroic, the other more humble and domestic. The Jacobin ideal of heroic

[31]Louis-François-René Portiez, *Sur l'instruction publique* (Paris: Convention nationale, 1793), p. 6.

virtue was largely based on episodes from classical history. For Jacobins the republican hero of antiquity was a moral giant with an unshakeable belief in the rightness of his cause, who like Brutus would sacrifice his own sons for the sake of a principle. Jacobins wanted the examples of this sort of heroism which had occurred during the Revolution transmitted to the public through works of art—Le Peletier, assassinated for demanding the death of a tyrant; Marat, martyred for the republican cause; Bara, dead at fourteen in the struggle against counter-revolutionaries in the Vendée; or Viala, mortally wounded at thirteen battling royalists near Avignon. Images of such acts of heroic virtue were expected to inspire others. Barère asked the Convention to commission an engraving of Bara to be distributed to all the primary schools in the country, "pour y retracer sans cesse à la jeunesse française l'exemple le plus pur de l'amour de la patrie et de la tendresse filiale."[32]

David has given us the best examples of the attempt to immortalize republican heroism through art. Both his picture of "Le Peletier au lit de Mort" and his "Marat assassiné" were presented to the Convention by the artist, who was himself a deputy. In offering the Assembly the first of these pictures, David said that he felt it was the duty of every citizen to enlighten his fellow citizens with symbols of heroism and virtue. He hoped that, if ever an ambitious dictator or tribune presented himself to the people, they would recall the example of Le Peletier, martyred for having voted death for a tyrant.[33] In his presentation speech for his republican *pietà*, the famous portrait of Marat slumped in the bathtub, David envisaged the people approaching his canvas and recalling the virtuous hero. It was as though the picture was speaking to them: "Il est mort, votre ami, en vous donnant son dernier morceau de pain; il est mort sans même avoir de quoi se faire enterrer."[34]

The Jacobins, as has been noted, also wanted art to celebrate the less dramatic virtue of everyday life, the domestic morality which Rousseau had preached in *La Nouvelle Héloïse*. In his report to the Convention on the Supreme Being Robespierre recommended not only the glorification of liberty, patriotism, and stoicism, but

[32]*Arch. parl.*, vol. LXXXII, p. 431; *Moniteur*, 10 Nivôse l'an II, le 30 décembre 1793, no. 100, p. 403.
[33]*Arch. parl.*, vol. LX, pp. 695–96; *Moniteur*, le 31 mars 1793, no. 90, p. 400.
[34]*Arch. parl.*, vol. LXXIX, p. 211.

also the exaltation of frugality, conjugal faithfulness, paternal love, motherly affection, filial devotion, hard work, and agricultural labour.[35] Genre painting was the obvious vehicle for such intentions and while some republican artists scorned it, others argued that it was the ideal form in which to depict these humbler virtues. Jacques Lebrun attacked Louis XIV for getting rid of genre paintings because as a monarch he could not be surrounded by pictures of peasants. Actually these paintings had depicted virtuous citizens— the robust farmer at his work which was so useful to humanity, the worthy shepherdess spinning flax and grazing her flock, the hardworking woodcutter uprooting a proud oak, or a loving mother feeding her young children.[36]

Republicans likewise intended to use allegorical works of art to recount the history of their new religion. As an example of republican allegory we might take the "Tableau révolutionnaire" by Jeaurat which was presented to the Convention by Gelé.[37] The picture represented the Revolution heralded by the events of July, 1789. Already in the middle of the storm are visible the ruins of the Bastille. Not far away toward the centre of the picture can be seen the holy Mountain. A radiant eye, shining out of the firmament unto the Mountain, symbolizes the divine surveillance of the Committee of Public Safety and the Committee of General Security over the preservation of France. Rays of light reveal the Crown of Immortality given by the people to their representatives as a reward for their work. On the crest of the holy Mountain rises a column dedicated to the Regeneration of France. At the foot of this column lies a copy of the Republican Constitution. Surrounding the central symbol of the Mountain are other figures and signs representing its various achievements.

Revolutionary allegories such as this one reveal that artists quickly evolved symbols to denote the new faith—the Level, token of equality; the Bonnet, indicator of liberty; the Cockade, emblem of the nation; the Pike, weapon of the free man; the Club, instrument of popular will; the Fasces, sign of revolutionary solidarity;

[35]*Décret de la Convention*, 18 Floréal an II.
[36]Détournelle, *Journal*, pp. 322–23.
[37]C-J. Gelé, *Tableau révolutionnaire peint et présenté par Jeaurat, avec la description de l'allégorie offerte et prononcée par Gelé, à la Convention nationale le 20 Messidor l'an II de la République* (Paris, n.d.).

the Oak, mark of rebirth and social virtue; and the Eye, symbol of divinity and watchfulness. At the same time, a new feminine trinity emerged—Liberty, often carrying a broken yoke or a pike capped with a bonnet; Equality usually portrayed carrying a level; and Fraternity, habitually carrying fasces.

Venus no longer reigned supreme and her playful Olympian companions had made way for sterner divinities: Virtue, winged with a crown on her head and a sun on her breast; Innocence, adorned with palms and with roses in her hands; Force, crowned with oak leaves and armed with a club; Probity, carrying a ruler often inscribed with the Golden Rule; Truth, normally nude and holding a mirror; Victory, bearing crowns, palms, and trumpets; Reason, carrying a sceptre tipped with an all-seeing eye; and Nature, pouring out her bounties to mankind. These formidable females confront the viewer in dozens of contemporary engravings, letter-heads, medals, coins, and playing-cards. Even in games there was no place for kings, queens, and knaves.

The Jacobin faith, like traditional Christianity, was going to employ art to convey its teachings. However, as successors of the Encyclopedists, radical republicans had even higher hopes for the arts than Churchmen had ever had. Many republicans believed in the natural goodness of man, a belief which encouraged confidence in the power of the arts to regenerate mankind. A good example is an essay on the arts dedicated to the Convention by one of its deputies, Boissy d'Anglas.[38] Although more moderate than those on the Mountain, the author shared many of the tenets of the new gospel. He believed that nature had placed within the human heart the germs of all the virtues, even though man had disregarded them. To cleanse the human heart all that was necessary was to revitalize these natural instincts. Now that the influence of vicious institutions had been destroyed by revolution, it was possible to restore man to his original purity:

C'est donc en instruisant l'homme, que vous le renouvellerez, pour ainsi dire, d'une manière absolue et complete; c'est en épurant sa raison et ses mœurs, c'est en lui faisant connoître l'influence et les dangers de ses

---

[38]F-A. de Boissy d'Anglas, *Essai sur les fêtes nationales suivi de quelques idées sur les arts et sur la nécessité de les encourager adressé à la Convention nationale* (Paris, an II).

passions et en lui enseignant à les diriger vers le bien, que vous le ramènerez à la simplicité primitive dont la nature l'avoit doté et qu'il n'a perdue que par l'ignorance ou par l'abus du faux savoir. (p. 7)

Boissy d'Anglas argued that an effective educational programme would have to appeal to the emotions as well as to the mind. He wanted the government to organize national celebrations in which symbols and images would be used to develop the principles of nature and to direct the mind towards noble ends (p. 17). The Romans had exploited symbols and festivities to inculcate a military spirit. The Greeks had utilized art and celebrations to cultivate civic virtues. The Egyptians had made their buildings and public squares a means of impressing certain ideas on citizens from the time they were infants. Likewise the Church had employed images and ceremonies to appeal to the masses, although its purpose had been to entrench its own authority rather than to make men better or to encourage virtue (pp. 20–37). Boissy d'Anglas wanted the Convention to refine these methods in order to encourage a sense of brotherhood, to engender the desire to serve others, and to kindle the love of equality. He wanted the state to use every institution and every ceremony to foster the practice of some virtue or the love of some duty, whether filial loyalty, paternal affection, or enthusiasm for one's daily work (pp. 38–46). Speaking to his fellow legislators he urged, "Ainsi vous ferez connoître aux citoyens que tout jusqu'à leur conduite intérieure et privée doit être sous la surveillance du corps social et se diriger vers son plus grand avantage . . ." (p. 75).

In establishing what Boissy d'Anglas called "cette religion civile" which the Republic would have to establish in France (p. 64), the visual arts would have an important role. On public squares and buildings they would provide models of virtue and glorify acts of heroism. At every instant the citizen would be confronted with the images of some noble deed or the likeness of some great man in bronze or stone (p. 153). Statues would immortalize men who had contributed to enlightening the nation: Fénelon, who had fought fanaticism and hypocrisy even though he might not have championed liberty; Voltaire, who had ridiculed the follies of kings and had prepared the way for freedom; and Rousseau, who had prescribed the true code of liberty for the nation (p. 156). Boissy

d'Anglas can be looked upon as a genuine disciple of the Encyclopedists. In order to regenerate the citizenry he too advocated the
mobilization of all the media capable of appealing to the senses.

As the revolutionary fever reached its peak in the years 1793–94
artists increasingly lent their support to the proposal of converting
art into a political weapon. Some of them were especially eager to
serve the republican cause. Young artists such as David, Gérard,
Sergent, Topino-Lebrun, Fleuriot-Lescot, Hennequin, and others
of their generation were often avid republicans. In fact painters
and sculptors played a role in various revolutionary bodies far out
of proportion to the number of artists in the population.[39] Many of
the younger artists including David had developed democratic
sentiments during their campaign to destroy the privileges of the
Academy, a campaign which developed into a prolonged ideological
battle and produced endless pamphlets and petitions by both the
officers of the Academy and their opponents. Artists had also been
prepared for their revolutionary activity by exposure to the progressive thought which had long been fashionable in intellectual circles.
Moreover as members of an educated elite many of them were confident that they could succeed in a society where careers were open
to talent.

Artists were now further subjected to a variety of pressures which
induced them to support the idea of art as propaganda. In his *Essai
sur les fêtes* Boissy d'Anglas spoke of widespread antagonism to the
arts and a tendency to question their value in a republic.[40] Some
avid republicans emphasized that the fine arts had pandered to
superstition and autocracy under the old régime. Other republicans
associated the visual arts with luxury which they thought undermined the strength of the state.[41] Like Rousseau they believed that
societies were born stoic and died epicurean. Moreover most patriots
now came to equate utility with goodness. It was a serious matter

[39]David L. Dowd, "The French Revolution and the Painters," *French Historical
Studies*, vol. I, no. 2 (1959), pp. 127–48.
[40]Boissy d'Anglas, *Essai sur les fêtes*, p. 128. In the *Société républicaine des arts*
Boizot refuted those who preached a false austerity and advocated destruction of
the arts; Détournelle, *Journal*, pp. 9 f.
[41]P.-T. Durand de Maillane, *Opinion sur les écoles primaires prononcée a la
Convention nationale le 12 décembre 1792* (Paris, n.d.), p. 3.

during a revolution thus to be accused of doing nothing to improve society. It was all the more serious at a moment when the new republic was menaced by enemies within and without. Confronted with such attitudes, it was imperative for artists to prove that the visual arts could be useful to the republic.[42]

At the same time the idea of using art for mass education provided a basis for appeals for government assistance. The revolutionary upheaval had swept away the patronage of those groups which to a large extent had sustained the arts in the past.[43] The monarchy and the court had been destroyed. The aristocracy had lost its privileges and had fled the country in large numbers. The Church was disunited and under bitter attack. As traditional patronage dried up artists became anxious to prove their usefulness to the republican government to which they now had to appeal for support. The promise that art would henceforth serve the republic was thus scarcely inspired by patriotism alone.

At first those artists who opposed the privileges of the Academy formed La Commune des arts. This association lasted for three years, but in time it became too much like an academy itself and was suppressed by the Convention. In the autumn of 1793 radical artists formed a rather amorphous organization called La Société populaire et républicaine des arts.[44] All members had to assert that they had not written anything anti-patriotic and had to affirm their allegiance to the republican constitution. Any artist who displayed immoral works or who wrote anything anti-revolutionary was excluded.[45] Boizot told the Convention that the welfare of the Republic was the foremost concern of the new Society of which he was president. "Aimer la république, une et indivisible, haïr les tyrans, sacrifier tout pour la *liberté* et l'*égalité*, placer son bonheur à bien mériter de la patrie et de ses frères," he asserted; "voilà ses sentimens et ses opinions."[46]

[42]"Preuves de l'utilité des Beaux-Arts," *La Décade philosophique*, vol. I, no. 7, 10 Messidor an II, pp. 401–10.

[43]M. Dreyfous, *Les arts et les artistes pendant la période révolutionnaire* (Paris, 1906), pp. 155 ff.

[44]Henry Lapauze, ed., *Procès-verbaux de la Commune générale des arts de peinture, sculpture, architecture et gravure, et de la Société populaire et républicaine des arts* (Paris, 1903), pp. xlviii ff.

[45]Détournelle, *Journal*, pp 5–6.

[46]*Ibid.*, p. 9.

The new Society behaved in a fashion similar to a Jacobin Club. Members tried to outdo each other in denouncing artists suspected of anti-republican sentiments. Wicar, pupil and disciple of David, denounced artists who remained in Italy, especially Xavier Fabre whom he accused of swearing allegiance to Louis XVII. Wicar suggested that the painting by this artist which hung in the former Academy should be dragged to the Tree of Liberty, mutilated by each member of the Society, and then burned amid cries of "Vive la République!"[47] Happily not all the members favoured such vandalism, but denunciations were quite common. The genre painter Boilly, for example, was accused of "ouvrages d'une obsénité [*sic*] révoltante pour les mœurs républicaines, lesquels [*sic*] obsénité salissent les murs de la République."[48] The accused appeared before the Society in an attempt to clear himself, and, explaining that he had renounced his previous mistakes, asked to be admitted to the Society. Boilly also tried to prove he had mended his ways by painting such themes as "Marat porté en triomphe."

La Société populaire et républicaine des arts constantly advocated the use of art as propaganda. Obviously the members of the Society were anxious to convince the government of their usefulness. Such was the purpose of the petition which Bienaimé read to the Convention on behalf of the Society in January 1794.[49] Praising the *courageux Montagnards* for destroying foolish monuments to tyranny, for restoring man to his proper dignity, and for laying the basis for public happiness, the petition claimed that the arts could be of great assistance in this sublime task by conveying useful lessons to the people. The petition urged the Convention to decree that heroic and virtuous actions be displayed everywhere, in all the departments, in all the sections, in all the public squares, in all the primary schools, so that the people would be exposed constantly to moral instruction. The artists suggested that useless statues should be removed from public parks and replaced with images of republicans who had died for their devotion to the public cause. The

---

[47]Lapauze, *Procès-verbaux*, pp. lii ff.
[48]*Ibid.*, p. lix.
[49]Détournelle, *Journal*, pp. 14-16. Détournelle says the petition was draughted by Bienaimé using suggestions from the sculptor Espercieux, the painter Désoria, and the architects Vignon, Balzac and himself. See Lapauze, *Procès-verbaux*, pp. 188, 190, 191, 192, 199, 204, and 206.

Convention should also erect impressive temples dedicated to Liberty and Public Happiness.

David replied to the petitioners on behalf of the Convention. He recalled that the arts had flourished along with republican virtues in classical times. These virtues were now reappearing and he urged artists to support them. After his speech the delegation of artists was admitted to the summit of the Mountain. When they had taken their places, Thuriot made a rousing speech in praise of the arts. He declared that in all revolutions staged on behalf of liberty there were those who argued that the arts and sciences were dangerous to republics. Too late the people learned that in fact the arts and sciences were the splendour of republics and their source of life. Thuriot called on the Convention to honour the arts and sciences and to proclaim their utility. "Je demande que le Comité d'instruction publique soit chargé de présenter un programme de concours entre tous les artistes pour immortaliser les actions vertueuses et tout ce qui peut développer l'amour de la liberté et de l'égalité."[50]

The Convention ordered its Committee of Public Instruction to plan for such a general contest among artists. Bienaimé and Balzac were given the task of reporting the ideas of La Société populaire et républicaine des arts to the Committee,[51] and they submitted their report late in January 1794. Once again the basic idea in the submission was that the fine arts could prove their utility by conveying lessons to the masses. "En effet, tout doit avoir un but moral chez un peuple républicain," the report argued: "il doit trouver des leçons jusques dans ses plaisirs."[52] The artists asked the government to complete the Palais National, to erect a Temple of Liberty, and to undertake other public works all of which were to be decorated with works of art dedicated to the Revolution. Other suggestions included amphitheatres for public celebrations and a temple to immortalize the victories of the Republic. The report urged the Committee of Public Instruction to draw up programmes for these projects and to invite all artists to begin work on them.

[50]*Arch. parl.*, vol. LXXXIII, pp. 422–24; *Moniteur*, 29 Nivôse l'an II, le 18 janvier 1794, no. 119, p. 480. Thuriot's speech is omitted in the *Arch. parl.*
[51]Lapauze, *Procès-verbaux*, pp. 206, 213; Détournelle, *Journal*, p. 152.
[52]*Ibid.*, pp. 155–57.

Some members of the Society were dissatisfied with the number of revolutionary works which had been displayed at the Salon in 1793. Landscapes, genre scenes, and portraits of ordinary citizens had dominated that exhibition.[53] There had been some revolutionary canvases such as Jacques Bertaux's *Le 10 août*, as well as quite a few portraits of *Conventionnels*, but on the whole the display had not been very different from those under the old régime. At a meeting of the Society Balzac proposed that for the next exhibition artists should be confined to patriotic subjects.[54] In addition he suggested that all members of the Society be required to submit within six months a work representing some patriotic or revolutionary subject. Some members protested that the first proposal was unnecessary since republicans did not have to be coerced into portraying revolutionary themes. Others opposed the second suggestion on the grounds that it recalled the regulations of the defunct Academy. After a heated discussion the two proposals were sent to a committee for further consideration. Finally the Society approved a resolution declaring that as good republicans members could treat only those subjects which would propagate virtue and liberty.

The Society was anxious for the public to understand the role which the fine arts could play in the Republic, and in February 1794 it set up a Committee of Instruction to inform the people about the proper function of art.[55] Early in April, Espercieux, a sculptor and enthusiastic republican, brought down a summary of the report which this Committee was preparing.[56] Like Boissy d'Anglas earlier, the Committee reviewed how governments since the time of the Egyptians had always made use of the arts to consolidate popular support and to commemorate important historical events. Under Louis XIV all the various arts had been concentrated on glorification of the monarch. As a result of their subservience the arts began to decline noticeably. Throughout succeeding reigns the arts had been prostituted to flattering worthless rulers or had been wasted on erotic boudoir scenes. Now the arts had been emancipated

[53]*Livret*, 1793.
[54]Détournelle, *Journal*, pp. 56 ff.; Lapauze, *Procès-verbaux*, pp. 212–13.
[55]Lapauze, *Procès-verbaux*, pp. 232–33; Détournelle, *Journal*, p. 135.
[56]Lapauze, *Procès-verbaux*, pp. 276; Détournelle, *Journal*, pp. 273 ff.

and a new route marked out for them. Henceforth they were to depict the accomplishments of the people and the virtuous actions of individuals. The report concluded with a suggestion that the legislature should be asked to divide one hundred thousand *livres* among artists who produced works of art which best conveyed a revolutionary or moral lesson.

The ideas of La Société populaire et républicaine des arts were vigorously supported by the art jury which the Convention set up to judge a contest among student artists. David explained to the Convention the grounds on which its Committee of Public Instruction had selected the jury.[57] The Committee believed that artists had to be *philosophes*: they had to propagate civic virtues and stir up devotion to public safety. Since artists needed to be inspired by patriotic ideals, it was vital that their works be judged by zealous citizens. If artists themselves were the only judges, the arts might remain in the same old rut where they had been left by despotism. Therefore, David announced, the Committee had chosen fifty men from various occupations to give the necessary impulsion to republican artists.

The proceedings of this jury, which met several times in February 1794 reveal that the Committee of Public Instruction had indeed succeeded in assembling a group of zealots.[58] The jury obviously cared more for republicanism than it did for aesthetics. For the sculpture contest competitors had been asked to execute low reliefs concerning the Faliscan schoolmaster who had tried to betray his town to the Romans by bringing some of the students entrusted to him into the Roman camp: "Camille, général de l'armée romaine, indigné de sa trahison, le renvoie aux parens des jeunes Falisques, chargé de liens, dépouillé de ses vêtements, et frappé par ces mêmes élèves que le perfide avoit voulu livrer." Dufourny, who chaired the first session, declared that the jury was to appraise art on a new basis. "Les artistes vont être jugés

[57]*Arch. parl.*, vol. LXXIX, pp. 280–81; *Moniteur*, 28 Brumaire l'an II, le 17 novembre 1793, no. 57, p. 231.

[58]*Procès-verbal de la première séance du jury des arts nommé par la Convention nationale et assemblé dans une des salles du muséum en vertu des décrets des 9 et 25 brumaire an II pour juger les ouvrages de peinture sculpture et architecture mis au concours 17 pluviose an II – le 25 février 1794* (Paris, n.d.). Détournelle's *Journal* also describes the proceedings, often much more completely than the minutes.

aujourd'hui autrement que par l'Académie," he announced; "il s'agit de savoir si la révolution leur a donné un caractère qui les distingue, s'ils sont vraiment révolutionnaires."[59] Fleuriot-Lescot, a disciple of David and a substitute for the Public Prosecutor, thought that all the reliefs lacked revolutionary spirit. He said he was not considering whether they were good art in themselves, but only whether they were useful to the Revolution. Some jurymen thought that the works lacked spirit. Others complained that the subject involved resistance to a mere schoolmaster rather than a tyrant.[60] In the end the jury agreed that none of the works deserved a prize.

The subject for painting was "La Mort de Brutus: l'instant où le corps du grand homme, de ce fondateur de la liberté de son pays, est rapporté dans Rome par les chevaliers romains, et reçu par le sénat qui vient au devant de lui."[61] Here results were considered better. "On a dit que les arts devoient prendre un caractère révolutionnaire," declared the writer Dorat-Cubières; "les sculpteurs l'ont négligé; ils n'ont pas eu de prix: ici les sujets sont républicains, et traités d'une manière républicaine, ainsi en donnant un prix il sera au moins mérité."[62] Other members of the jury were less enthusiastic although they all looked for republican zeal more than artistic skill. The actor Monvel, for instance, liked the third painting because the soldiers expressed a profound sorrow and the body of the dead hero revealed the noble character of a man who had died for his country. Topino-Lebrun, a pupil of David and juror on the Revolutionary Tribunal, thought none of the paintings revealed sufficient revolutionary fervor, although he saw some signs of it in the third painting. The actor De Lays preferred the same painting because it depicted the deep austerity of the Romans and the sad blow which struck them when their firmest defender was killed. The painter Caraffe thought the second painting was the best expression of republican sentiments.[63] After prolonged discussion the jury awarded an encouragement to Harriet, a seventeen-year-old pupil of David.[64]

---

[59]Détournelle, *Journal*, p. 29.
[60]*Ibid.*, pp. 31–33.
[61]*Procès-verbal*, p. 6.
[62]Détournelle, *Journal*, p. 37.
[63]*Ibid.*, pp. 337–50.
[64]*Procès-verbal*, p. 7. The reasons for each member's decisions are printed in the record, pp. 8 ff.

The jury devoted another session to judging the designs for a cavalry school, submitted by student architects. Dufourny, who was presiding, claimed that architecture too would have to serve an educational function in the new society. "Les grands monuments doivent faire de grandes impressions," he exclaimed; "les murs doivent parler; des sentences doivent rendre nos édifices des livres de morale."[65] Fleuriot-Lescot, usually one of the most outspoken jurors, declared that the real purpose of the jury was not just to decide on a prize, but to regenerate the arts. He thought that all the designs expressed an academic rather than a revolutionary spirit. Some of the jury thought that this judgment was somewhat severe.[66] The vote split evenly on whether or not to give a prize. Fleuriot-Lescot, somewhat milder than usual, declared that in case of a deadlock a jury ought to give the benefit of the doubt to the accused. This suggestion was adopted, and a second rather than a first prize was given to a young gunner named Protin.[67] On March 1, 1794, the jury sent a report of its decisions to the Convention.

When this extraordinary art jury had completed its official business it transformed itself into Le Club révolutionnaire des arts to continue its work for the regeneration of the fine arts.[68] Le Sueur suggested that the revolutionary fervor of the group might be weakened if they admitted members who did not share their determination. Fleuriot-Lescot agreed that it was absolutely necessary to maintain their zeal. "Il ne faudra pas seulement être artiste," he declared, "mais aussi avoir un caractère vraiment républicain, nous ne voulons pas raisonner sur le métier mais sur l'utilité et le rapport qu'il a avec la république."[69] The new Club decided that it would admit members only on the recommendation of four existing members and the unanimous approval of the group. At their meetings in the spring of 1794 the Club discussed how the fine arts might be transformed. Various members of the Club—Balzac, Le Sueur, Chaudet, Lussault, Hassenfratz and others read papers suggesting how the fine arts could be converted into revolutionary weapons. The suggestions of Hassenfratz illustrate the sort of ideas which

[65]Détournelle, *Journal*, p. 71.
[66]*Ibid.*, p. 74.
[67]For the explanation of each juror's vote, see *Procès-verbal*, pp. 45 ff.
[68]Détournelle, *Journal*, pp. 100, 120, 177 ff.
[69]*Ibid.*, p. 262.

were propounded at Le Club révolutionnaire des arts. He contended that the fine arts would have to demonstrate their usefulness before they could expect to receive national support. "On n'encouragera les arts que quand on saura qu'ils sont utiles . . ."[70] Previously they had catered to the taste of human parasites, but now they would have to serve the labouring masses by portraying noble exploits. The arts were better weapons for spreading ideas than either festivals or books; festivals lasted but a moment and books were read once or twice at the most. Hassenfratz thought that the government would be more than willing to subsidize the arts once they had demonstrated their utility. Another member, a painter named Belle, agreed that the arts ought to propagate republican lessons, but he felt that incentives were necessary to compel art to serve virtue.[71] The Club appointed Prud'hon, Belle, Chaudet, Talma, Neveu, and Le Sueur to convey these various ideas to the Committee of Public Instruction.[72]

Thus at the height of the Revolution the government was bombarded with appeals to employ the fine arts in the service of the republic. The Committee of Public Safety responded to these appeals even though it was toiling in an effort to crush counter revolutionaries, mobilize the citizenry for war, regulate economic activity, and cope with recurrent political crises. It took some of its hard-pressed time to attempt to direct artistic activity because it was anxious to spread the republican gospel by every available means. It realized that the ultimate success of its sacred cause depended on remaking men's minds. "Le Comité," Barère told the Convention, "s'occupe d'un vaste plan de régénération dont le résultant doit être de bannir à la fois de la République l'immortalité

[70]*Ibid.*, p. 282.   [71]*Ibid.*, p. 287.

[72]Le Club revolutionnaire des arts came to an end with the overthrow of Robespierre. Fleuriot-Lescot, who had been its guiding spirit, followed Robespierre to the guillotine. La Société populaire et républicaine des arts managed to survive until 1795 by dropping "populaire" from its title and ceremoniously smashing its bust of Marat. It continued to demand government aid by stressing the value of art as propaganda: Etienne Eynard, *Considérations sur l'état actuel des arts, sur les concours de peinture, sculpture, architecture, et gravure, et sur le mode de jugement, publiées par la Société républicaine des arts et présentées à la Convention nationale* (Paris, n.d.). See the pamphlet of one of the members of the Society, Jean-Baptiste-Pierre Le Brun, *Essai sur les moyens d'encourager la peinture, la sculpture, l'architecture et la gravure* (Paris, an III).

et les préjugés, la superstition et l'athéisme."[73] Consequently in the spring of 1794, at the very height of political crisis, the Committee approved an ambitious scheme to conscript the fine arts. It launched a series of contests for works of art dedicated to the Revolution.[74] On the Place des Victoires there was to be a monument erected to the memory of those who had given their lives on August 10.[75] At the western end of the Ile de Paris there was to be a colossal bronze monument depicting the French people trampling down fanaticism, royalism, and federalism.[76] The government announcement for this latter contest in the newspapers proclaimed that the arts would no longer corrupt the public mind, but would regenerate it: "Pénétrez-vous de l'esprit qui doit vous animer," the artists were told; "faites respirer dans vos ouvrages la haine du despotisme et des vices qui l'accompagnent; qu'ils paroissent sous les traits hideux qui les caractérisent, et représentez le Peuple avec la majesté qui lui convient."[77]

Sculptors were also called upon to compete in designing monuments commemorating the glorious epochs of the Revolution which had been celebrated at the great Fête de la Réunion the previous August. Objects of this contest were to be a monument representing Nature Regenerated, to be placed on the ruins of Bastille; an arch of triumph commemorating the October Days, for the Boulevard des Italiens; a statue of Liberty to be shown rising from the wreckage of the statue of Louis XV, for the Place de la Révolution, and a figure portraying the French People crushing Federalism.[78] In addition the Committee of Public Safety called on sculptors to compete in designing other monuments: a column to be erected at the Panthéon in honour of soldiers who had died for the Republic, and a bronze statue of Rousseau to be placed on the Champs Elysées. Painters were not asked to compete for any specific project, but to submit themes of their own choice honouring the Revolution.

[73]*Moniteur*, 12 Germinal an II, le 1er avril 1794, no. 192, p. 775.
[74]*Arrêtés du Comité de Salut public relatifs aux monuments publics, aux arts, et aux lettres* (n.d.) signed by Robespierre, Carnot, Prieur, Barère, Couthon, Lindet, Billaud-Varenne, and Collot d'Herbois. Arch. Nat. AF. II. 80, dossier 591.
[75]*Ibid.*, Arrêté du 12 Floréal an II.
[76]*Ibid.*, Arrêté du 5 Floréal an II.
[77]*Journal de Paris*, no. 507, 3 Prairial an II, p. 2048. Signed by Le Camus, Rondolet, and Dupin of the Commission of Public Works.
[78]*Arrêté . . . relatif aux monuments*, Arch. Nat. AF. II. 80, dossier 591, Arrêté du 5 Floréal an II.

Likewise the Committee of Public Safety called on architects to create monuments and buildings suitable for the Republic. They were to compete in designing a Temple of Equality to be erected on the Champs Elysées.[79] Later they were urged to develop plans for other buildings and monuments such as Temples décadaires, Assemblées primaires, and covered arenas for public celebrations.[80] In its announcement the government warned competitors that regenerate architecture ought to express the influence of republican freedom by a severe and lofty style. No longer would the fine arts cater to the pride of one man and the taste of a corrupt society:

La République les appelle à des travaux plus utiles, à des conceptions plus vastes, à une gloire plus méritée. De petits travaux, d'après de petites données, voilà ce qu'ils avoient à attendre du despotisme; mais dans le siècle de la liberté, les arts liés à la morale, agrandis comme les âmes, ont une destination plus relevée, une utilité plus générale.[81]

At the same time the Committee of Public Safety commissioned the engraver Tassaert to produce prints of the Jacobin hero, Joseph Chalier, as depicted by the artist Caresme.[82] In Lyons, early in 1793, Chalier had shown Paris the way to Jacobin dictatorship. Organizing an armed following, he had announced his intention of purging his city of those whom he considered aristocrats, moderates, speculators, and priestly fanatics. After a long struggle his party had won control of the city government. With his "revolutionary army" he carried out his programme by arresting, and sometimes murdering, the richer and more reactionary citizens. But his opponents had organized themselves in the sections and overthrown the Jacobins in May; Chalier and one of his followers were executed. The print depicted the republican martyr in his prison cell, his arm raised, ready to depart with his executioner: "Pourquoi pleurez-vous?" read the inscription. "La mort n'est rien pour celui dont les intentions sont droites et dont la conscience fut toujours pure . . . Chalier saura mourir d'une manière digne de la cause qu'il a soutenue."[83] As Aulard remarked, the artists had tried to turn the Jacobin martyr into the Socrates of the Revolution.

[79]*Ibid.*, Arrêté du 12 Floréal an II. [80]*Ibid.*, Arrêté du 28 Floréal an II.
[81]*Journal de Paris*, no. 541, 7 Messidor an II, pp. 2184–85. Announcement signed by Le Camus, Rondolet, and Dupin of the Commission of Public Works.
[82]Alphonse Aulard, "L'Art et la politique en l'an II" *Etudes et leçons sur la Revolution française*, 1ère série (Paris, 1893), vol. I, p. 252.
[83]*Ibid.*, p. 253.

The Committee of Public Safety also ordered prints depicting the heroism of Claude Fabre and François Bara. Fabre was a member of the Mountain who had been sent on mission to the army in the Pyrénées-Orientales. He died trying single-handed to defend a gun battery in a battle with the Spanish in December 1793. Bara was the young boy who became famous as the "Décius de treize ans." After a year fighting in the Vendée he died in action supposedly shouting at the enemy around him. "Vive la République!" The revolutionary government likewise subsidized artists to celebrate the heroism of Roman patriots. Such Romans as Brutus, Decius, and Scaevola provided examples of stoic virtue which appealed to the Jacobins. The engraver Audouin, for example, was ordered to print a thousand copies of an engraving of Junius Brutus. And the artist Mirys was told to continue work on a pictorial history of the Roman Republic.[84] "Il en sera déposé un exemplaire gravé dans chaque bibliothèque de district pour servir à l'instruction publique."[85]

Popular societies, local authorities, and representatives on mission also commissioned works of art as propaganda. For example, an artist by the name of Reattu demanded assistance from Maignet who was on mission to Marseilles.[86] The artist requested ten thousand pounds to finance an allegorical painting depicting the "Triumph of Liberty." He proposed to show Liberty carried in triumph by the Warriors who had vanquished the priests and kings allied against her. These Warriors would be portrayed trampling underfoot royalism, fanaticism, and atheism. On one side Philosophy would guide Liberty and help to disperse the clouds hiding her foes. Equality, along with Law and the various Virtues, would follow Liberty while the regenerated people gave thanks to her for having broken their chains. Maignet granted the artist three thousand pounds to begin work.[87] Other payments totalling seven thousand pounds were to come later. Reporting to the Committee of Public Safety, the representative justified his grant on the grounds that it

---

[84]*Ibid.*, p. 258–59.　　　　　　　　　　[85]*Ibid.*, p. 260.

[86]Jacques Reattu, *Petition au citoyen Maignet, Représentant du peuple en mission, le 1er Messidor an II*, Arch. Nat., F17 1065, dossier 16.

[87]Etienne Christophe Maignet, *Rapport par Maignet, Représentatif dans les départements des Bouches-du-Rhône et du Vaucluse*, Arch. Nat. F17 1056, dossier 16.

was urgent to propagate republican ideas by using every medium available.

Meanwhile the Committee of Public Safety approved plans for a grandiose national park surrounding the Palais national, as the Tuileries Palace had come to be called.[88] The plans were the work of the architect Hubert, brother-in-law of David. Atop the dome of the palace there was to be a bronze statue representing Liberty standing erect with the tricolour in one hand and the Declaration of the Rights of Man in the other. The courtyard of the palace was to be enclosed by a circular stylobate on which the Declaration and the Constitution were to be inscribed in gilt letters. Figures representing the republican virtues were to be erected on pedestals all supported by a common base symbolizing the unity of the Republic. On the face of each of these pedestals toward the courtyard there was to be a flaming star which would illuminate the palace by night. At the entrance to the courtyard there were to be imposing statues of Justice and Public Happiness holding suspended the level of Equality. On the other side of the palace there was to be a terrace with twin gateways decorated with statues and low reliefs on revolutionary themes.

Beyond the palace there was to be a magnificent Jardin national stretching to the Champs Elysées. Part of this park was to be converted into an outdoor gymnasium with a long portico decorated with scenes capable of arousing liberal ideals in youths. Another area was to be transformed into a vast esplanade suitable for staging mass festivals. Among other embellishments was to be a large fountain representing the rivers of France with smaller fountains on either side representing Liberty and Equality. The riverside entrance to the park was to be flanked by colonnades retracing the most important events of the Revolution.

The Place de la Révolution was to feature a huge erect figure of Liberty on the site of the former statue of Louis XV. On either side of this central figure were to be spurting fountains decorated with revolutionary symbols. An arch in honour of the victories over tyranny would lead off the square toward the church of the Madeleine, now destined to become a Temple to the Revolution. On the

[88]*Arrêtés . . . relatifs aux monuments*, Arch. Nat. AF. II. 80, dossier 591. Arrêté du 25 Floréal an II.

opposite side of the square toward the river another arch would commemorate the great Festival of Unity on August 10. The approach to the Champs Elysées was to be decorated with the famous horses of Marly and colonnades matching those leading into the garden and likewise decorated with revolutionary themes. The Committee of Public Safety ordered the architects to give as much of a Greek quality as possible to their work "de donner à l'architecture française un caractère particulier et analogue à une grande République Démocratique."[89]

The Government was intent on using every available instrument to communicate the republican gospel to the masses. It called on poets to celebrate the deeds of republican heroes such as Bara and Viala. "Poètes, vous tous dont l'âme est embrasée du double enthousiasme des vers et du patriotisme," said one government appeal, "saisissez vos lyres; quels plus riches tableaux offrit-elle jamais aux muses?"[90] Dramatists were urged to create republican plays publicizing the valiant deeds of the apostles of liberty. Literary men were exhorted to tell of the regeneration of the nation in an austere style suited to such a theme.[91] Musicians too were invited to create civic songs and martial music which would fill republicans with the memories and passions of the Revolution.[92] Thus the short rule of the Jacobins brought the modern state to the threshold of the totalitarian society in the fullest sense of the phrase. As in the utopian society which Mercier had pictured in *L'An 2440* all the arts were to be directed towards a single moral and political purpose.

Throughout the eventful spring of 1794, in the midst of political crisis, the Committee of Public Safety pressed ahead with its artistic plans with the same note of urgency which it devoted to military matters. Those in charge of supervising the project of the Jardin national were ordered to overcome all obstacles which hindered progress and to report to the Committee any way in which the work

---

[89]Letter to Hubert, Moreau, Bernard, and Lannoy from the Committee, 4 Messidor an II, Arch. Nat. AF. II. 80, dossier 591.

[90]*Journal de Paris*, 9 Thermidor an II, no. 573, p. 2313. Appeal by the Committee of Public Instruction signed by Payan and Fourcade.

[91]*Arrêtés . . . relatifs aux monuments*, Arch. Nat. AF. II, dossier 591, Arrêté du 27 Floréal.

[92]*Ibid.*, Arrêté du 28 Floréal an II.

could be accelerated. At the same time the Commission of Public Works was ordered to furnish all the men, material, and funds necessary for the rapid execution of the plan.[93] Then, at the end of a series of urgent directives, there came an abrupt order calling a halt to the work. The date, 16 Thermidor, is explanation enough. The guillotine had intervened.[94] David, one of the leading exponents of the Jacobin conception of art, barely escaped the same fate as Robespierre.

Prior to 9 Thermidor artists had submitted more than four hundred models, plans, and sketches in response to the contests announced by the Committee of Public Safety.[95] Painters had presented more than a hundred drawings and sketches for canvases glorifying the Revolution. Some had depicted the great mass upheavals such as the storming of the Bastille or the overthrow of the monarchy. Others had portrayed feats of individual courage or sacrifice by republican soldiers or zealous citizens. Still others had offered allegorical scenes illustrating the blessings of the Revolution or the triumph of the Mountain. And quite a number had idealized the humble republican virtues of everyday life such as a mother instructing her children in the basic principles of morality.

Robespierre and his followers had gone to their fate, but something had to be done with the large number of works which had been submitted. Both La Société républicaine des arts and the previous Jury des arts urged the Committee of Public Instruction to draw up plans for a jury to judge the contests.[96] Finally four months after the contests had closed the Committee decided to select twenty-seven judges from a list of forty non-contestants chosen by the competitors themselves.[97] This jury did not begin its deliberations until early the following year, and it did not get approval of its decisions until September 1795.[98] Even though the political

[93]Arch. Nat. AF. II. 80, dossier 590. Arrêtés dated 25 Floréal, 25 Prairial, and 4 Messidor an II.

[94]*Ibid.*, dossier 591, Arrêté du 16 Thermidor.

[95]*Notice des ouvrages de sculpture, architecture, et peinture exposés aux concours qui ont eu lieu en vertu des décrets de la Convention nationale et des arrêtés du Comité de Salut Public* (Paris, n.d.).

[96]Guillaume, *Procès-verbaux du Comité d'instruction publique*, vol. V, pp. 168, 175.

[97]*Ibid.*, p. 255: Text of the Decree, pp. 258–59 (Annex A); *Loi portant qu'il sera nommé un jury....* 9 *Frimaire an III*, Arch. Nat., AD. VIII. 12.

[98]Guillaume, *Procès-verbaux*, vol. VI, pp. 293, 596, and 606 ff.

climate had changed drastically during the previous year, the jury was still anxious to see art put to work as propaganda. It called on artists and art lovers to submit memoranda suggesting how the fine arts could be regenerated.[99] And it supported one of its members who suggested that in future contests those whose projects were almost as good as the winners should be given commissions to do monuments for provincial cities. In its final report the jury reminded the Committee of Public Instruction that "il importe de remplacer, sur tous les piédestaux vacans de la tyrannie, les effigies de la liberté, ou tous autres sujets analogues à la Révolution. . . ."[100]

Despite these intentions and though the jury awarded prizes totalling 442,800 *livres*, the contests in the end failed to produce art with a revolutionary message.[101] In the painting contest Gérard won first prize worth twenty thousand pounds with a sketch for a huge painting representing the triumph of the people on August 10. Vincent won second prize of ten thousand pounds with a sketch depicting a republican heroine of the Vendée. The jury instructed both these artists to finish their proposed paintings on a large scale suitable for decorating public buildings and for making a powerful impression on the public mind. Twenty-three other prize winners were awarded expenses to complete revolutionary or moral paintings on as large a scale as possible. Finally sixteen lesser prize winners were given purely monetary encouragements even though the jury would have preferred to commission actual paintings. Very few of the prize-winning artists ever completed the revolutionary themes which they had sketched.

The jury had asked most of the prize winners to execute paintings of their choice dealing with either revolutionary themes or moral subjects which would contribute to public education.[102] The uncertain value of prizes payable in *assignats* had prevented many

[99]*Avis aux artistes et aux amateurs d'envoyer des mémoires au jury des arts*, 11 Messidor an III; *Deloynes*, vol. LVI, Item 1733.

[100]*Extrait du procès-verbal des séances du jury des arts ou rapport fait au Comité d'instruction publique sur les prix que le jury a décernés aux ouvrages . . . soumis à son jugement en vertu de la loi du 9 Frimaire*, Arch. Nat., F17 1057, dossier 3.

[101]*Prix décernés aux esquisses de peinture présentées au concours ouvert par la Convention Nationale et soumises au jugement du jury des arts en vertu de la loi du 9 Frimaire an III* (Paris, n.d.).

[102]*Extrait du procès-verbal des séances des arts ou rapport fait au Comité d'instruction publique*, p. 12.

of the artists from setting to work until a jury had clarified the value of the awards more than eighteen months after they had been announced.[103] When the artists did begin work most of them ignored the intention of the jury and treated subjects very different from those for which they had been given awards.[104] Prud'hon completed a painting of "La Sagesse et la Vérité descendant sur le globe" and Vanderburch finished his "Trait de courage et de vertu de Philippe Rouzeaud," but most other prize winners changed their subjects completely. Instead of "L'instruction publique" and "Toulon rebelle ramené par la Victoire à la République," Fragonard junior did a painting of Psyche and one of a slave dealer concluding the sale of a woman. Instead of "La République française rend hommage à l'Etre suprême," Garnier did a painting of the family of Priam. In place of "Le Dévouement d'une citoyenne de la Vendée," Bidault portrayed Orpheus leading animals with the melodies of his lyre. In place of "L'Atrocité de Lambesc le 12 juillet 1789," Thevenin depicted Oedipus and Antigone. For "La Liberté ramène au peuple la justice et la vertu," Taillasson substituted a painting of Leander and Hero. And for "L'Epoque du 10 août," La Grenée junior substituted a picture of Ulysses saved from a shipwreck. One could multiply examples. Perhaps artists felt that their original themes were no longer appropriate. Or perhaps they felt free to return to traditional themes once political pressure was relaxed.

The projects for great monuments and public buildings also failed. The jury thought that some of the monuments proposed by the Committee of Public Safety had been badly conceived.[105] The proposed statue of the people for the point near Pont Neuf offered technical difficulties which restricted artists. The idea of a statue of Liberty rising from the ruins of the statue of Louis XV

[103]Within a few months of making its decisions values had already changed so much that the jury suggested supplementary grants to be paid when the paintings were finished: *Extrait du procès-verbal de la dernière séance du jury des arts du 11 Vendémiaire an IV*, Arch. Nat., F17 1056, dossier 5. Later a special session of the jury converted the awards into cash payable in installments as work progressed: *Rapport présenté au ministre de l'intérieur le 3 Ventôse an V*, Arch. Nat., F17, 1057, dossier 7.

[104]*Rapport sur les travaux d'encouragements faits au ministre de l'intérieur ans V–VIII*, Arch. Nat., F17 1057, dossiers 6, 7, 8, 9, 10, 12, 13, 14, 15, 16.

[105]*Extrait du procès-verbal des séances du jury des arts*, Arch. Nat., F17 1057, dossier 5, pp. 14 ff.

was bizarre and presented many artistic problems. The column for the Panthéon was not suitable to inscribe with names or to erect among a forest of other columns. The project of Nature Regenerated rising from the ruins of the Bastille was too abstract and metaphysical for visual representation. And, as for the "Statue du Peuple terrassant le Fédéralisme," the jury pointed out the Convention had decreed that all monuments relative to federalism were to be destroyed. The jury did award a number of monetary prizes to enable sculptors and architects to submit further models to new contests,[106] but, in his report to the Convention on behalf of the Committee of Public Instruction, Louis Portiez admitted that the monuments were too expensive to be completed under existing circumstances.[107] Thus the bold plans of the Year II collapsed.

[106]*Prix décernés aux esquisses de sculpture* . . . (Paris, n.d.). *Prix aux projets d'architecture.* . . . (Paris, n.d.).

[107]Louis-François-René Portiez, *Rapport fait au nom du Comité d'instruction publique sur les concours de sculpture, peinture, et architecture ouvert par les décrets de la Convention nationale* (Paris, n.d.). The Committee of Public Instruction did order Moitte to complete the statue of Rousseau for the Champs Elysées. Guillaume, *Procès-verbaux*, vol. V, p. 514.

The Sterility
of the Idea of
Art as Propaganda

6.

Artistes, songez-y. Prenez garde que l'avenir
républicain ne vous demande compte de
l'emploi de vos talens. On a publié les traits de
l'héroïsme national sous le titre d'Annales
françaises. Cette histoire n'appartient pas à la
plume, mais au pinceau, au ciseau, au burin.
      PIERRE CHAUSSARD, *Décade philosophique*[1]

THE MEN RESPONSIBLE for 9 Thermidor had been united only in
their hatred of Robespierre. Some had disapproved of the narrow
course down which he and his colleagues had tried to steer the
Revolution. Others had hoped to seize the machinery of the Terror
simply in order to establish themselves in power. Most had feared
that for one reason or another they themselves were in the shadow
of the guillotine. Those who had conspired to strike down the Incor-
ruptible did not realize that they were opening the way to reaction;
indeed some thought that they were carrying the Revolution forward as had been done when the Girondists were expelled. But the
death of Robespierre and his associates had opened the way for a
mounting revulsion against the Terror: Jacobin leaders were

[1]Pierre-J-B. Chaussard, "Exposition des ouvrages . . . dans les salles du
Muséum," *Décade philosophique*, an VI, vol. XVIII, no. 34, p. 418.

arrested, their followers were dispersed, and the terrorist machinery was gradually dismantled.

This reaction against the Terror stopped short of restoration of the monarchy. The brothers of the guillotined King were too closely associated with foreign invasion and counter-revolution to be acceptable as rulers, and the death from tuberculosis of the infant son of the late King and Queen ended any chance of reviving constitutional monarchy. After hesitating for more than a year, the Thermidoreans drew up a new constitution to replace the radical democratic one which the Convention had kept in storage. Real political power was by it confined to a small group of propertied citizens. The National Assembly was divided into two chambers: a Council of Five Hundred which could frame but not approve laws, and a Council of Elders which could approve or reject but not amend legislation; to safeguard its members the Convention ruled that two-thirds of the new Assembly was to be made up of *Conventionnels*. Executive authority was to be divided among five Directors chosen by the two chambers. The rump Convention had attempted to guard against both democracy and dictatorship; what it did was to design a cumbersome constitution.

Of the original five Directors four—Reubell, Larevellière-Lépeaux, Carnot, and Le Tourneur—were stolid bourgeois and sincere republicans. The fifth, Barras, was an hedonistic ex-noble; scarcely a typical republican, he owed the prestige he had won to his defence of the Convention against mob violence and he was the only Director to retain office as long as the system survived. The officials of the new régime attempted to defend republican institutions against enemies on both the left and the right. As one means of stability they persisted in attempting to establish a civic cult to supersede the Roman Church. Secular education provided one means by which they hoped to undermine old beliefs and transfer loyalty to the state, and the *culte décadaire* was intended to serve a similar purpose. The government insisted on the sole use of the republican calendar in which the tenth day was endowed with all the privileges of Sunday, and the patriotic festival every tenth day thus was aimed at establishing a sort of national religion.

During the four years of the Directory there were repeated appeals for art which would impress the masses and help to attach men to republican institutions. The social role of art was the topic of innumerable articles, speeches, essays, petitions, poems, and government communications. Proposals for republican monuments, for civic temples and for arches of triumph, were exceptionally common. There was, for example, the suggestion as to how the government might use the four bronze horses which the army had confiscated in Venice.[2] They were to be attached to a chariot carrying Liberty attended by Justice and Wisdom in a whole allegorical complex erected on the Place de la Révolution. Victory was to hover above, holding a crown over the head of Liberty. In front of the horses Renown was to stand, blowing her trumpet. At the four corners of the monument would be Tyranny, Anarchy, Terror and Egoism, in chains, "ce dernier, comme étant le poison de la philosophie et de tous gouvernemens," the author of the scheme suggested, "doit être placé au nord-ouest, c'est-à-dire, dans le point le plus correspondant à l'Angleterre." Discord, Envy, and Treason, along with their infernal attributes, were to be shown downtrodden and crushed by the wheels of the chariot.

Newspapers featured extensive discussion of the social influence of the fine arts. The *Journal de Paris*, for instance, published a long series of letters on the subject. Mercier had provoked this controversy by assailing the visual arts in a speech to the Council of Five Hundred. He had begun his attack by claiming that literature was far more expressive than painting or sculpture, and then had proceeded to charge that these arts were the product of luxury and its accompanying vices.[3] When he repeated these opinions in the press he was met by a chorus of protest. Some reminded him that in his utopian novel he had shown how art might serve to idealize virtue. Others, while admitting that the visual arts had done a great deal of harm in the past, insisted that they could do just as much good in the future by serving as "lois muettes."[4] In the end Mercier

[2]*Journal de Paris*, 16 Thermidor an VI, no. 316, pp. 1323–24. For other examples in the same newspaper see 19 Pluviôse an VI, no. 139, pp. 577–78, and 16 Pluviôse an VII, no. 136, pp. 599–600.

[3]Louis-Sebastien Mercier, *Corps législatif. Conseil des Cinq-Cents. Rapport et projet de résolution au nom d'une commission sur la pétition des peintres, sculpteurs, graveurs, architectes relativement au droit de patentes.* Séance du 25 Vendémiaire an V.

[4]*Journal de Paris*, 12 Nivôse an V, no. 102, pp. 409–10; 21 Germinal an VI, no. 201, pp. 837–38.

seems to have been forced to call a halt to his campaign against the
fine arts, but only on condition that they began to communicate
noble ideas and produce useful monuments.[5]

The notion of using art to diffuse republican ideals was still the
theme of many speeches. It was the refrain every year of the president of the Institut national as he handed out the grand prizes to
the best students in painting, sculpture and architecture.[6] Similar
orations were common in the legislatures. Typical was the speech
by Trouille when he presented the Council of Five Hundred with
an engraving by a Swiss artist symbolizing the liberation of the
Cisalpine region by the French. Liberty, which has just freed the
inhabitants of the Alps, is bringing peace to the people of Italy. The
Sciences, the Arts, and Commerce were honouring Liberty with a
sacrifice. Religion, unveiled by Truth, was depicted listening to
Peace who was asking for Tolerance. Fanaticism, realizing she was
finished, was extinguishing her torch and throwing away her
poisons. France was shown, crowned by Nature, sitting near an
arch of triumph consecrated to July 14, 1789. Trouille thought that
this work of art was an example of the value of engraving. "Son
utilité rivalise avec celle de l'imprimerie," he asserted. "Par elle on
peut multiplier, à peu de frais, des sujets patriotiques et moraux,
dont la vue doit influer, plus qu'on ne pense, sur l'opinion
publique."[7]

Under the Directory there were also numerous essays on the
social utility of the fine arts.[8] One group of essays deserves special
mention: the painting section of the Institut national sponsored an
essay contest on the topic, "Quelle a été et quelle peut être encore
l'influence de la peinture sur les mœurs et le gouvernement du

[5]*Ibid.*, 26 Thermidor an VI, no. 326, p. 1367.
[6]See the speech by Jussieu in October 1798: *Discours prononcé par le président
de l'Institut national dans la séance du 15 Vendémiaire, an VII, aux élèves qui
ont remporté les grands prix de peinture, de sculpture et d'architecture de l'an
VI*; in *Deloynes*, vol. I, Item 1377. For a similar speech by Camus a year earlier
and Buache a year later see Items 1373 and 1392 respectively.
[7]Jean-Nicolas Trouille, *Discours prononcé en faisant hommage d'une estampe
à la gloire de la liberté triomphante; ouvrage posthume de Vincent Vangelisty,
artiste cisalpin*. Séance du conseil des Cinq-Cents, 17 Germinal an VII (Paris,
an VII), p. 3.
[8]Space does not allow us to analyse all the works which discussed the educational value of art, e.g., F. R. J. de Pommereul, *De l'art de voir dans les beaux-
arts* (Paris, an VI), and T. B. Emeric-David, *Musée olympique de l'école
vivante des beaux-arts* (Paris, 1796).

peuple libre." In April 1798 the judges announced that the best essay was by a young officer by the name of Allent, and gave honourable mention to the painter Robin and the history teacher Raymond. Unfortunately all the manuscripts submitted to this contest were destroyed during the uprising of the Paris Commune in 1871. Only one of the essays was published and thus preserved for the student of the history of ideas. However, we are able to get a fairly adequate picture of the content of the other essays from the long report submitted by the judges[9]—Vien, Vincent, David, Dufourny, Mongez, Leblond, and Andrieux—who summarized the various essays and included long quotations from them.

All the essays which had been submitted argued that painting ought to idealize not only heroic deeds, but examples of unselfishness, fairness, filial piety, and other public and private virtues. The judges reported that they gave the essay by Allent first prize because he alone had seen that painting was as likely to be influenced by social conditions as vice versa; he had emphasized the fact that only in unison with other social institutions could art effectively influence morals and government. The essayist had begun by examining the influence of art among ancient and modern peoples. In his opinion only the Greeks and the Church had made full use of art, the former to honour the champions of liberty, the latter to establish its authority. He had concluded that, in conjunction with other social institutions, art could help to shape national character: "Puisque la peinture parle à l'imagination des peuples c'est au Législateur à faire en sorte qu'elle ne lui donne que d'utiles leçons; c'est à lui de la faire servir à la conservation des mœurs, à la propagation des vertus qui doivent composer le caractère national."[10]

The other essayists likewise emphasized the value of art for propagating republican virtues. The judges praised Robin for developing the idea of using vast frescoes on public buildings to portray republican themes. The judges also liked many similar ideas in the discourse by Raymond (although they found it somewhat

---

[9]*Rapport au nom de la commission nommée pour examiner les discours envoyés sur cette question proposée par la section de peinture "Quelle a été et quelle peut être encore l'influence de la peinture sur les mœurs et le gouvernement d'un peuple libre," lu dans la séance publique de l'Institut national.* 15 Germinal an VI; in the Archives of the Académie française.

[10]*Ibid.,* p. 4.

verbose—when printed it ran to nearly three hundred pages). This author indeeed went further than almost anyone else in repudiating art for its own sake. He bitterly assailed works of art which drew attention primarily to the technique of the artist. Such works misled men into looking for nothing in pictures but painting. Better to have a moral theme and mediocre art.[11] He also went further than most other writers in advocating government controls. He wanted the government to establish unalterable codes of taste and to direct the arts toward a common political goal, although he was vague as to how it was to be done: "Non, les lois ne doivent pas limiter la carrière des lettres et des arts, mais elles doivent frapper l'ennemi des mœurs qui abuse de son talent pour détruire la morale publique; elles ne doivent pas guider froidement le pinceau de l'artiste, mais le lui arracher des mains quand il le prostitue."[12]

The idea of art as propaganda occasionally even inspired poetry in this period. The poem entitled *Sur la peinture: sur les tableaux dont l'armée d'Italie a enrichi le muséum et sur l'utilité morale de la peinture* which Lavallée read to the Société philotechnique was an excellent example of the attitude toward art prevalent among republicans.[13] The poet was pleased that the nation had acquired so many masterpieces from Italy, but he hoped that in future art would serve a better purpose than these famous works. He called on artists to dramatize the rule of law and civic morality, but above all he wanted them to paint the simple domestic virtues which he considered the basis of society:

> Peignez surtout, peignez, le respect filial,
> Et l'amour paternel, et l'amour conjugal,
> Pour guider les humains aux vertus héroïques,
> Faites-leur traverser les vertus domestiques.

In view of this endless reiteration of the call to mobilize art the amount of art actually produced to serve as propaganda from the

[11]George-Marie Raymond, *De la peinture considérée dans ses effets sur les hommes en général et de son influence sur les mœurs et le gouvernement des peuples* (Paris, 1799), p. 169.

[12]*Ibid.*, p. 237.

[13]Joseph Lavallée, *Poème sur la peinture: sur les tableaux dont l'armée d'Italie a enrichi le Muséum et sur l'utilité morale de la peinture lu à la Société philotechnique*, 20 Floréal an VI, Deloynes, vol. I, Item 1375.

meeting of the Estates General to the *coup d'état* by Napoleon seems meagre indeed—no great monuments, and only about five per cent of the works exhibited in the Salons. This relative sterility of the idea of art as propaganda demands explanation.

In part the ineffectiveness of the concept of art as propaganda was the result of unstable political conditions. This instability during much of the revolutionary decade made it difficult for governments to turn monumental plans into real accomplishments. The overthrow of Robespierre and his colleagues, for instance, rendered useless their grandiose plans to employ the fine arts. Moreover, rapidly changing revolutionary doctrines made the creation of political art a problem, for revolutionary saints enjoyed none of the permanence of those of the traditional Church. It was no accident that David never completed "Le Serment du Jeu de Paume": many of those who took the Tennis Court Oath had ceased to be suitable heroes for the Jacobins by the Year II. And it was probably fortunate for Le Barbier that he did not finish his painting of Captain Desilles until after Thermidor: the hero who died trying to suppress a mutiny in 1791 came to be considered a reactionary a year or so later.

The Directory too lacked the stability needed to carry out an ambitious programme for the fine arts. From the first, political conditions remained perilous. Within seven months the government had to crush Gracchus Babeuf and his followers who planned an insurrection to introduce some sort of socialism. As the economy continued to languish, resurgence of Jacobinism on the left posed a more serious threat. Meanwhile an equal menace arose on the right: returning *emigrés* and priests succeeded in arousing royalist sentiments, especially among the peasants. In fact, in the partial elections of 1797, the first really free elections in republican France, so many royalists of various hues were returned that three of the Directors decided to call in the army to purge the Assemblies. Two Directors —Carnot and the newly elected Barthélemy—were ousted, elections in forty-nine departments were quashed, opposition papers were suppressed, and the main opponents of the government were deported or executed. And in the next two years there were more insurrections, more elections quashed, more purges.

This shaky republic tried without success to redirect the fine arts. The advice which Bénézech, the Minister of the Interior, gave to artists about the forthcoming Salon of 1796 typifies the attitude of this government's officials.[14] The Minister began by praising the number of good works which artists had displayed at the previous exhibition despite lack of peace and leisure. Then he proceeded to urge artists to make themselves worthy of government support by choosing new themes. He appealed to them to transmit to posterity those deeds which would honour the nation and would efface the memory of deplorable crimes committed by individuals. In his opinion French artists ought to feel the need to celebrate the power and the grandeur with which the nation had controlled events and shaped her destiny. There were already enough paintings dealing with the history of ancient peoples. Such classical themes were no longer appropriate for the French who concerned themselves with the future happiness of mankind.

In a proclamation that same year Bénézech appealed to artists to compete in designing a series of republican monuments. He attacked the way in which art had been used under the old régime to fill public squares with images of despotism and slavery.[15] Inspired by flattery, these monuments had lacked an air of true grandeur. When the people overthrew tyranny they had obliterated these vile symbols of their long servitude. Now the squares which had been rid of kings awaited monuments dedicated to liberty: "Qu'ils s'élèvent simples et majestueux; qu'en frappant les yeux ils parlent à la pensée et au sentiment; qu'ils offrent de grands exemples, qu'ils donnent de grandes leçons, que leur aspect laisse de grands souvenirs." On behalf of the Directory, Bénézech invited artists to submit plans for an Altar of the Motherland and monuments for all the principal squares in the capital. This was supposed to be the first stage in a more general plan to create civic monuments.

The models which artists submitted to the competition were displayed in the Louvre and later were turned over to the literature and fine arts division of the Institut national.[16] A panel of judges

14*Avis du ministre de l'intérieur relatif à l'exposition qui s'ouvrira le 1er Vendémiaire an V*, 22 Septembre 1796; *Deloynes*, vol. I, Item 1368.
15Ministère de l'intérieur, *Appel aux artistes* (Paris, an IV).
16"Des Sciences et des arts," *Mercure français*, 30 Nivôse l'an V, pp. 345–53.

was selected and it handed down its judgment in October 1796.[17] The judges decided that none of the plans were good enough to be completed as public monuments, but they granted some of the models encouragement—those by Balzac, Faivre, Stouf, Dardel, Le Vasseur, Le Mercier, and Tardieu. Since the full report by the judges cannot be found, we know very little about the sort of works which artists submitted in response to this appeal by the Minister of the Interior, but we have other confirmation that the models submitted were inferior. In an open letter to the Directory, Charles Corbet claimed that the plans displayed in the Louvre had been quite poor, and that much of the fault lay in the manner in which the contest had been conducted. The government ought to have laid down specific themes instead of merely asking artists to submit their ideas. Also he thought it had been a mistake to stage a contest which was open to all artists. Better results would have been achieved had a few skilful artists been asked to compete for commissions.[18]

Corbet went on to complain that the government was doing very little to assist the arts, especially in the field of sculpture. He concluded by challenging the government to commission revolutionary art on a grand scale.[19] His plea was in vain. The Directory did not sponsor any more ambitious projects to mobilize the fine arts. Financial difficulties were partly to blame for this, since of the money that might have been available for art much was being spent to pay off the debts of the previous government.[20] During Year VI the government had 350,000 livres for cultural encouragements of all kinds, but it still owed 174,000 livres to artists who had won awards in the Year III and who were entitled to payment as their

[17]Marcel Bonnaire, ed., *Procès-verbaux de l'Académie des beaux-arts: la classe de littérature et beaux-arts de l'Institut national an IV–an VIII* (2 vols., Paris, 1937), vol. I, p. 35.

[18]Charles-Louis Corbet, *Lettre au Citoyen Lagarde, secrétaire-général du Directoire exécutif, sur les esquisses et projets de monuments pour les places publiques de Paris, suivie d'une réponse au rapport contre les arts et les artistes fait par le citoyen Mercier au Conseil des Cinq-Cents* (Paris, an V), pp. 8–12.

[19]*Ibid.*, pp. 15–23.

[20]*Rapport au ministre de l'intérieur sur les travaux d'encouragement dans les arts de peinture, sculpture et architecture*, 9 Nivôse an VI, Arch. nat. F17 1056, dossier 8. During Year VI the government had 350,000 livres for cultural encouragement of all kinds, but it still owed 174,000 livres to artists who had won awards in the Year III and who were entitled to payment as their work progressed.

work progressed. But in the final analysis there also seems to have been a lack of vigour and imagination in applying the idea of art as propaganda.

This did not mean that the government abandoned attempts to redirect art altogether. François de Neufchâteau, the Minister of the Interior after the Year V, did not launch any great projects for republican monuments, but he was anxious to turn art into a political force. His instructions concerning the special contest announced in December 1798 illustrate his attitude toward art. This contest was called after he received a petition from artists pleading for government assistance.[21] These artists claimed that the fine arts could still perform a valuable educational service as they had done in classical times, but that now only the government had the means to employ the arts in this way. They asked for execution of the law passed by the Constituent Assembly for the support of the arts and called for the launching of competitions like the one staged by the Convention. In response to this petition the Minister asked artists to submit the best works which they had exhibited in the various Salons since 1794.[22]

In February 1799, François de Neufchâteau revealed his own philosophy of art in a directive which he sent to the jury elected by the competitors to judge their works. The jury had balked at the idea of the government dictating subjects to artists who won encouragement, and the Minister replied that it was necessary thus to direct artists because they had done nothing in return for the benefits they had received from the Revolution. He pointed out that not more than one out of every hundred subjects which had been treated by artists dealt with a republican theme. The jury would therefore have to indicate to artists a new moral direction for the visual arts. At a time when the problem was to lay a firm foundation for republican institutions, it was essential to rally all the forces which could influence the human mind. If artists did not realize this fact, then it was the responsibility of the government to give them directions. "Ce n'est pas un problème difficile à résoudre,"

21"Les artistes professant les art du dessin au Ministre de l'Intérieur," *Journal de Paris*, 9 Vendémiaire l'an VII, no. 9, pp. 34–35.
22*Ministère de l'Intérieur. Musée central des arts. L'administration du musée aux artistes*, 27 Nivôse an VII; *Deloynes*, vol. LVI, Item 1754.

he wrote, "que de savoir si les arts doivent être dirigés de manière à répandre les principes et les institutions du gouvernement qui les salarie et les honore."[23]

François de Neufchâteau went on to discuss the question of the value of the various awards which the jury was to hand out. He proposed that the awards ought to be directly related to the utility of the genre in question. Historical paintings and sculpture, which were valuable for propagating ideals, were to be given much more than genre paintings which simply imitated some beauties of nature. However, military paintings which portrayed glorious epochs in the history of the nation, and genre paintings which dealt with moralistic subjects, both deserved more valuable prizes than other kinds of genre painting. "En un mot l'utilité dont peut être une production de l'art, son influence sur les mœurs, voilà ce que le gouvernement se propose particulièrement de considérer, en couronnant les talens,"[24] wrote François. The moment had arrived to give art the new compulsion it required. If this moment was allowed to pass, the chance to make art a moral and political force would be lost. These were the reasons behind the *arrêté* which he was sending the jury.

The order to which he seems to have been referring was not issued until July when the jury had already decided which works were best.[25] It opened with a declaration stating that in a republic all the arts had to contribute to public education and should converge to inspire noble and liberal sentiments, devotion to the motherland, respect for the laws, and hatred for traitors and perjurers. His order then outlined how the government intended to use encouragement as a means of redirecting art toward this purpose. Artists receiving awards were to treat only patriotic and moral themes, and were to submit their plans for paintings or statues to the Minister of the Interior for his approval. In addition, the artists who had been awarded first prizes for painting and for engraving were ordered to portray the assassination of the French plenipotentiaries

[23]*Le Ministre de l'Intérieur aux citoyens composant le jury des arts séant au muséum*, 30 Pluvôse an VII; Arch. Nat., F17 1059, dossier 28, p. 3.
[24]*Ibid.*, p. 7.
[25]*Ministère de l'Intérieur. Extrait des registres du Directoire exécutif du 14 jour du mois Messidor l'an VII de la République française*; Arch. Nat. F 1056, dossier 5.

at Rastadt by the Austrians. Girodet was later commissioned to do a painting of the assassination, and Bervick an engraving.[26]

The jury had been ordered to award prizes according to a scale based on utility, but this advice was not very practical simply because artists had not submitted many didactic works.[27] The two top prizes in the first class for painting went to Girodet for a picture of "Le Sommeil d'Endymion" and Lethiers for one of "Philoctète sur l'Ile de Lemnos." In the second class awards went to Regnault for "Le Génie de la Liberté," to Garnier for "Dédale et Icare," and to Topino-Lebrun for "La Mort de Caius Gracchus." In other divisions awards were given to Serangeli for "La Mort d'Eurydice," to Bidault for "Un Lever de Soleil," to Boilly for "Une Réunion des artistes," to Mme Chaudet for "Une Femme à sa toilette," to Mérimée for "Une Bacchante jouant avec un faune," and to others for similar works. In sculpture perhaps more of the works had a philosophic message. In the first class Chaudet was given a prize for "Une Statue de Cyparisse" and Espercieux for "Une Statue de la Liberté." In the second class Blaise won an award for "Une Statue de Cléopâtre" and Petitot for "Le Génie de la Guerre." In the third division Lorta won a prize for his "Statue de la Paix" and Castellier for his "Statue de l'Amitié." From this list of prizes it is clear that the jury had been forced in many cases to give awards to traditional subjects. When it had completed its deliberations, it issued a warning to artists that henceforth it would be advisable to treat patriotic subjects.[28]

As the period of the Directory drew to a close the government was still trying to persuade artists to idealize civic virtues. In April 1799 the Minister of the Interior issued a communication to artists stating that he expected them to produce more republican themes for the Salon opening in August than they had for previous exhibitions.[29] Once again he reminded artists of what the government had done for the arts. Among other benefits it had collected

[26]*Rapport presenté au Ministre de l'Intérieur sur les travaux d'encouragement* 20 Messidor an VII, Arch. Nat., F17 1056, dossier 13.

[27]*Distribution des prix par le jury des arts*, 23 Ventôse an VII, 13 Mars 1799; *Deloynes*, vol. LVI, Item 1755.

[28]Procès-verbaux du jury des arts, 28 Ventôse an VII, 18 Mars 1799; *Deloynes*, Item 1757.

[29]*Le Ministre de l'Intérieur aux artistes 1799, ibid.*, Item 1757.

masterpieces from different countries and various centuries. In this way it had opened up possibilities for genius which had been unknown in earlier times. Now it remained for the government to give artists works to do which would have a philosophic and moral purpose. "Artistes," he urged, "honorez une Nation qui vous honore!"

Clearly it had not been enough to issue eloquent appeals and to dictate themes to a handful of prizewinners. Part of the explanation for this sterility of the idea of art as propaganda can undoubtedly be found in the ineffectiveness of the government programme. However, part of the explanation lies in certain tensions in this attitude toward art which had been evident from the time of Diderot and the Encyclopedists and the advocates of art as an educational weapon had never managed to resolve.

Perhaps the most important of these tensions was that between the affirmation of artistic freedom and the possibility of government regulation. We have already noted that during the Revolution rebellious artists had overthrown the Académie royale de peinture et sculpture in the name of artistic freedom. The Academy had been organized on an hierarchical basis with control concentrated in a privileged group of officers. These officers had been willing at the time of the Revolution to allow the ordinary members more influence, but they had been unwilling to abandon all idea of special rank.[30] They had accused their opponents of misusing the words *liberté* and *égalité*: "Nous sommes égaux, et nous voulons l'être, s'écrient ceux qui, ne pouvant s'élever de leurs propres aîles, veulent remettre tous les hommes sur la même ligne."[31] The officers had claimed that the existence of various ranks encouraged artists to work their way up by doing their best possible work. To bring everyone down to the same level would destroy the whole system of administration on which the body was founded.[32] Furthermore, the

[30]*Projet des statuts et règlemens pour l'Académie royale de peinture et sculpture par les officiers et plusieurs Académiciens de la dite Académie* (Paris, 1790).

[31]Antoine Renou, *Esprit des statuts et règlemens de l'Académie royale de peinture et sculpture pour servir de réponse aux détracteurs de son régime* (Paris, 1790), p. 2.

[32]Antoine Renou, *Précis motivé par les officiers de l'Académie royale de peinture et sculpture, et plusieurs Académiciens qui s'y sont joints, pour servir*

officers had argued, the Academy was a college in which it was essential to have a permanent group of professors who had demonstrated their ability.

The rebellious faction had protested that the whole structure of the Academy was alien to the spirit of liberty which was transforming France. As early as the autumn of 1789 the artist Restout had called for replacement of the Academy.[33] He protested that it was the creation of a man who had forced genius to serve the insulting vanity of Louis XIV, and who had helped to create that irritating and pompous monument, Versailles. Restout complained that the Academy bore the earmarks of its origin, that it was an hierarchical organization which forced some members to bow down to others. To achieve artistic liberty it was necessary to sweep away all pretensions, distinctions, and ranks, and to create a simple assembly of all artists. In this assembly the officers and professors would be elected for limited terms and rotated in office. The Commune des arts, formed in the autumn of 1790 by opponents of the Academy led by David, poured out similar arguments in the following years.[34]

The attack on the Academy had been more than an attempt to destroy an hierarchical organization. It had involved a revolt against the teaching methods of the Academy on the grounds that they cramped the free development of artistic talent. In a petition to the National Assembly on behalf of the Commune des arts, Dufourny had complained that the system of education administered by the Academy restricted artistic freedom, ". . . que l'organisation actuelle des écoles, loin de produire l'émulation, la détruit, loin de développer le génie, la force à suivre l'ornière de la routine, ou l'enferme dans les limites du système de quelque secte."[35] We find that over

---

de réfutation à un projet de statuts pour l'Académie centrale par quelques Académiciens (Paris, 1791), p. 6.

33Jean-Bernard Restout, Discours prononcé dans l'Académie royale de peinture et sculpture le 19 décembre, 1789 (Paris, 1790), p. 3.

34Mémoire sur l'Académie royale de peinture et sculpture par plusieurs membres de cette Académie (Paris, 1790); Deloynes, vol. LIII, Item 1464; Assemblée générale de la Commune des arts: résultats des arrêtés, Septembre 1790, Item 1474, Adresses, mémoires et observations presentés à l'Assemblée nationale, Avril 1791 par la commune des arts, Item 1497.

35Léon Dufourny, Pétition motivée de la Commune des Arts à l'Assemblée nationale pour en obtenir la plus entière liberté de génie par l'establissement de concours dans tout ce qui intéresse la nation, les sciences, et les arts (Paris, n.d.), p. 5.

and over again artists had asserted their right to develop their talents without restraint. The basic assumption was that genius had to be absolutely free to develop according to its own dictates. Speaking during the final debate in the Convention about the Academies, David had claimed that under the academic system the young artist was not free to develop his talents. The professors were in a position to force their taste upon the student, or to make him an outcast if he dared to provoke their jealousy.[36] As a result of arguments such as these all the Academies were abolished in August, 1793.

Under the Directory the Academies were brought back, disguised as subdivisions of the Institut national. Artists nevertheless continued to assert their right to that freedom which they felt genius deserved. Today we associate the idea of art as propaganda with controls over creative work, and we may be surprised to find artists and art lovers demanding complete artistic freedom precisely at the moment that they elaborated the notion of art as a republican weapon. The fact is that most of the exponents of the notion of art as propaganda believed that art could be redirected on purpose without any restriction of artistic freedom. For instance, in his *Essai philosophique sur la dignité des arts*, Pierre Chaussard argued that the arts provided a forceful language which the state would have to employ to gain control over men's minds, but he insisted that this could be done without violating artistic freedom:

Observons que les lois hâteront cette régénération, moins par la rigueur que par la bienfaisance des dispositions; qu'il ne s'agit point de règlemens coërcitifs, mais d'une police d'encouragement; que loin de comprimer l'essor libre, la marche indépendante du génie, le gouvernement se proposera de le favoriser, de réchauffer, de révéler ses ailes, et non de les livrer aux ciseaux d'une censure d'autant plus arbitraire, qu'elle s'exercerait sur des ouvrages de sentiment, sur les productions d'imitation.[37]

Chaussard spoke of regulation by encouragement. Many republicans thought that commissions and other forms of encouragement could be used to direct art toward government service. This was the

---

[36]*Arch. parl.*, LXX, p. 523–24.
[37]Pierre-J-B. Chaussard, *Essai philosophique sur la dignité des arts* (Paris, an VI), p. 28.

method advocated by Allent, the essayist crowned by the Institut national.[38] Allent saw that the problem was to prevent the artist from simply following his own immediate interest by catering to the taste of patrons rich enough to buy his works. He admitted that the government would never have enough revenue to commission a large number of works itself, but he proposed that what revenue there was available for art ought to be spent on patriotic works. In addition patriotic artists could be provided with studios, they could have their works displayed in national buildings, and they could be given public honours. Student artists could be encouraged to treat national subjects, they could be asked to compete in portraying republican themes in contests, and they too could be honoured for combining talent with patriotism. Allent and others like him did not view this sort of government guidance as a real threat to artistic freedom.

Many of the advocates of the idea of art as propaganda thought that, even apart from government encouragement, artists would be eager to serve the republican cause. For instance, in an article in the *Décade philosophique*, Pommereul contrasted the traditional subjects which artists had been forced to depict with the interesting new themes provided by the Revolution.[39] In Italy the arts, he said, had been forced to serve a despotic religion. Nearly all subjects had been taken from religious history or the Bible—everlasting Madonnas, all sorts of martyrs, and countless miracles. All these subjects were too similar to serve as a good basis for creative work, and had already been treated in a hundred different ways. "La révolution," he asserted, "a ouvert au génie une carrière nouvelle, et bien préférable à celle qu'offraient la mythologie ou la bible."[40]

Republicans thus believed that artists had a natural penchant for lofty themes, which had been thwarted by the corruption and despotism of the old régime.[41] They argued that the monarchical system had depraved morals and hence degraded taste. It had

[38]*Rapport au nom de la commission*, pp. 6–7.
[39]F-R.-J. de Pommereul, "Des institutions propres à encourager et perfectionner les beaux-arts en France," *La Décade philosophique*, vol. IX, no. 71, 20 Germinal an IV, pp. 78–87; and no. 72, 30 Germinal, pp. 140–48.
[40]*Ibid.*, p. 143.
[41]Charles Alexandre Amaury-Duval, "Première lettre de Polyscope sur les ouvrages . . . exposés dans le grand Salon de Muséum," *Décade philosophique*, 30 Vendémiaire an IV, no. 54, pp. 139 ff.

encouraged luxury with its corrupting influence and frivolous inclinations. Above all the artist had been forced to grovel before the king and a few rich parasites. "Des mains esclaves, un esprit forcé d'obéir aux volontés d'un homme puissant," wrote the republican Amaury-Duval, "ne produira jamais rien que de vil, de mesquin, de bizarre."[42] Now under republican institutions genius would be free to produce noble works. Instead of serving a few despotic patrons, the artist would be able to work for the whole people. Amid the struggle for liberty, his soul would be ennobled and he would be inspired to depict the great events which he saw on every hand.

But directing art toward republican themes was not in practice as easy as many republicans anticipated. Artists seem to have been less than enthusiastic about treating political subjects. Their experience during the turbulent period of the Revolution must have convinced many of them that it was a risky business to become too closely involved in politics or to idealize some revolutionary hero whose popularity might prove all too brief. David, who had painted "Le Peletier au lit de mort" and "Marat assassiné," had barely escaped the guillotine following the overthrow of Robespierre. A number of radical young painters had been less fortunate, and had ridden the tumbrels to their fate. As we have seen, even those who won prizes in the great art contests preferred to treat traditional themes rather than complete the revolutionary sketches which they had submitted. Under the Directory, when artists were under much less pressure than they had been during the Terror, most of them produced the same sort of works as they had before the Revolution.

Even if artists had been eager to serve the Republic, the advocates of art as propaganda did not show them how to escape economic realities. In spite of all the talk about how artists had been freed from the tyranny of kings and aristocrats, painters and sculptors were still forced to please the customer. The catalogues of the exhibitions show that artists continued to turn out genre paintings, landscapes, and portraits, rather than revolutionary pictures. The obvious reason was that the *bourgeoisie*, the newly rich, wanted easel paintings, and above all portraits. The *Journal de Paris* pointed out in 1796 that portraits were crowding out the great

[42]*Ibid.*, p. 142.

historical paintings and claimed the reason for this was that artists had to live, and consequently had to paint what their patrons demanded. Soon, the journal lamented, there would be nothing on display but *le père, la mère, la fille,* et *grand papa!* Three years later this same newspaper reported that at the recent exhibition there were only twelve historical paintings compared with about two hundred portraits.[43]

Government encouragement on a vast scale might have succeeded in procuring republican themes. However, the government had very little money to spend in this way, and it did not make the best use of what it had. In 1799 Chaussard complained that the government had just handed out one hundred thousand pounds in prize money, without much visible result.[44] We have seen how François de Neufchâteau, the Minister of the Interior, having already reached a similar conclusion, informed the art jury that henceforth the government would dictate subjects to artists who won commissions as prizes. Government patronage was thus to be used to force artists to portray useful subjects. This would have involved a kind of regulation of the arts, but only in a limited sphere. "On ne blesse point par cette mesure leur liberté," wrote François. "Les artistes peuvent refuser de concourir et s'exercer volontairement sur d'autres sujets."[45] It is significant that the Minister of the Interior felt obliged to show that he was not infringing upon artistic freedom. But even extensive government patronage would still have left most artists dependent on the open market.

Another unresolved tension was that between views of art as an aesthetic object and art as a useful instrument. Chaussard, one of the leading advocates of art as propaganda, protested that in modern times men had made a serious error by relegating the arts to the sphere of mere aesthetic pleasure. "On confondit," he complained, "leur *moyen,* qui consiste à plaire, avec leur *objet,* qui consiste à être utile."[46] Apparently, from this point of view what was labelled

43*Journal de Paris,* 21 Brumaire an V, no. 51, pp. 204–206; *ibid.,* 23 Fructidor an VII, no. 361, pp. 1581–82.
44Pierre-J-B. Chaussard, "Exposition des ouvrages . . . dans le Salon du Musée central des arts," *Décade philosophique,* vol. XXII, an VII, no. 36, p. 544.
45Arch. Nat. F17 1059, dossier 28, letter dated 30 Pluviôse an VII.
46Chaussard, *Essai philosophique,* p. 2. Chaussard was the author of a number of other pamphlets in which he discussed art as propaganda: *Fête des arts* (Paris,

the means, the aesthetic qualities of art, had no value by themselves without some didactic content. Even the revolutionaries, however, found it difficult to be consistently utilitarian in their approach; their actions and their comments reveal that for them art still had value simply as art. Like Diderot and the Encyclopedists before them, even doctrinaire republicans seemed unable to abandon the tradition of art for the sake of art.

One intriguing example of this survival of aesthetics can be seen in the ambivalent attitude of the revolutionaries toward the art of the old régime. From a republican point of view much of this art was not only useless but a menace because it exalted tyrants, flattered aristocrats, and transmitted superstitions. Since republicans believed art could make a lasting impression on the public mind, the logical course of action was to remove these pernicious images, to purge the nation of all anti-republican symbols. Actually the Revolution did destroy innumerable works of art—statues of kings, portraits of aristocrats, tapestries with feudalistic designs, and a large number of religious images. Iconoclastic fervour reached a climax when, following the insurrection of August 10, 1792, the Legislative Assembly ordered that all "monuments élevés à l'orgueil, au préjugé, et à la tyrannie," whether in public places or private homes, be destroyed in the name of liberty.[47] Widespread destruction of pre-revolutionary art continued throughout the period of the Terror, with artists themselves sometimes assisting in eradicating symbols of the old order.[48]

At the same time an attempt was made, however feeble at first, to preserve works of art from the old régime which had some special value. First the Commission of Monuments, and then its successor, the Temporary Commission on the Arts, collected masterpieces with a view to preserving them in museums. We must credit the Convention with creating an art gallery in the Louvre, establishing the Museum of Monuments, and laying the foundation for various regional museums. One scholar has argued that this

---

an VI); *Monumens de l'héroïsme français* (Paris, n.d.); and *Coup d'œil sur l'intérieur de la république française* (Paris, an VII).

[47]Law passed August 14, 1792. Representatives of the Communes were to oversee temporary preservation of works of art.

[48]Stanley J. Idzerda, "Iconoclasm during the French Revolution," *American Historical Review*, vol. LX (October, 1954), pp. 13–26.

preservation of symbols from the former régime does not necessarily mean that republicans were inconsistent in their attitude towards art. He contends that when these works were seen in a museum, torn out of their normal social context, they ceased to be symbols and became merely *objets d'art*.[49] This may be true in the case of a monument lifted from a public square and immured in a gallery, but the argument is not convincing in the case of paintings which were displayed in a museum in the same way as they would have been in an ordinary exhibition. In fact many of these symbols of royalty, aristocracy, and traditional religion were probably seen by more common citizens now that they were displayed in an art gallery than when they were in their original setting during the old régime.

A report made during the Terror to the Committee of Public Instruction of the Convention by one of the members of the conservatory of the new National Museum of the Arts further reveals some curious tensions in the republican attitude toward the art of the *ancien régime*. The spokesman of the conservatory, Varon, waxed enthusiastic over the artistic masterpieces which were then being gathered and classified in the Louvre. Then he admitted that an involuntary regret intruded on the pleasure of organizing such a rich collection. Because art had served superstition, flattery, and debauchery for centuries past, it could not convey any lofty lessons to a regenerated nation:

... il ne retrace point au peuple régénéré les fières leçons qu'il aime; il n'est rien pour la liberté; on seroit tenté de briser tous ces hochets du délire et du mensonge, si l'on ne comptoit pas sur sa force d'en éviter les prestiges. Mais du moins est-il quelque adresse à voiler ses fautes, quelque moyen détourné de lui arracher ses préceptes. Voilà notre tâche et nous essaierons de la remplir.[50]

Evidently this republican curator was anxious to preserve pre-revolutionary art despite its seductive influence. Why did he want to preserve such art unless it had aesthetic values apart from its content? If revolutionary artists could cull from it techniques to put to better use, why did he want to display it in a public gallery? And

---

[49]*Ibid.*, p. 24.
[50]*Rapport du Conservatoire du Muséum National des Arts fait par Varon l'un de ses membres au Comité d'instruction publique*, I Prairial l'an II, Arch. nat. F 1057, dossier 3, pp. 10–11.

did not the very ambiguity of his closing pronouncement suggest that the aesthete and the republican were not entirely of one mind? Under the Directory the government expanded its collections with works of art plundered by the army. At the very time the government was promoting the *culte décadaire* and other movements aimed at undermining traditional religion, it was also filling its galleries with masterpieces of Christian art. Many republicans were well aware that these famous paintings were ideologically unsound. In the *Journal de Paris* Barbault-Royer stated that three different groups came to view the great Italian paintings in the Museum: those who came to nourish their religious feelings by viewing the powerful images of the sufferings of a mysterious God; artists who were indifferent to the religious sentiments of the devout onlookers and who came to study the rendering of lines and colour by the great masters; finally, the philosophers who came to meditate about how puerile mysteries had been assisted by the powerful influence of art.[51] Another republican confessed that when he entered the Museum he was shocked to find that artists had employed their talents to portray the fallacies of twenty centuries.[52] Both these republicans exhorted artists to portray virtue and patriotism in future, but neither demanded that the pernicious masterpieces of the past be removed from public view.

The difficulty in being consistently utilitarian is also evident in art criticisms which republicans produced. Even during the Terror, doctrinaire republicans occasionally found it hard not to respond to beauty itself. For example, Détournelle, editor of the *Journal de la Societé républicaine des arts* and an ardent advocate of art as propaganda, sometimes revealed his enthusiasm for purely aesthetic values. On one occasion Détournelle accompanied a delegation sent by the Society to see a collection of reproductions of classical works possessed by Giraud,[53] and he devoted considerable space in his journal to an enraptured description of these reproductions. His enthusiastic appreciation of such classical masterpieces as Venus de Medici, Apollo Belvedere, and Laocoön centred on their aesthetic

[51]P-F. Barbault-Royer, "Aux auteurs du Journal," *Journal de Paris*, l'an VI, no. 201, 21 Germinal, pp. 837–38.
[52]Lavallée, *Poème sur la peinture*, 20 Floréal an VI; *Deloynes*, vol. I, Item 1375, p. 16.
[53]Détournelle, *Journal*, pp. 159–69.

qualities. The beauties of these famous works led him to condemn young men who tried to become artists despite the fact that they lacked the talent to produce sublime works. For a moment Détournelle had enjoyed contour, form, and expression, but most of the time he and his colleagues were too busy discussing ideology to enjoy art. Only when the Terror ended did the persistence of *l'art pour l'art* become more evident.

Under the Directory the survival of aesthetics can be illustrated by reviews of exhibitions written by exponents of the theory of art as propaganda. An example is the review of the Salon of 1795 which Amaury-Duval wrote under the pseudonym "Polyscope" for the *Décade philosophique*.[54] Polyscope had gone to the exhibition expecting to find that artists had treated new themes in keeping with the new political system. He had expected artists to have portrayed the great events of the Revolution and the courageous men who had taken part. Also, he hoped that artists would have created some ingenious allegories which would have provided onlookers with clear lessons and moral maxims.[55] Instead, the exhibition contained some huge classical canvases, drawing-room paintings, domestic scenes, landscapes, still lifes, and a mass of portraits. "O! mes belles espérances, comme vous avez été déçues!" exclaimed Polyscope. "Où est ce goût pur et simple que je désirais trouver dans la plûpart des ouvrages exposés aux yeux du public?"[56]

A few of the works on display pleased Polyscope both by their content and by their style. He admired such a painting as "Hippocrate refusant d'employer ses talents à aidèr les ennemis des Grecs" because it held promise of a noble republican style.[57] Among the works of sculpture he liked "L'Instruction publique" by Chaudet and "La Tendresse maternelle" by Julien because they had a moral message and were well executed.[58] However, Polyscope also enjoyed many works which had no didactic intention. Even though he rebuked David for submitting nothing but portraits, this republican

[54]Charles Alexandre Amaury-Duval, "Lettres de Polyscope sur les ouvrages exposés dans le grand Salon du Muséum," *Décade philosophique*, 30 Vendémiaire an IV, vol. VII, no. 54, pp. 139–46; 10 Brumaire, no. 55, pp. 205–10; 20 Brumaire, no. 56, pp. 273–81; 30 Brumaire, no. 57, pp. 333–39; 10 Frimaire, no. 58, pp. 412–18.

[55]*Ibid.*, IV, vol. VII, no. 54, pp. 144–45.

[56]*Ibid.*, IV, vol. VII, pp. 145–46.

[57]*Ibid.*, IV, vol. VII, p. 281.

[58]*Ibid.*, IV, vol. VII, p. 414.

critic was won over by a painting of a young girl. "Ce n'est qu'un petit ouvrage," he exclaimed, "mais il fera un nom à l'artiste. Comme il est bien pensé: comme il est exécuté dans un bon esprit! La simplicité gracieuse de la pose répond parfaitement à la naive physionomie de la jeune fille. Tout est traité avec justesse et vérité."[59] Such enthusiasm for pure art constantly lured him into praising works of art with no ideological implications. He arrived at the exhibition in search of republican themes, but he lingered to enthuse over landscapes and still life.[60]

The dualism in the republican attitude towards art was also evident in the reviews of the exhibition of 1798 which appeared in the *Mercure français.*[61] The critic opened his account with an imaginary debate between a royalist and a republican about whether or not art could thrive under any other form of government than a monarchy. The royalist contended that the arts had only flourished under such monarchs as Augustus, Leo X, and Louis XIV. The republican replied that the arts had prospered under republican régimes in Carthage, Athens, Venice, and contemporary France. Thereupon the royalist pointed out that the destruction of religion under republican rule had robbed the arts of a great deal of patronage. "Je conviens, citoyen," remarked the republican spokesman, "que les richesses déposées entre les mains des prêtres ont servi à exercer le pinceau et le ciseau des artistes. Mais une nouvelle carrière va s'ouvrir pour eux: les faits glorieux de nos armées, les traits généreux des républicains, tout ce qui tient à notre histoire républicaine."[62]

The republican obviously spoke for the author of the reviews. Whenever he found a painting with a republican theme he became ecstatic. He lauded "La Fidélité des hussards français" by Vernet which he thought portrayed the disinterested valour of republican soldiers and the sort of heroism inspired by France.[63] He also approved "La Mort du Général Marceau" by Le Barbier the elder who had shown the dying commander surrounded by his mourning fellow generals. The painter had captured this inspiring scene in

---

[59]*Ibid.*, IV, vol. VII, p. 210.
[60]*Ibid.*, IV, vol. VII, pp. 334 ff.
[61]"Sur l'exposition des tableaux et sculptures de l'an VI," *Mercure français,* an VII: no. 1, 10 Vendémiaire, pp. 155–63.
[62]*Ibid.*, no. 1, p. 26.   [63]*Ibid.*, p. 32.

a suitable style. "C'est encore un peintre national," exclaimed the critic, "et qui honore son pinceau et son crayon."[64] "Un Portrait d'un ex-représentant des colonies" by Girodet, who had portrayed the coloured man leaning on a bust of Raynal, likewise won the critic's praises.[65] Over and over again the reviewer reasserted his conviction that art ought to portray heroic deeds and civic virtues. Nevertheless, he was often attracted to paintings with no utilitarian justification. For instance, coming to the "Portrait de Mme Gérard" by Mme Chaudet, he praised the brushwork, the truthfulness of the effect, the finish of the various accessories, the mirror at which the subject fixed her hair, the table on which the mirror was sitting, and the flowers decorating the table.[66] This admiration for pure art was evident again when the critic stayed to enjoy some of the better landscapes on display.[67]

The best examples of this tension in the republican attitude toward art are the reviews of the Salons of 1798 and 1799 by Pierre Chaussard. For his *Essai philosophique sur la dignité des arts* Chaussard had asserted that the fine arts ought to be considered essential instruments for shaping the very foundation of the social order.[68] In his reviews he emphasized this thesis repeatedly and praised those artists who treated republican themes.[69] In his view historical painting ought to serve *la politique*, genre paintings ought to support *la morale*, and portraits ought to immortalize those who served the Republic.

Les arts doivent être un *langage d'expression morale*. Hors de ce point de vue ils ne sont qu'une imitation stérile. Ne cessons de le répéter, les arts deviendront un jour une *institution sensible*, une *législation muette et toujours éloquente*.[70]

Following Chaussard around the Salons, we learn what he means. Whenever he found a painting with a patriotic message

64*Ibid.*, p. 33.   65*Ibid.*, no. 2, p. 95.   66*Ibid.*, p. 92.
67*Ibid.*, no. 3, pp. 157 ff.
68Chaussard, *Essai sur la dignité des arts*, p. 2.
69"Exposition des ouvrages . . . exposés dans le Salon an VI," *Décade philosophique*, vol. XVIII, an VI, no. 32, pp. 274 ff.; no. 33, pp. 335 ff.; no. 34, pp. 410 ff.; no. 35, pp. 465 ff.; no. 36, pp. 535 ff. "Exposition des ouvrages . . . exposés dans le Salon an VII," *ibid.*, vol. XXII, an VII, no. 36, pp. 542 ff.; vol. XXIII, an VIII, no. 1, pp. 36 ff.; no. 2, pp. 94 ff.; no. 3, pp. 312.
70*Ibid.*, vol. XVIII, no. 34, p. 417.

he responded enthusiastically. He praised the ardent patriotism of "Le Triomphe du Peuple français le 10 août" by Hennequin, in which the colossus Royalty topples under the feet of a giant symbolizing the People, while overhead Philosophy drives away Crime, Fanaticism, Credulity, Discord, and Envy.[71] Likewise he praised a classical theme such as "La Mort de Caius Gracchus" by Topino-Lebrun because it depicted wicked patricians, with daggers ready, attacking republicans, while a soothsayer, representing superstition, urges them on.[72] He saluted the patriotic brush of Thevenin who had painted "Augereau sur le pont d'Arcole" because it showed a republican general, flag in hand and defying the crossfire of the enemy, leading his troops to victory—although Chaussard wondered whether the general should have been distinguished so clearly from the other brave republicans.[73] "La Patrie en danger" by Lethiers, "La Mort du Général Marceau" by Le Barbier the elder, and "La Fidélité des hussards français" by Vernet also met his demand for art with a political impact. On the whole he was disappointed at the small number of artists who had produced republican paintings. He suggested that the government should use its patronage to guide art toward its proper purpose.[74]

Chaussard thought that genre paintings should give moral lessons useful to a republic, and it is interesting to observe how he responded to this type of painting. Like Diderot, he approved of works which illustrated homely moral truths such as "Retour à la vertu" by Drolling, which shows a young girl, respectable but humiliated, embracing the knees of her old father while the mother stands with tear-filled eyes. However, as an offspring of the Enlightenment, the republican critic disapproved of the prayer-book lying near the young girl on the grounds that virtue inspired by sentiment was superior to that dictated by religion.[75] A few other titles, "Une Mère expliquant Emile à sa fille" by Pajou, "Un Ecolier étudiant sa leçon" by Bonnemaison, or "Une Leçon d'agriculture" by Vincent suffice to show what was meant by la morale en peinture. As an austere republican Chaussard disapproved

[71]*Ibid.*, vol. XXII, no. 36, p. 548.
[72]*Ibid.*, vol. XVIII, no. 32, pp. 280–81.   [73]*Ibid.*, no. 34, p. 341.
[74]*Ibid.*, vol. XXII, no. 36, p. 545.   [75]*Ibid.*, vol. XVIII, no. 35, p. 466.

heartily of "L'Atelier d'une imprimerie" by Senave because, instead of idealizing the printing trade, the artist had made the shop look like a tavern. *Un peintre philosophe* would have made the most of such a subject. In the foreground a man of genius would have been shown meditating over a proof, while in the rear workmen would have been intent on their respectable task. A bust of Franklin would have been included, and on the floor would have been the Almanach Royal with its list of censors torn and lying in the dust.[76]

Despite this republican enthusiasm, Chaussard could not remain consistent to his utilitarian theories. The critic who in theory dismissed as "sterile imitation" all art without a political or moral message ends up his tour admiring classical themes with absolutely no political message, pretty genre paintings with no didactic intent, and even still life and landscapes whose only merits were those of pure art. In one case Chaussard even confesses without realizing how it shatters his theories, that art can be a relief from politics:

Ah! Trop souvent affligé par le spectacle de ces assassinats pieux ou héroïques que le peintre d'histoire est condamné à retracer, ne venez-vous pas rêver avec une plus douce émotion devant un beau site, devant une scène sentimentale que le peintre de genre vous présente; oui, souvent j'ai préféré des pâtres à des héros, et un paysage à une bataille.[77]

Here was an unwilling tribute to a wider significance for art than mere preaching. Other republican critics also usually finished up by admiring art simply for its beauty of form and splendor of colour. As the need to defend their work became less urgent, is it any wonder that artists continued to paint traditional subjects? And since there was no control over what the artist produced, is it any wonder that the public demanded art rather than propaganda?

One other major tension impeded application of the concept of art as a means of civic instruction: the conflict between mobilization of art to educate Frenchmen and patronage of artistic activity to impress the rest of Europe. Since the middle of the seventeenth century France had set the artistic fashions and had exported her

76*Ibid.*, p. 471.
77*Ibid.*, vol. XXIII, no. 3, p. 213.

art all over Europe. Louis XIV had patronized art, not only so that his greatness could be portrayed directly, but so that it might also be reflected indirectly through the cultural pre-eminence of France. Many republicans were anxious to maintain this cultural hegemony, if only to prove that republicanism did not involve a reversion to barbarism. Moreover, the upsurge of nationalism during the Revolution made revolutionary leaders all the more determined to uphold France as the cultural leader of the West.

Both the demand for didactic art and the desire for national prestige were utilitarian attitudes, but they did not necessarily coincide. At the peak of the Terror, the government was more lenient toward suspect artists than most other groups. Contemporaries estimated that two-thirds of the officers and members of the Academy of Painting and Sculpture were royalists, yet only four academicians out of more than a hundred were imprisoned and not a single one was guillotined before Thermidor. Most academicians were allowed to continue living in the Louvre and to retain their posts in the former royal manufacturing establishments. The zealous Jacobin David, who as a member of the Committee of General Security and a friend of Robespierre was in an ideal position to crack down on his fellow artists, actually protected Vien, the director of the former Academy, and Fragonard, the master of rococo painters. Not only does this show an admirable lack of vindictiveness on the part of David, but it suggests that he and his fellow Terrorists were willing to temper ideology with concern for French artistic leadership.[78]

Determination to perpetuate French cultural hegemony compromised ideological consistency in other ways. Concern over the quality of the works in the Salons probably prevented the government from excluding paintings and sculptures which had no moral or political message. Desire to maintain artistic prestige led the Convention to found the Art Gallery in the Louvre, set up the Museum of Monuments, and decreed the establishment of regional

[78]Professor Dowd points out that for the sake of prestige the Terrorists were willing to forgive the artists their political errors short of outright treason, but he does not concede that this compromised the effort to revolutionize the arts: D. L. Dowd, "Structure sociale et activité politique: les artistes engagés de la Révolution," *Actes du 86ᵉ Congrès National des sociétés savantes, Montpellier, 1961* (Paris, 1962), pp. 528–29.

art collections, all of which would contain masterpieces of the old régime.[79] Anxiety to sustain the artistic heritage of France also seems to have inspired the stopgap assistance totalling about seven hundred thousand *livres* which the Convention granted to writers and artists in the year and a half following the overthrow of Robespierre. More than sixty grants went to artists, most of whom were former officers or members of the Academy. Although all the advocates of governmental aid spoke of binding the arts to the cause of liberty, they did not attach any strings to the grants.[80]

Desire to perpetuate artistic pre-eminence also helps to explain some of the policies of the Directory which encouraged artistic activity without doing much to turn art into propaganda. This desire explains subsidization of the former Academy of Painting and Sculpture as a division of the Institut national, the enthusiastic acquisition of great art masterpieces which were ideologically suspect, and continued aid to artists despite their lack of responsiveness to republican appeals. In the last exhibit before Napoleon seized power only a handful of paintings or sculptures had any political or moral message, yet the jury selected to judge these works made nearly fifty awards.[81] Throughout the Revolution most leaders wanted art to be propaganda, but they also wanted France to remain the Greece of the modern world.

[79] In an open letter to David in 1792, Roland, who was then Minister of the Interior, argued that the Louvre would provide one of the most powerful means of making the French Republic illustrious. *Journal de Paris*, no. 298, le 24 octobre 1792, pp. 93–94.

[80] H-B. Grégoire, *Rapport sur les encouragements . . . séance du 17 Vendémiaire l'an III* (Paris, an III); P-C-F. Daunou, *Rapport sur les récompenses . . . séance du 27 Germinal l'an III* (Paris, an III); N-G-L. Villar, *Rapport et projet de décret présentés a la Convention nationale dans la séance du 18 Fructidor l'an III . . .* (Paris, an III).

[81] *Deloynes*, vol. LVI, Item 1761.

Conclusion

*Il est très peu de nations où l'union des arts avec
la philosophie et la liberté, leur influence sociale,
leur rapports avec la perfectibilité de l'homme et
du citoyen, aient été mieux sentis, plus profondément
étudiés, plus clairement développés que parmi les
Français.* JOSEPH-MARIE DESSAIX, *the Council of
Five Hundred.*[1]

THIS SURVEY of the idea of art as propaganda indicates that neither
the *philosophes* nor the revolutionaries ignored the importance of
emotion in human affairs. It was in fact their awareness of the
power of emotion which made them wish to conscript the fine
arts in the service of their cause. Diderot was convinced that the
arts could convey a philosophic message because their appeal to
the emotions was so much more powerful then mere verbal argument. The *Encyclopédie* contended that philosophy alone could
never lead the people along the route to happiness; it needed the
compelling force of the various arts. Some of the articles came
very close to advocating what we would call "motivational research"
so that the greatest possible utility could be derived from the
emotional power of the fine arts. The revolutionaries were also
aware that they would have to use the emotional appeal of *all* the
arts—drama, poetry, prose, painting, sculpture, and engraving—
to inspire the masses with the new political ideals.

In many ways the eighteenth-century radicals remind us of the
Churchmen of previous centuries: they were filled with a kind of

[1] Joseph-Marie Dessaix, *Motion d'ordre tendante à honorer les talens des artistes
républicains qui ont exercé leur génie à célébrer les principaux événements de la
Révolution, la souveraineté et les triomphes du peuple.* Conseil des Cinq-Cents,
3 Vendémiaire, an VIII.

religious zeal which culminated in the republican faith of the Revolution. Even before the Revolution the *philosophes* thought of themselves as members of an intellectual priesthood working, not just to obtain some social or political reforms, but to achieve a moral transformation. Mercier made this clear in his vision of a future utopia where writers and artists were united in propagating a civic gospel. At the height of the Revolution radical republicans thought of themselves as harbingers of a new faith struggling to convert or destroy those who were not in a state of grace. The art which they hoped to create was to be essentially religious—it was to idealize domestic morality and heroic virtue, commemorate revolutionary saints and republican martyrs, recount the history of the new religion in historical scenes and allegories, and raise up national altars and civic temples.

Like traditional Christianity, the new secular faith was to employ art to convey its teachings, but the reformers and revolutionaries had higher hopes for the arts than Churchmen had ever had. The *philosophes* and republicans shared a belief in a beneficent order of nature. They did not conceive of nature as contaminated by sinfulness or deprived of God, and therefore evil. Nor did they picture nature as viewed by science, shorn of the concepts of right and wrong, and therefore without moral significance. For most of them nature, including human nature, was something essentially good. This conception of nature explains why both the *philosophes* and the republicans believed that the arts, apart from any supernatural agency, could regenerate the human heart, provided of course that the arts were properly guided. As educational weapons the arts would not have to overcome any innate sinfulness, but would only have to revitalize the seeds of virtue implanted deep in the human heart.

This discussion about the role of art provides an illustration of the continuity between the old régime and the Revolution, a continuity which was very marked even though the *philosophes* did not advocate revolution and did not usually favour democracy. Both the *philosophes* and revolutionaries aimed at moral transformation rather than mere administrative change. The debate over the moral influence of luxury, for instance, ran through the whole period. The *philosophes* thought that the evil effects of luxury on the fine arts could be avoided by a wider distribution of wealth. The revo-lutionaries thought they could rid luxury of its baneful conse-quences by turning it over to the public—by making buildings, monuments, paintings and other works of art serve the whole people. Both reformers and revolutionaries made utility their basic touchstone of value. When Espercieux told the Société populaire et républicaine des arts that a thing was good only when it was useful, he was merely issuing a radical statement of the viewpoints expressed in the *Encyclopédie*.[2] When the revolutionaries de-manded national subjects for arts they were continuing a demand made by art critics under the old régime. And when republicans tried to turn art toward virtuous themes, they were simply express-ing their version of an idea propounded earlier by royal officials.

Unfortunately for the advocates of arts as propaganda, not all the traditions they inherited were consistent with their programme. Failure to discard certain legacies of the old régime, combined with political instability and financial difficulties, helped to frustrate their plans. Creation of public collections in the Louvre and other museums fulfilled a dream of Saint-Yenne, d'Angiviller, and other pre-revolutionaries,[3] but it involved displaying works which ran counter to republican ideology and exposed artists to a great variety of influences. The desire inherited from the Bourbons to maintain the cultural hegemony of France also led to contradictory policies. Above all the continuing liveliness of the Renaissance spirit impeded the effort to turn the arts into political weapons. Concern for freedom of expression inspired abolition of academic controls and made republicans reluctant to dictate to creative spirits. And lingering interest in *l'art pour l'art* demonstrated how difficult it was for even doctrinaire republicans to be consistently utilitarian. It was little wonder that the public, tired of being bombarded by political arguments, favoured art rather than propaganda.

The French revolutionaries failed to mobilize the arts effectively, but their intention remains significant. They brought the modern

[2]Détournelle, *Journal*, p. 330.
[3]J. L. Connelly, "The Movement to Create a National Gallery of Art in Eighteenth-Century France" (unpublished Ph.D. thesis, University of Kansas, 1962), shows that the idea of a national gallery displaying royal collections went back to the 1740's and that royal officials actively planned such a museum in the 1770's and 1780's.

state to the threshold of totalitarianism in the fullest sense of the word—mobilization of every available instrument for impressing ideas on the minds of men so that, as Boissy d'Anglas put it, citizens would be guided "jusqu'à leur conduite intérieure et privée."[4] Many of the totalitarian features of the Terror—the dictatorship of the Mountain, the regimented economy, the mass mobilization, and the summary justice—were considered temporary expedients by zealous Jacobins. But they intended even after victory over their enemies to continue employment of schools, festivals, plays, music, and art in order to regenerate the masses. In his long report to the Convention on April 20, 1794 concerning the foreign policy of the Committee of Public Safety, Billaud-Varenne envisaged a post-war republic in which all the mass media would continue to propagate republican principles.[5] Evidently he did not expect peace to bring cultural demobilization. Indeed the Directory did continue much of the Jacobin cultural programme, although rather ineffectively.

Since the French Revolution various totalitarian régimes have taken up the idea of the total mobilization of mass media in order to indoctrinate the masses—Bolshevik Russia, Red China, and Castro's Cuba, not to mention régimes on the right since Napoleon. But our analysis makes it clear that in order to mobilize the visual arts successfully a régime must have more stability than existed during most of the French Revolution. Moreover, such a régime must also be much more ruthless in sacrificing whatever cultural prestige it may have had among rival states, in suppressing the creative freedom of the artist, and in repudiating art for art's sake. In short it must break decisively with the conception of art and the artist which we owe to fifteenth-century Italy.

[4]Boissy d'Anglas, *Essai sur les fêtes*, p. 75.
[5]J. N. Billaud-Varenne, *Rapport fait* . . . *dans la séance du 1er Floréal an 11* . . . *sur le but politique de la guerre actuelle, et sur la nécessité d'inspirer l'amour des vertus civiles.* . . . (Paris, s.d.).

An Essay on Sources

THIS ESSAY does not attempt to list all the individual items which were utilized in this study, rather it attempts to indicate the varieties of material which proved useful. For individual items the reader is referred to the detailed bibliographies cited below or to specific footnotes in the text. Unless indicated otherwise, the place of publication is Paris.

BIBLIOGRAPHICAL AIDS

There is no need here to list all the standard guides to sources on later eighteenth-century French history and the Revolution, most of which are listed in the American Historical Association's *Guide to Historical Literature*, but a few special bibliographies deserve mention. On the general movement of ideas before the Revolution the principal guide is D. C. Cabeen (ed.), *Critical Bibliography of French Literature*, vol. IV: *The Eighteenth Century* (Syracuse, 1951). Also very valuable is G. Lanson, *Manuel bibliographique de la littérature française* (5 vols., 1909–1914). On artists and critics before the Revolution, C. du Peloux, *Répertoire biographique et bibliographique des artistes au XVIIIᵉ siècle* (1930, supp., 1941), is useful but badly marred by errors and omissions. For sources on art during the Revolution, M. Tourneux, *Bibliographie de l'histoire de Paris pendant la Révolution* (5 vols., 1890–1913), is especially valuable because of its topical arrangement and index. A. Monglond, *La France révolutionnaire et impériale, annales de bibliographie méthodique* (8 vols. [to 1810], 1930–), lists publications topically by year of appearance but omits many items on art. A. Tuetey, *Répertoire général des sources manuscrites de l'histoire de Paris pendant la Révolution* (11 vols., 1890–1914) helps to locate some manuscript evidence. G. Walter, *Catalogue de l'histoire de la Révolution française: écrits de la période révolutionnaire* (5 vols.), lists items according to author. A. Martin and G. Walter, *Répertoire de l'histoire de la Révolution française: travaux publiés de 1800 à 1940* (2 vols., 1941–   ), to date covers persons and places but not subjects. Recent publications are listed topically in the *Bibliographie annuelle de l'histoire de France* (1955–   ).

There are rich, mostly unpublished, sources on French art in various archives. The Archives nationales of France contain much material on art to which there is a handy, if incomplete, guide by Mireille Rambaud, *Les Sources de l'histoire de l'art aux Archives nationales* (1955). The print department of the Bibliothèque nationale has a large collection of items on art from the closing years of the *ancien régime* and the Revolution assembled by Deloynes and others at the time. This collection includes original printed items plus numerous manuscript copies of other items all catalogued by G. Duplessis, *Catalogue de la collection des pièces sur les beaux-arts...recueillie par M. Deloynes* (1881). Other useful archival material, often poorly catalogued, is located in the Ecole des beaux-arts, the Musée du Louvre, the Bibliothèque historique de la ville de Paris, and the Institut de France. For a study of this sort pictorial archives are naturally indispensable. The print department of the Bibliothèque nationale, the Musée Carnavalet, and the British Museum have especially rich collections of revolutionary prints. Paintings and sculptures of the period are scattered in various national and regional museums and collections, but they are often difficult to trace for lack of any central catalogue.

A number of printed collections are invaluable evidence of artistic activities in France before the Revolution. For almost a century the Société de l'histoire de l'art français published documents from various collections in the *Archives de l'art français* and the *Nouvelles archives de l'art français*. Especially valuable for this study are the volumes of correspondence of Marigny and d'Angiviller in vols. XIX–XXII (1904–1906) in the third series of the latter publication. Other publications of the Society are listed by J-J. Marquet de Vasselot, *Répertoire des publications de la Société de l'histoire de l'art français* (1930). For the activities of the powerful academy the basic source is A. de Montaiglon (ed.), *Procès-verbaux de l'Académie royale de peinture et de sculpture 1648–1793* (10 vols., 1875–92, Table, 1909). For the French School at Rome, important for the neoclassical cult, there is A. de Montaiglon and Jules-J. Guiffrey, *Correspondance des directeurs de l'Académie de France à Rome avec les surintendants des bâtiments* (17 vols., 1887–1912). For the Salons of the Old Régime and the Revolution the indispensable source is Jules-J. Guiffrey (ed.), *Collection des livrets des anciennes expositions depuis 1673 jusqu'en 1800* (42 vols., 1869–72). Information on royal commissions and purchases is contained in F. Engerand (ed.), *Inventaire des tableaux commandés et achetés par la direction des bâtiments du roi 1709–1792* (1900).

Several printed collections, in addition to those above which extend beyond 1789, tell of the activities of various artistic groups during the Revolution. H. Lapauze (ed.), *Procès-verbaux de la Commune générale des arts de peinture, sculpture, architecture, et gravure, et de la Société populaire et républicaine des arts* (1903) should be supplemented by A. Détournelle, *Aux armes et aux arts! Peinture, sculpture, architecture et gravure. Journal de la Société républicaine des arts séant au Louvre* (n.d.), which is livelier and fuller than the official minutes for the briefer period it covers. On the Academy partially restored after 1795 see M. Bonnaire (ed.), *Procès-verbaux de l'Académie des Beaux-Arts : la classe de la littérature et beaux-arts de l'Institut national, an IV–an VIII* (2 vols., 1937). On bodies set up to save works of art from iconoclasm and vandalism, and to create museums, we have Jean Guiffrey and A. Tuetey (eds.), *La Commission du Muséum et la Création du Musée du Louvre 1792–3* (Paris, 1909), and Louis Tuetey, *Procès-verbaux de la Commission des monuments* (2 vols., 1902–1903), and his *Procès-verbaux de la commission temporaire des arts* (2 vols., 1912–18).

The printed proceedings and enactments of various political bodies during the Revolution often touch on artistic matters. The most readily available source for legislative debates is of course J. Mavidal, E. Laurent, and others *Archives parlementaires*, 1ère sér.

(84 vols., 1867–1914 and 1961–), covering the period up to early 1794. Since this collection is not always dependable, I have also used the *Moniteur* (*Gazette nationale, Moniteur universel*, 152 vols., 1789–1868), including a rather inadequate table for the Revolution period. As a further check I have consulted the official printed versions of important speeches and reports, although to save space these are usually not cited in the footnotes. Laws and decrees related to art are found in J-B. Duvergier, *Collection complète des lois, décrets, ordonnances* . . . *de 1788 à 1824* (24 vols., 1825–28, Table, 2 vols., 1834–38). The contemporary collection compiled by the printer of the National Assembly is, however, more complete: F-J. Baudoüin (ed.), *Collection générale des décrets.* . . . [May 1789–Nivôse an VIII] (79 vols., 1788–89). The proceedings of the propaganda committees of the assemblies have been edited, along with a lot of supporting evidence, by J. Guillaume, *Procès-verbaux du Comité d'instruction publique de l'Assemblée législative* (2 vols., 1889), and *Procès-verbaux du Comité d'instruction publique de la Convention* (6 vols., 1891–1907), both sets lacking indexes. Since A. Aulard's well-known *Recueil des actes du Comité du salut public* (27 vols., 1889–1933), is not invariably complete or accurate, one is well advised to consult the archives directly using Aulard as a guide.

Periodicals and newspapers are naturally invaluable for a study of the history of ideas of this sort. Helpful introductions to this material are L-E. Hatin, *Bibliographie historique et critique de la presse périodique française* (1866), and G. Lebel, *Bibliographie des revues et périodiques d'art parus en France de 1746 à 1914* (1951). Scores of periodicals have been examined for this study, but only some of these carried much art news. Three literary newsletters are especially valuable: Grimm, Diderot, Raynal, and others, *Correspondance littéraire, philosophique et critique 1747–1793*, ed. Tourneux (16 vols., 1877–82); L. P. de Bachaumont and others, *Mémoires secrets pour servir à l'histoire de la république des lettres depuis 1762 jusqu'à nos jours* (36 vols., Londres, 1777–89); and M-C-C. Pahin-Champlain de la Blancherie, *Nouvelles de la république des lettres et des arts* (1779–87). The important Jesuit journal, *Mémoires pour servir à l'histoire des sciences et des arts* [*Mémoires de Trévoux*] (1701–67), was continued by the *Journal des sciences et des beaux-arts* (1768–74; Table, 1701–75 by Le P. Carlos Sommervogel, 1864), by another periodical with the same title (1776–78), and by the *Journal de littérature, des sciences, et des arts* (1779–83). Since periodicals proliferate with the outbreak of the Revolution, only some of the most useful for this study can be mentioned: *L'Année littéraire* (1754–90); *La Chronique de Paris* (1789–93); *La Décade philosophique* (1794–99); *La Gazette de France* (1750–92); *Le Journal d'instruction publique* (an II–III); *Le Journal de Paris* (1777–99); *Le Journal général de France* (1785–97); *Le Magasin encyclopédique* (1792–99); *Le Mercure de France* (1750–91); *Le Mercure universel* (1791–98); *Révolutions de Paris* (1789–95); *Tribut de la Société nationale des neuf sœurs* (1790–92). Détournelle's revealing journal has already been mentioned.

Among the innumerable memoirs and diaries of the period a number deserve mention for the light they cast on the world of art before and during the Revolution. For the period before 1789 we have the Comte d'Angiviller, *Mémoires*, ed. L. Bobé (Copenhagen, 1933); C-N. Cochin, *Mémoires inédits*, ed. C. Henry (1880); C. Collé, *Journal et Mémoires*, ed. H. Bonhomme (3 vols., 1868); and the Baron de Besenval, *Mémoires*, ed. Didot (4 vols., 1857). Unfortunately, the great revolutionary artist, Jacques-Louis David, did not leave memoirs. The so-called *Mémoires de David*, ed. Miette de Villars (1850), are made up of recollections by those who knew him. E-J. Delécluze, *Louis David, son école et son temps: souvenirs* (1855), and *Souvenirs de soixante années* [1789–1849], contain reminiscences by one who during the Revolution was a young student of David. A-L. Girodet-Trioson, *Œuvres posthumes* (1829) and P. A. Hennequin, *Mémoires* (1933), contain recollections by two members of the Davidian movement. A-F. Sergent, *Reminiscences of a Regicide*, ed. M. C. M. Simpson (London, 1889), is by an engraver who like David was an ardent Jacobin and active politician. J-G. Wille, *Mémoires et Journal* (2 vols., 1857), is especially valuable for the insights it provides into the struggles within the Academy in the first phase of the Revolution. Mme L-E. Vigée-Lebrun, *Souvenirs* (3 vols., 1835), is the story of the most celebrated *artiste-émigré* of the age. C. Nodier, *Souvenirs épisodes, et portraits . . . de la Révolution et l'Empire* (1831), is valuable because of the author's associations with young artists and writers.

SECONDARY WORKS

Among many good studies of eighteenth-century French art are A. Michel (ed.), *Histoire de l'art* (9 vols., 1905–29, vol. VIII); R. Schneider, *L'Art français 1690–1789* (1926); L. Réau, *Histoire de la peinture au XVIIIe siècle* (2 vols.; 1925–26); A. Leroy, *Histoire de la peinture au XVIIIe siècle* (Fontenay-aux-Roses, 1934); and Louis Hourticq, *La peinture française, XVIIIe siècle* (1939). Jules and Edmond Goncourt, *L'Art du dix-huitième siècle* (1859–75), offers a lyrical but penetrating series of studies of the major artists of the period. On the rise of the neoclassical style the principal authorities are L. Bertrand, *La Fin du classicisme et le retour à l'antique dans la seconde moitié du XVIIIe siècle et les premières années du XIXe en France* (1897), and L. Hautecœur, *Rome et la Renaissance de l'antiquité à la fin du XVIIIe siècle* (1912). The early Russian Marxist G. Plekhanov, wrote a suggestive essay on the relationship between French art and social structure near the end of the Old Regime, translated in *Art and Society* (London, 1953). Especially valuable for this study is J. Locquin, *La Peinture d'histoire en France de 1747 à 1785: étude sur l'évolution des idées artistiques dans la seconde moitié du XVIIIe siècle*, part of which discusses official attempts to redirect art. P. Marcel, "Les peintres et la vie politique en France au XVIIIe siècle," *Revue du dix-huitième siècle*, no. 4 (1913), pp. 345–65, discusses the neglect of political art from Louis XIV to the Revolution, but fails to do justice to the efforts of Marigny and d'Angiviller.

On Diderot's ideas about art there are a number of useful works. A. Fontaine, *Les Doctrines d'art en France: peintres, amateurs, critiques de Poussin à Diderot*, 1909 and the recent article, R. Desné, "La Font de Saint-Yenne, précurseur de Diderot," *La Pensée*, n.s., no. 73 (1957), pp. 82–96, both provide essential background. The unpublished dissertation by D. L. Hamilton, *The Aesthetic Theories of Diderot* (Chicago, 1941), which has been ignored by most recent scholars, is excellent although it strains too hard to render Diderot consistent. F. Vexler, *Studies in Diderot's Aesthetic Naturalism* (Columbia dissertation, New York, 1922), deals only with drama, but has some illuminating passages on the *philosophe's* notions of the social utility art. The second volume of K. Rosenkranz, *Diderot's Leben and Werke* (Leipzig, 1866), contains what is still one of the best treatments of Diderot's aesthetics. W. Folkierski, *Entre le classicisme et le romantisme; étude sur l'esthétique et les esthéticiens du XVIIIᵉ siècle* (Cracow, 1925), sees the philosophe as embodying all the various aesthetic currents of the age. Other useful studies of Diderot's theories on art can be found in Eleanor Walker, "Toward an Understanding of Diderot's Esthetic Theory," *Romanic Review*, XXXV (1944), pp. 277–87; Yvon Belaval, *L'Esthétique sans paradoxe de Diderot* (1950); and L. G. Crocker, *Two Diderot Studies—Ethics and Esthetics* (Baltimore, 1952). On Diderot as a working critic rather than an aesthetician see F. Brunetière *"Les Salons de Diderot," Etudes critiques sur l'histoire de la littérature française* (1882); A. Dresdner, *Die Entstehung der Kunstkritik* (München, 1915); J. Seznec, "Les *Salons* de Diderot," *Harvard Library Bulletin*, vol. 5, no. 3 (Autumn, 1951), pp. 267–87; and Gita May, *Diderot et Baudelaire* (Genève, 1957). Two recent editions of Diderot's writings on art contain useful notes: *Œuvres Esthétiques*, ed. P. Kernière (1959); and the *Salons*, ed. J. Adhémar and J. Seznec (Oxford, 1957–   ), 3 volumes to date including the exhibit in 1767.

For the aesthetic theories of the Encyclopedists there is nothing like the wealth of material available on Diderot's ideas on art. J. Morley, *Diderot and the Encyclopedists* (2 vols., London, 1878), is still a lively introduction. L. Ducros, *Les Encyclopédistes* (1900), is fairly useful although now outdated in some respects. The recent study by P. Grosclaude, *Un audacieux message—L'Encyclopédie* (1951), is very brief and superficial. Probably the best general view of the great enterprise is provided by the series of papers delivered at the Sorbonne on the 200th anniversary of the first volume, *Annales de l'Université de Paris*, 22ᵉ année, N° spécial N° 1 (octobre, 1952). On the aesthetic theories proper of the Encyclopedists we have J. Rocafort, *Les Doctrines littéraires de l'Encyclopédie* (1890), and A. R. Roger, *The Encyclopedists as Critics of Music* (New York, 1947), but no comparable work on their ideas about the plastic arts. The paper by Mario Roques, "L'Art et l'Encyclopédie," delivered in the series at the Sorbonne cited above, says nothing about the views of the Encyclopedists on the social utility of art although these were clear already in the volumes edited by Diderot. Since Roques was discussing the first edition, he naturally does not examine the supplementary volumes. To date the section entitled "L'Encyclopédie et l'art en général" in Rocafort, *Les Doctrines littéraires de l'Encyclopédie*, is the best commentary available. Professor G. Boas kindly provided me with a suggestive paper on the arts in the *Encyclopédie* intended for a bicentennial study of the work which unfortunately never appeared.

Among recent studies of art during the French Revolution the works of D. L. Dowd, S. J. Idzerda, and Colette Caubisens-Lasfargues are of outstanding importance. Dowd's major work, *Pageant-Master of the Republic: Jacques-Louis David and the French Revolution* (Lincoln, Nebraska, 1948), deals mainly with festivals, touching only briefly on other artistic activities. Two of Dowd's articles, both very similar in content, deal directly with the concept of art as propaganda: "Art as National Propaganda in the French Revolution," *Public Opinion Quarterly* (Fall, 1951), pp. 195–214; and "L'art comme moyen de propagande pendant la Révolution française," *Actes du 77ᵉ Congrès des sociétés savantes, Grenoble, 1952* (1952). While these articles are useful they do not examine the psychological theories which encouraged confidence in the effectiveness of visual propaganda, the tensions in the Revolutionaries' attitude toward art which they inherited from the Old Régime, the reasons for the relative sterility of the notion of art as propaganda, nor its *dénouement* in the last phase of the Revolution. Five other articles by Dowd deal mainly with the political activities of artists during the Revolution: "Jacques-Louis David, Artist Member of the Committee of Public Safety," *American Historical Review*, vol. LVII (July, 1952), pp. 871–92; "Jacobinism and the Fine Arts: the Revolutionary Careers of Bouquier, Sergent, and David," *Art Quarterly*, vol. XVI, no. 3 (1953), pp. 195–214; "Art and Politics during the French Revolution: a Study of Three Artist Regicides," *Studies in European History in Honour of Franklin Charles Palm*, ed. F. J. Cox *et al.* (New York, 1956), pp. 105–28, virtually repeating the above article; "The French Revolution and the Painters," *French Historical Studies*, vol. I, no. 2 (1959), pp. 127–48, which analyses the reasons for the remarkable political activity of artists during the Revolution; and "Structure sociale et activité politique: les artistes engagés de la Révolution," *Actes du 86ᵉ Congrès national des sociétés savantes, Montpellier, 1961* (1962), pp. 513–29, which simply elaborates the main points of the previous article. See also Dowd's "Art and the theatre during the French Revolution: the Rôle of Jacques-Louis David," *Art Quarterly*, vol. XXII, no. 1 (Spring 1960), pp. 2–22.

S. J. Idzerda's unpublished doctoral dissertation, "Art and the French State during the French Revolution 1789–1795" (Western Reserve, 1952), is a valuable study despite the fact that the author was apparently confined to sources available in North America. Idzerda's provocative article "Iconoclasm during the French Revolution," *American Historical Review*, vol. LX (October, 1954), pp. 13–26, is in my opinion an unsuccessful attempt to show that the Revolutionaries resolved the tension between aesthetics and ideology by neutralizing pre-revolutionary art in museums. Colette Caubisens-Lasfargues, "Les Salons de peinture de la Révolution française," *L'Information de l'histoire de l'art*, a. 5, No. 3 (1960), pp. 67–73, demonstrates the paucity of great civic paintings in the exhibits of the period 1789–99. Her article "Le Salon de Peinture pendant la Révolution," *Annales historiques de la Révolution française*, n.s. 33, no. 164 (avril 1961), pp. 191–214, analyses the liberating effect of Revolutionary legislation on the art exhibits.

A few other recent works must be mentioned. The text of L. Hautecœur, *L'Art sous la Révolution et l'Empire* (1953), contains nothing new, but the illustrations are good. A Marxist account, M. W. Brown, *The Painting of the French Revolution* (New York, 1938), exploits only a small fraction of the sources available. Another Marxist study by J. Billiet, "The French Revolution and the Fine Arts," *Essays on the French Revolution*, ed. by T. A. Jackson (London, 1945, translated by W. Zac from *Cahiers du Communisme*, 1939), oddly enough emphasizes the work of the Revolution in opening the Salons, limiting vandalism, and creating museums, rather than its efforts to use art as an ideological weapon. L. Hautecœur, "Pourquoi les académies furent-elles supprimées en 1793?" *Académie des beaux-arts* (1959–60), pp. 27–35, is a brief undocumented study of a question which deserves fuller treatment. A. Mabille de Poncheville, "Comment Boilly 'peintre de boudoir'

se convertit à 'la vertu'," *Ibid.*, pp. 83–90, examines the effects of Jacobin pressure on one minor artist. G. de Blatz, "History, Truth, and Art: the Assassination of Marat," *Art Quarterly*, no. 4 (1945), pp. 249–60, investigates the problem of truth in historical paintings using David's Jacobin *pietà* as a starting-point. My own paper, "The Idea of Art as Propaganda during the French Revolution," *Canadian Historical Association Annual Report* (1959), pp. 30–43, is a preliminary statement of the findings embodied in this present study.

Some older studies of Revolutionary art are still useful, although none of them offers a thorough treatment of the notion of art as propaganda. J. Renouvier, *Histoire de l'art pendant la Révolution considéré principalement dans les estampes* (1863), lists the revolutionary engravings of various artists and analyses revolutionary iconography, but does not attempt to appraise the effectiveness of these works. S. Blondel, *L'Art pendant la Révolution* (1887), provides a good summary of developments in all the plastic arts during the Revolution. F. Benoît, *L'Art français sous la Révolution et l'Empire, les doctrines, les idées, les genres* (1897), examines the ideas and institutions which influenced art from 1789 until the overthrow of Napoleon, but focuses attention mainly on the rivalry between the neoclassicists and their opponents. M. Dreyfous, *Les arts et les artistes pendant la période révolutionnaire* (1906), sketches developments in the plastic arts, music, theatre, and festivals. A. Aulard, "L'art et la politique en l'an II," *Etudes et leçons sur la Révolution française*, 1ère série, vol. I (1893), is a brief pioneer study of the use of images in the effort to create a Republic of Virtue. On revolutionary iconoclasm and efforts to curb it is E. Despois, *Le Vandalisme révolutionnaire. Fondations littéraires, scientifiques et artistiques de la Convention* (1868). See the comments by J. Guiffrey, *Le Vandalisme révolutionnaire . . .* (1868). The effects on European art collections of plunder by the French army are discussed by C. Saunier, *Les Conquêtes artistiques de la Révolution* (1902).

Finally, a few biographies of artists, connoisseurs and officials must be mentioned. E. Campardon, *Madame de Pompadour et la cour de Louis XV au milieu du dix-huitième siècle* (1867) and G. Pawlowski, *La Marquise de Pompadour, bibliophile et artiste*

(1888), both still cast considerable light on the age of rococo. C. Mauclair, *J. B. Greuze, sa vie, son oeuvre, son époque* (1905) is valuable both for the text and plates. J. Silvestre de Sacy, *Le comte d'Angiviller, dernier directeur général des bâtiments du roi* (1953), the only biography of this minister of fine arts, provides much information about the world of art at the close of the Old Régime and the beginning of the Revolution. R. Schneider, *Quatremère de Quincy, et son intervention dans les arts 1788–1830* (1910) is important because of Quatremère's advocacy of art as propaganda and his role in the creation of the Panthéon. Biographies of David are especially useful because of his leading role in the artistic developments of the Revolution. Jules David, *Le Peintre Louis David* (2 vols., 1880–82) contains a lot of information, but does not cite sources, and is totally uncritical. Other studies of David by C. Saunier (1903), L. Rosenthal (1905), W. R. Valentiner (New York, 1929), R. Cantinelli (1930), Agnes Humbert (1936), and K. Holma (1940), are all worth consulting.

Appendix

AN ANALYSIS OF THE WORKS OF ART
EXHIBITED AT THE SALONS FROM
1789 TO 1799

THIS ANALYSIS is based on the *Livrets* or guide-books for each exhibit, supplemented by contemporary reviews. We have classified items enumerated in the guide-books rather than individual works of art which sometimes appeared under the same number. This procedure seemed advisable in view of the fact that the exact number of minor works grouped together often is not revealed. Absolute precision is impossible too, because of the difficulty of classifying particular works on the basis of brief titles. Current reviews do not always help out in such cases since they usually mention only a small fraction of the works displayed. Also we have not tried to classify all the minor types of art on display such as miniatures, imitation low reliefs, sketches of animals, anatomical studies, and so on. Despite these limitations, the following tables do make clear the relative sterility of the idea of art as propaganda during the Revolution.

TABLE A
PAINTINGS AND DRAWINGS

	1789	1791	1793	1795	1796	1798	1799	Whole decade
Total on display	218	617	760	536	522	442	392	3487
Classical themes	35	81	94	62	81	48	33	434
Classical scenes of civic virtue	4	9	9	8	8	4	6	48
Contemporary political events or allegories	2	10	20	17	8	8	16	81
Landscapes, seascapes and interiors	60	167	230	139	132	105	76	909
Portraits	50	169	144	134	129	154	154	934
Portraits of political leaders, generals or *philosophes*	7	22	19	14	12	10	9	93
Genre paintings and familiar scenes	21	31	99	48	85	60	53	397
Didactic genre paintings	0	1	9	3	3	6	1	23
Still lifes	11	27	23	21	15	11	11	119
Religious themes	14	23	23	13	4	3	0	80

The efforts of pre-revolutionary art ministers to encourage didactic classical compositions and historical painting in general proved futile. Although grand classical canvases and drawings continued to be important, they were swamped by the *petit genre* which these officials had sought to discourage—landscapes, portraits, familiar scenes, and still lifes. A flood of landscapes and portraits followed the opening of the Salons to all artists in 1791.

Some classical compositions did convey a civic message: David's painting, "J. Brutus, premier Consul, de retour en sa maison, après avoir condamné ses deux fils, qui s'étoient unis aux Tarquins et avoient conspiré contre la Liberté Romaine, des Licteurs rapportent leurs corps pour qu'on leur donne la sépulture" (88),[1] which won the admiration of patriots at the Salon in 1789; Naigeon's canvas, "Une Lacé-démonienne voyant, au siège d'une ville, son Fils ainé, qu'on avoit placé dans un poste, tomber mort à ses pieds, qu'on appelle son Frère pour le remplacer, s'écrie-t-elle. Le sujet est l'instant où le Frère arrive" (530), exhibited in 1793; Lethiere's drawing, "Virginius, capi-taine de légion, tue sa fille pour lui sauver le déshonneur de servir au plaisir d'Appius Clodius. Cet événement amena la chute du décemvirat" (354), shown in 1795; or Potain's sketch, "Fermeté des vieillards Romains, qui aimèrent mieux périr que d'abandonner Rome" (378), displayed in 1796. Such civic themes were, however, greatly out-numbered by scenes of Venus emerging from the sea, Œdipus left to die on Mount Cithaeron, Orpheus lamenting the loss of Eurydice, the love of Paris for Helen, the painter Zeuxis choosing the most beautiful Athenian women as models, Narcissus admiring his reflection in the brook, Hercules felling a lion, or other classical subjects devoid of political relevance.

Advocates of visual propaganda were not very successful in their attempts to encourage production of contemporary political paintings and revolutionary allegories. The number of such works did mount from two in 1789 to twenty in 1793 in a Salon which opened in August about a month before the real commencement of the Terror. The latter exhibit featured scenes of revolutionary events such as Thevenin's "Prise de la Bastille" (541), Demachy's "La Fédération des Français, le 14 Juillet 1790" (159); Bertaux's "La Journée du 10 Août" (125); and Hauer's "La Mort de Marat" (supp. 447). There were also a number of revolutionary allegories such as Balsac's "Le Triomphe de la Liberté" (531), Desfonts' "Le Siège des Tuileries par les braves Sansculottes, qui, conduits par la Liberté, renversent la Tyrannie, malgré les efforts du Fanatisme" (595); and Genillon's "Tempête allégorique. Le Vaisseau, nommé le Despote, se brise au pied du rocher de la Liberté, et s'engloutit à l'instant où la foudre le frappe. La figure de la Liberté, fille chérie de

[1]Numbers following the titles denote items in the *Livret*.

la Nature, du haut du rocher, tient, d'une main, l'étendard national formé des couleurs de l'arc-en-ciel; et de l'autre, embrassant le globe terrestre" (280). Following the fall of Robespierre such themes continued to appear, plus a few commemorating the end of the Terror such as Mouchet's "Le 9 Thermidor, ou le triomphe de la Justice, allégorie. Le Génie de la France, après avoir précipité la Terreur dans le fleuve de sang qu'elle-même avait fait couler, rétablit l'empire de la justice et la couvre de son égide; il tient le livre de la Constitution ouvert à cet article: La Loi est la même pour tous, soit qu'elle protège, soit qu'elle punisse" (235) exhibited in 1799. Under the Directory there was an increase in the number of canvases depicting French military exploits. But political themes constituted only a small fraction of the paintings and drawings on display during the revolutionary decade: 81 out of 3487 items, or 2.32 per cent.

Portraits could, of course, have an ideological significance. Likenesses of revolutionary leaders, republican generals, or *philosophes* who had fought for social reform might be considered propaganda pieces. Vestier's portrait of Latude, with the Bastille being demolished in the background, had obvious political implications in the summer of 1789. The *Livret* for that year describes this work: "Jean-Henri Masers, Chevalier de la Tude, Ingénieur, retenu, pendant 35 ans, dans les prisons d'Etat dont il s'est échappé plusieurs fois, et entr'autres de la Bastille, avec deux échelles, l'une de bois, et l'autre de corde, toutes deux faites par lui et son compagnon, sans le secours de personne que de leur industrie; ils y ont employé leur bois de chauffage et leur linge qu'ils ont filé" (111). In the same Salon Le Barbier displayed his portrait, "Henri, dit Dubois, Soldat aux Gardes-Françoises qui est entré le premier à la Bastille" (99). The number of likenesses of deputies in the Assembly, leaders of the National Guard, and eighteenth-century social critics reached a peak in the Salon of 1791 when there were twenty-two. There were not quite so many in the following exhibit, perhaps because many outstanding deputies had been purged a few months earlier. After the Thermidorean reaction portraits of victims of the Terror appeared in the Salons. In 1795 Suvée displayed four such portraits done while he himself was imprisoned (460–63). In the next Salon Laneuville exhibited his painting of the lovely Citoyenne Tallien, now "Our Lady Thermidor," as she supposedly had appeared in prison at La Force, holding the hair cut from her head (244). But portraits with any kind of political significance formed less than 10 per cent of the total number on display, and many of these were simply representations of celebrities rather than conscious efforts at propaganda.

A few genre paintings and familiar scenes conveyed some political or moral message. Take, for example, Petit-Coupray's "Le Départ pour les Frontières" described in the guide-book to the Salon of 1793:

Deux jeunes Citoyens, le havre-sac sur le dos, font le serment, devant leur Père, de défendre la Patrie. Le Père remercie le Ciel de lui avoir donné des Enfans pleins de courage. Une jeune Fille éplorée représente à ses Frères le chagrin que causera leur départ à leur Mère. Un Adolescent tient le bonnet de son Frère, et regrette de ne pouvoir partir; un plus jeune se jette sur sa Mère, et reste dans l'étonnement. Une vieille Gouvernante, qui a élevé cette famille, est dans l'admiration pour leur dévouement. La chambre est ornée des armes de Vétérans qui appartiennent au Père. (103)

That same exhibit included Mallet's "Sacrifice à la Patrie, ou le départ d'un Volontaire" (35), Defrance's "Des Couturières occupées à faire des guêtres pour des Volontaires Français" (328), Pourcelli's "Fête des Sansculottes sur les ruines de la Bastille" (514), and Lejeune's "Le Père arme son Fils pour la défense de la Patrie, la Liberté, et l'Egalité" (736). In 1795 Haver displayed "Une Forge Nationale. On y fabrique des canons de fusils et les ouvriers y chantent des airs patriotiques" (241) along with "Une Ferme. L'on y voit le départ d'un Dragon. Son père lui montre la charrue qu'il va conduire, pour procurer des subsistances à nos déffenseurs (sic) tandis que son fils va combattre l'ennemi" (242), and there were two or three other such didactic genre paintings. Canvases or drawings depicting some humane or charitable act have also been included in our total. But the great majority of familiar scenes on display conveyed no political or moral message.

Old Testament and Christian themes constituted only a small fraction of the works shown at the Louvre during the revolutionary decade. Nevertheless in the Salon of 1793 when the Revolution was reaching fever pitch there were still more religious paintings and drawings than contemporary political themes. Indeed during the decade as a whole there were almost as many religious compositions as revolutionary themes. During the Directory, however, the number of religious works fell off sharply. The persistent anti-Christian policies of the Republic seem to have taken their toll.

TABLE B

SCULPTURE

	1789	1791	1793	1795	1796	1798	1799	Whole decade
Total on display	109	121	184	89	50	50	44	647
Civic themes	0	6	24	13	2	4	6	55
Statues and busts	45	35	57	22	12	22	17	210
Statues and busts of political figures or *philosophes*	4	13	18	2	0	5	2	44

Civic themes among works of sculpture were more common than in the case of paintings and drawings, but still fell far short of what one might expect in light of the endless reiteration of the idea of art as propaganda. The number of civic themes increased from zero in the first Salon of the decade to twenty-four in 1793. The exhibit that year included Desfonds' "Projet de Colonne triomphale, pour être placée sur les ruines de la Bastille" (18), Morgan's "Le 10 Août, ou la France rompant le joug du Despotisme, et foulant aux pieds le Sceptre de fer" (23), Boisot's "Un Républicain maintenant l'Union et l'Egalité" (51), Jacob's "Projet de Monument à la reconnaissance de l'Etre Suprême et de la Liberté" (110), Milot's "Le Peuple Souverain" (147), Ricourt's "J. J. Rousseau, montrant le Contrat Social comme base de la Constitution" (167), and Chaudet's "Le Dévouement à la Patrie" (supp. 631). But such revolutionary and patriotic works were greatly outnumbered by figures of Cupid crowning Friendship, an African bitten by a serpent, Hymen asleep, a young girl surprised while undressing, Œdipus and Antigone, a Bacchante sleeping, a Nymph emerging from her bath, and similar apolitical pieces. Also the proportion of civic themes dwindles markedly under the Directory. Over the whole decade there were 55 civic themes out of 647 sculptured works on display, or 8.5 per cent.

The percentage of works with some political significance is increased if one includes all the statues and busts of revolutionary leaders, military heroes, and *philosophes*. There were a considerable number of these in the Salons of 1791 and 1793, after which the total fell off sharply. Over the whole ten years busts and statues of political personnages were outnumbered almost five to one by sculptured likenesses which had no political relevance whatsoever. Civic themes and busts of political figures together comprised only 15.3 per cent of all the works of sculpture on display.

TABLE C

ENGRAVINGS

	1789	1791	1793	1795	1796	1798	1799	Whole decade
Total on display	23	47	81	48	50	26	29	304
Related to the Revolution	2	4	8	4	2	5	1	26
Portraits of political personalities	2	2	1	2	1	1	0	9

In view of repeated statements by revolutionary leaders that engravings offered an ideal means of disseminating propaganda, it is surprising to find that only a small number of the prints exhibited conveyed any moral or political message. The Salon of 1793 displayed Helman's "Serment du Jeu de Paume" (423), "Fédération générale des Départements français, au Champ-de-Mars, 1790" (424), "La Journée du 10 Août 1792" (424), Lépine and Niquet's "Tableaux gravés de tous les principaux événemens de la Révolution française" (436 and 436 *bis*), Dupréel's "La Liberté assise sur les débris du trône . . ." (457), and two others for a total of eight—less than 10 per cent of the prints on display. There were very few engraved portraits of revolutionary leaders or *philosophes* shown at any of the Salons. Revolutionary themes plus political portraits made up less than 12 per cent of all the engravings exhibited in the Louvre during the decade.

TABLE D

ARCHITECTURE

	1789	1791	1793	1795	1796	1798	1799	Whole decade
Total on display	0	9	24	63	20	11	23	150
Related to the Revolution	0	7	7	12	8	2	7	43

Architectural models and plans formed only a small part of the Salons, but more than 28 per cent of these were devoted to revolutionary projects, a higher proportion than in the case of any of the other visual arts. Perhaps this was because architects were more dependent on state patronage for completion of their most ambitious schemes than were any other group of artists. These projects included commemorative columns, civic shrines, public squares, legislative buildings, and temples to Liberty or other revolutionary ideals. These were, of course, only models and plans which would have had to be built in order to have their full ideological impact.

Taking all the paintings, drawings, statues, engravings, and models with any conceivable political connotation—classical compositions idealizing civic virtue, depictions of recent events, political allegories, didactic genre paintings, portraits of leaders, and plans for revolutionary edifices—we get a total of 422 out of 4588 items, that is just over 9 per cent of the works on display. But if we count only these works consciously conveying some revolutionary message—excluding many classical works, portraits of celebrities, moralistic genre scenes, and engravings which simply recorded events—the total would certainly not exceed 250 items or about 5 per cent. Revolutionary leaders had not succeeded in turning the Salons into schools of patriotism.

Index